The Subversive Tradition in French Literature
Volume I. 1721–1870

Twayne's World Authors Series
French Literature

David O'Connell, Editor

Georgia State University

TWAS 810

The Subversive Tradition
in French Literature
Volume I: 1721–1870

Leo Weinstein

Stanford University

Twayne Publishers
A Division of G. K. Hall & Co. • *Boston*

The Subversive Tradition in French Literature
  Volume I: 1721–1870
Leo Weinstein

Copyright 1989 by G. K. Hall & Co.
All rights reserved.
Published by Twayne Publishers
A Division of G. K. Hall & Co.
70 Lincoln Street
Boston, Massachusetts 02111

Copyediting supervised by Barbara Sutton
Book production by Gabrielle B. McDonald
Book design by Barbara Anderson

Typeset in 11 pt. Garamond
by Huron Valley Graphics, Ann Arbor, Michigan

Printed on permanent/durable acid-free paper
and bound in the United States of America

Library of Congress Cataloging-in-Publication Data

Weinstein, Leo.
    The subversive tradition in French literature, 1721–1870 / Leo
Weinstein.
        p.   cm.—(Twayne's world authors series ; TWAS 810-
French literature)
    Bibliography: p.
    Includes index.
    Contents: v. 1. 1721–1870.
    ISBN 0-8057-8248-6 (v. 1 : alk. paper)
    1. French literature—History and criticism. 2. Protest
literature, French—History and criticism. 3. Revolutionary
literature, French—History and criticism. 4. Opposition (Political
science) in literature. 5. Politics and literature—France.
6. Literature and history. I. Title. II. Series: Twayne's world
authors series ; TWAS 810- III. Series: Twayne's world authors
series. French literature.
PQ145.4.P73W4 1989
840'.9'358—dc 19   88-30089
                                                                             CIP

Contents

About the Author

Leo Weinstein, professor of French, emeritus, at Stanford University, fled his native Germany in 1938, served in the Psychological Warfare Service of the U.S. Army during World War II, and obtained his Ph.D. in 1951 from Stanford University, where he taught French and comparative literature until his early retirement in 1985. He is the co-author of *Ernest Chausson: The Composer's Life and Works* (University of Oklahoma Press, 1955; rpt. Greenwood Press, 1973) and the author of *The Metamorphoses of Don Juan* (Stanford University Press, 1959; rpt. AMS Press, 1967), *Hippolyte Taine* (Twayne, 1972), and articles on Franz Kafka, Stendhal, Flaubert, and Jules Laforgue. He also edited *The Age of Reason: The Culture of the Seventeenth Century* (Braziller, 1965) and translated *Pelé* by François Thébaud (Harper & Row, 1976).

This book represents both the synthesis and the culmination of much of his previous work, since he draws on experience gained in treating large subjects (Don Juan), interdisciplinary study (*The Age of Reason*), and the combination of history and literature employed by Hippolyte Taine.

Acknowledgments

Grateful acknowledgment is made to the following for permission to quote previously published material:

Paul Valéry, *The Collected Works in English,* Bollingen Series 45, vol. 10; *History and Politics,* trans. Dénise Folliot and Jackson Mathews. © 1962 by Princeton University Press. © 1962 by Associated Book Publishers (U.K.) Ltd. Illustrations in this volume by permission of Bibliothèque Nationale, Paris.

Introduction

L'Art de rouspéter

The French have a long tradition of protest literature; in fact, if there is one characteristic that distinguishes the French from other people, it is not their being great lovers or their being frivolous (as Americans perceive them), but a particular manner of expressing dissent, discontent, or disagreement. *Rouspéter* and *bougonner,* to protest and to grumble, are the two inalienable traits of the French character. A count of vocabulary used in everyday language would no doubt reveal a far greater number of pejorative than laudatory terms.

No wonder one hears rumors that the French are ungovernable, but these claims must be exaggerated, since there seems to be no lack of candidates to assume that ungrateful burden.

This does not mean that the French cannot be, and are not indeed, very charming and witty people, nor should the foregoing remarks be taken as a negative view of them. It means, quite to the contrary, that the French will not suffer injustices and wrongs in silence. Let others swallow their resentment, get ulcers, and have to drink milk. The French prefer to speak out and drink wine, even at the risk of suffering eventually from cirrhosis of the liver.

Added to that risk must be the fact that, during most of their colorful history, the French have been under all sorts of dictatorships that did not look kindly on criticism and that set up a more or less severe censorship to deal with unfavorable publicity. It was all right to drink wine, but criticism or ridicule of the authorities was likely to incur punishment all the way from being imprisoned to having a hand or head (or both) cut off, to perhaps being burnt, depending on the gravity of the offense and the susceptibility of those in power.

It is the fascinating and often dangerous game of matching wits between the *rouspéteurs* and the censors that will occupy a great deal of our attention, and we shall have occasion to admire the ingenuity of great writers who managed not only to remain alive and free but also to produce masterworks of literature in the process.

Although Albert Camus is generally correct in assigning the literature of revolt to the nineteenth and twentieth centuries (he might well have added the eighteenth),[1] the expression of criticism and resentment goes back to the early days of French recorded literature.[2] From the medieval farces, which attacked and ridiculed pretentious professions and authorities (e.g., *La Farce du Maître Pathelin,* about 1469), to the *Roman de Renart,* which condemned the privileges and excesses of the powerful and the noble; from Rutebeuf, who, in the thirteenth century, aimed his satires against the materialism of the mendicant orders, to Jean de Meung's completion of the *Roman de la rose* (about 1277), where even the origins of royalty are questioned ("they elected among themselves a *peasant,* the most robust they could find, the one with the broadest shoulders, in short: the biggest, and they made him a prince and a lord"), recurrent traits can be observed which make a French scholar conclude that "the art of seizing ridiculous features and vices appears in our history as a typically French quality."[3]

La Satire de Menippé (1593–94), which parodies the pompous speeches given during the meeting of the Estates-General in 1593; the accusations of Agrippa d'Aubigné, in *Les Tragiques* (1616), against the Catholic party during the religious wars; and the satires of Vauquelin de la Fresnaye (published in 1605), of Mathurin Régnier, of Saint-Amand, and of Boileau continue the tradition right through the seventeenth century.

Written primarily by educated middle-class authors, these works are the only means at the disposal of the weak to protest, to be heard, to make those who are abusing their power feel bad. Unable to resort to an armed struggle, the clever but powerless writer acts the way Renart does: he uses his intelligence, his ruse, and his wits not only to let off steam but to bring about change, either by shaming those in power into remedial action or by creating a consciousness of injustice in the minds of the abused majority. Despite widely varying conditions, across the centuries protests and ridicule are directed at common targets.

In religious institutions: the "absurdum" of cult and creed, the unnaturalness of celibacy and asceticism in general, in individual and corporate hypocrisy respecting what is and what is not of this world. In the upper classes: social parasitism, the prerogatives of status, the extravagances of etiquette, courtly love, chivalry, heroism. In philosophy: the claims of abstract systems, the refinements of dialectic. In the learned professions: display, legal, medical, academic costume, jargon, prolixity, and general ostentation. In moral code: contemplativeness, otherworldliness, fatalism, social otiosity, pseudo-idealistic impostures.[4]

Frequently these protests are pervaded by *l'esprit gaulois,* that mocking, down-to-earth tone which critics trace from the medieval farces to

Rabelais, Molière, and Voltaire. Every nation has its particular phobia, the accusation it fears most. For the English and the Americans it is immorality; for the French it is ridicule and ugliness. That is why satire flourished in France and why judgments tend often to be aesthetic.

The present study examines opposition literature in France during the 250 years between 1721 and 1971, beginning with the grandfather of modern works of the genre, Montesquieu's *Lettres persanes,* and ending at the moment when the Fifth Republic had to pass one of its severest tests during the May 1968 uprisings and de Gaulle's subsequent resignation.

For each historical period or important event one or two literary works of opposition have been chosen. As a general rule, the following criteria guided that choice: (1) The work had to be an important literary creation, successfully combining a fictional account or poetry with a representative expression of opposition; (2) it had to be written during the period in question or shortly after; (3) it had to attack specific conditions or acts rather than general vices of the times and it had to intend to motivate the reader to join in the author's opposition.

While not always adhering slavishly to these principles,[5] the aim of this study is twofold: (1) to present, not the official or academic history of France from the death of Louis XIV to the resignation of de Gaulle (kings, rulers, battles, dates, changes of government and of social conditions), but a sort of concave mirror image of that history: those eventful and changing patterns of French life seen through the eyes of the literary opposition, often distorted, always subjective, but depicted as living history through more or less fictional characters speaking the language of their time, eating, drinking, hating, loving, enjoying, and suffering like their contemporaries; (2) to examine the ways in which the authors expressed their opposition, to examine their art of combining fiction and political views, and to supply the background and the information necessary for a fuller appreciation of their works. To this end, a brief introduction has been provided for each historical period or event. Although primarily concerned with factual information, these sections also contain personal views, which should be taken seriously only by those who agree with them.

Even though the criteria used severely restrict the number of works suitable for this study, some difficult choices still had to be made. What is likely to strike the reader immediately is the absence of Balzac for the Restoration and the July Monarchy, and of Flaubert's *Education sentimentale* (1869) for the period surrounding the 1848 revolution. As for the latter, having been published twenty years after the events, it seemed too remote to qualify.

Balzac presents a more difficult problem. He has definite criticisms about government and about economic and social conditions. But these views are not expressed by his major characters (Rastignac, Lucien de Rubempré, Vautrin). Rather, Balzac usually inserts them in authorial comments, and even these do not quite add up to outright opposition to a particular government. Of course, the Restoration kings and Louis Philippe failed to satisfy his dream of a medieval monarchy, "but he makes no attempt to draw his reader actively into the debate in order to persuade him to take sides."[6] In this case, the songs of Béranger and Stendhal's *Le Rouge et le noir* were judged to be a more effective representation of opposition literature.

Good arguments can also be made for the inclusion of writers such as Léon Bloy, Alphonse de Lamartine, Charles Maurras, Charles Péguy, Paul Nizan, Emile Augier, Alfred de Vigny, Alexandre Dumas fils, and Marcel Proust; but the criteria used, an effort to avoid duplication, or literary judgments resulted in other choices. The subject is so rich that another study could be done using these and other authors.

Obviously, the writers studied can also be called committed, but in the framework of this study it seemed more appropriate and practical to refer to their works as opposition, or protest, literature. The terms *committed* and *engagé* have been used so loosely and in so many ways that the necessity of defining and defending their particular application here would have required considerable space that could be more usefully devoted to the subject at hand.[7]

Suffice it to say that what primarily interests us is the quality of the work and the effect it is likely to produce, rather than the author's personal readiness to do battle, although that trait is indispensable in a committed writer. Some of our authors indeed resorted to action in one way or another, while others watched the world go by in frustration, anger, or philosophical amusement.

Voltaire rallied to the defense of the unjustly condemned, as did Zola; Victor Hugo risked his life in street battles; Aragon and Sartre faced danger in the Resistance movement against the German occupation of France during World War II. But Montesquieu had no intention of fighting in any revolution, and although Crébillon fils risked and actually experienced imprisonment, he was not really an enemy of the government beyond satirizing what he considered stupid stubbornness. And Stendhal, a model opposition writer, not only accepted employment from the government he criticized but never committed an overt act against it. This emphasis on the effect of the work explains why relatively little space is devoted to the authors' biographies. On the other hand, in the Conclusion, in Volume II, an attempt has been made to measure the influence their works may have exerted.

Equally as important as effectiveness is literary excellence, and in this respect opposition literature has met, in its turn, with a great deal of opposition. "Introducing politics into the realm of imagination is like firing a pistol shot during a concert." [La politique au milieu des intérêts d'imagination, c'est un coup de pistolet au milieu d'un concert.][8] Stendhal knew the pitfalls inherent in that enterprise better than most of its critics. Many works that had excited contemporary readers or spectators made later generations yawn, either because the problems they dealt with had been solved or because they were no longer considered important.

The plays of Voltaire and of Dumas fils are unknown today to all but literary specialists (except for the latter's *La Dame aux camélias,* which appeals to great dramatic actresses with a special propensity for coughing), yet they were considered among the greatest of their times. Voltaire's thinly disguised references to contemporary events were certainly clever, but we do not recognize them any more, and even if we did, we would not care, because they are too closely tied to what are now considered minor events of his times. The subjects Dumas fils deals with (legalizing divorce, the fallen woman, gold diggers, among others) are no longer pressing matters, and as the problems disappear, so do the plays.

The three-year military service, the effect on France of the papal bull *Unigenitus,* an election campaign during the July Monarchy—even though of historical importance, these matters are not of overwhelming interest to posterity. Indeed, it takes a great artist to make them interesting, and we shall attempt to examine how several authors overcame such awesome odds.

But for the few who succeeded there were hundreds of failures. The large number of works that appeared during the French Revolution about young girls forced to live in a monastery make for painful reading, and even the more skillfully written plays that led to controversy and governmental interdiction, such as Marie-Joseph Chénier's *Charles IX; ou, L'Ecole des rois* (1789) or Charles Collé's *La Partie de chasse de Henri IV* or Jean-Louis Laya's *L'Ami des lois* (1793), offer no more than historical interest today.

No wonder there exists a widespread view, supported by major figures, that denies any literary merit to works incorporating a political point of view. It should come as no surprise that Théophile Gautier, the advocate of *l'art pour l'art,* rejects all "useful" literature. "The only truly beautiful things are those that can serve no useful purpose; anything that is useful is ugly." [Il n'y a de vraiment beau que ce qui ne peut servir à rien; tout ce qui est utile est laid.][9] Baudelaire espouses a similar view in criticizing poetic inspiration derived from particular events. "The poetry of [Auguste] Barbier was *adapted* to the 1830 Revolution and to the spiritual and social upheavals following it, . . . *adapted* to circumstances, and, however beautiful it may be, it bears the pitiful stamp of circumstances and fashion." [Les poésies de Barbier étaient *adaptées* à la révolution de 1830 et aux troubles spirituels et sociaux qui la suivirent, . . . *adaptées* à des circonstances, et, si belles qu'elles soient, marquées du misérable caractère de la circonstance et de la mode.][10] Even Stéphane Mallarmé, who wrote a great number of circumstantial poems, expresses a dislike for literature inspired by events, stating that he felt "the need to write poems in opposition to everchanging circumstances."[11]

The war cry against event-inspired literature was taken up by Julien Benda who, in *La Trahison des clercs* (1922), belabors the point by admonishing writers, scholars, and intellectuals to stick to their trade and not neglect their disinterested calling in favor of party politics.

While the foregoing criticism of circumstantial literature is not unexpected, Balzac's attack, even though primarily directed at the motives of such authors, comes as somewhat of a surprise.

Too often, in Paris, in their eagerness to obtain more promptly than via the natural path that celebrity which means fortune for them, artists embark on the wings of circumstance. They believe they will be greater by espousing a cause, by supporting a system, and they hope they can turn a coterie into a general public.

[Trop souvent, à Paris, dans le désir d'arriver plus prompt que par la voie naturelle à cette célébrité qui pour eux est la fortune, les artistes empruntent les ailes de la circonstance, ils croient se grandir en se faisant les hommes d'une chose, en devenant les souteneurs d'un système, et ils espèrent changer une coterie en public.][12]

Against those who favored putting a silencer on the political pistols we find an equally great number who felt that politics not only has its legitimate place in literature but that it is the stuff that great literature is made of. One need not go so far as Jean-Paul Sartre, who limits valid works to those which are militantly committed to the extension of freedom, to discover that political thought and literature can blend to produce masterworks. "What is good art does not necessarily make good politics. On the other hand, much bad art does unquestionably grow from bad political thinking and much of the greatest literature of the nineteenth century is produced by writers whose long, difficult, and profound contemplation of political ideas finds proper expression in their works."[13]

Flaubert, who oscillated between "pure" and political literature, aptly summarized the arguments of the affirmative side when he praised Hippolyte Taine for having gotten rid of the uncritical notion that books drop like meteorites from the sky.[14]

While there is no lack of people to point out what politics can do for literature, far less attention has been paid to what literature can do for politics. Most political manifestos and party platforms make for dull reading and are usually ignored or quickly forgotten. Conveyed through the medium of literature by an imaginative writer, these ideas will not only reach a far larger audience but create a stronger and more lasting impact. It is not so much that the medium is the message; rather, it is the medium that makes the message come to life and renders it meaningful.

Shot out of the pen of the literary warriors, dry and dusty history passes movingly before our eyes, statistics are replaced by feeling and suffering individuals, abstract ideas turn into concrete events, and the characters we encounter and come to understand force us to the realization that, whether we agree with them or hate them, they are so much like ourselves, so human, so alive, that we cannot ignore their appeal by ordering them back into their graves; rather, we feel compelled to enter into their battles and embrace them in recognition of our common humanity.

I wish to express my gratitude to my friends and colleagues, professors Marc Bertrand of Stanford University and Henri Mitterand of the University of Paris, for advice and references; to Sidney D. Swartz, who typed a draft of the first three chapters for me; to the Bibliothèque Nationale in Paris, the Fifth Avenue Public Library in New York City, and the Stanford University Libraries for courteous and helpful services; for financial aid to obtain illustrations to Stanford University's Department of French and Italian and the Office of the Dean of Humanities and Sciences, which also placed an IBM computer at my diposal for preparing the manuscript; to Malcolm Brown and Margaret Tompkins, both of Stanford University, for technical and moral aid; and to Beth Avary, who urged me to carry my study up to the Fifth Republic rather than stop at the end of World War II, as I had originally intended (although I am not quite sure what I am thanking her for, since it meant a great deal of additional work).

Finally, I would like to remember my teacher and colleague, the late Professor Georges E. Lemaître, who, when I asked him a long time ago what he thought of my project, replied with Gallic politeness something to the effect that he thought I was crazy—and I had never known him to be wrong.

Unless otherwise indicated, all translations into English are mine, for better or for worse. As a rule, French quotations are cited only for primary sources.

Leo Weinstein

Stanford University

Part 1

From Louis XIV to Louis XVI

Chapter One
A Persian in Paris

The Last Years of Louis XIV and the Regency, 1685–1723

On the surface, no period of French history has basked in the glow of greater public approval than has the long reign of Louis XIV (1661–1715).

Ascending to the throne at the age of five, in 1648, and beginning his personal reign in 1661 on the death of Cardinal Mazarin, his protector and the morganatic husband of his mother, Louis XIV corresponded ideally to the hopes and ambitions of the French people, if one excepts the aristocracy.

After a turbulent period of disorders and civil wars that had plagued France since the deaths of Louis XIII in 1643 and of his minister Cardinal Richelieu one year earlier, the country was longing for peace, security, and stability. Louis XIV not only provided these, but he added a splendor that catapulted France into a model of artistry and taste, which European sovereigns strove to imitate.

What the French call their classical literature reached its apex in the years between 1660 and 1685 with writers of gigantic stature: the critic Boileau, who defined classical doctrines; Molière and his immortal comedies; Racine, whose tragedies continued and perfected those of his predecessor Corneille; the fables of La Fontaine; the maxims of La Rochefoucauld; Mme de Sévigné's letters; and Mme de Lafayette's *La Princesse de Clèves*, the first modern French novel, are just some of the giants and masterpieces produced during a period that offered glittering festivities at the Chateau of Versailles, which Louis XIV had constructed as his residence.

Balance, reason, observance of rules, good taste, propriety—these are the key terms of the period. "Follow nature," Boileau advised, and he meant especially human nature. And men and women of genius proved that one can create lasting masterworks within the limits imposed by rules and without describing quaint characters or resorting to wild flights of fancy.

Louis XIV showed good judgment not only in patronizing the best artists of the time but also in the choice of his principal minister. Colbert, a commoner, worked unceasingly to improve the French economy by encouraging new industries, trading companies, and artisans. And the king himself devoted his considerable energy to governing his country, paying attention to even the slightest details. His subjects easily forgave him his mistresses, especially when they were as charming as Louise de La Vallière or as impressive as Mme de Montespan.

The greatest problem facing Louis XIV was how to handle the nobles, who had never resigned themselves to accepting unlimited royal power and whose last attempt to assert their influence had resulted in the civil wars, called "La Fronde," that had lasted from 1648 to 1653. The king resorted to a simple and effective solution: he bought off the ambitious nobles by obliging them to live at Versailles, where they received princely emoluments for such perfunctory but highly prized services as handing the king his nightgown. But neither royal service nor promotion could be obtained unless the candidate was within the range of Louis XIV's sight.

This expensive manner of keeping the nobility under control was to result eventually in dire consequences, but for the time being it brought to Versailles a large number of nobles with little else to do but crave entertainment or gather in salons for witty or chatty conversations. It is they who applauded Molière and Racine, and in the salons an elegant tone prevailed that taught those gathered there to understand allusions, undertones, and the subtleties of irony and satire. Louis XIV would have been horrified had he suspected that he was preparing the future readers of Montesquieu's Lettres persanes and of Voltaire's Candide.

Louis XIV's wars began auspiciously but ended in disaster. The first one, called the War of Devolution, concerned a matter of territorial heritage from Spain to which Louis XIV laid claim upon the death of Philip IV, asserting the rights of his queen Marie-Thérèse, daughter of the deceased Spanish sovereign. In 1667 his troops marched into Flanders, and the peace of Aix-la-Chapelle in 1668 awarded some fortified towns to France. But the second war brought Holland into the conflict, and from 1672 to 1678 William of Orange proved a difficult opponent. Still, the Treaty of Nimwegen gave to France a portion of Flanders and the province of Franche-Comté, to which Louis XIV added Strasbourg by simple annexation.

About halfway through his long reign the king's luck turned. In 1684, after the death of Marie-Thérèse, he secretly married the pious and prejudiced Mme de Maintenon, the widow of Paul Scarron, a writer of low-life novels. In 1685, largely due to her influence and that of his confessor, Louis XIV, who had defended Molière against attacks from religious bigots, revoked the 1598 Edict of Nantes, which had granted French Protestants religious and civil rights. While the Jesuits acclaimed the king's action, the Huguenots left the country in droves, thus depriving France of some four hundred thousand of its most capable artisans, tradesmen, and technicians.

About that time the king's wars also took a turn for the worse. Worried about French power, a coalition of England, the Empire, Holland, Spain, and Sweden opposed Louis XIV in a third war (1688–97), which ended in the Treaty of Ryswick, under the terms of which the French had to abandon the Netherlands and to recognize the house of Orange in England. Worse still, Louis XIV became entangled in the War of the Spanish Succession (1701–14), and France consequently lost its conquests in Belgium and was reduced to about its present frontiers, while England began its long period of domination.

A brilliant court of lavishly kept but useless nobles, along with protracted but unproductive wars, is an expensive luxury. Add to this an economic crisis in Europe, and the picture becomes dark. Famines raged in France in 1693–94 and again in 1709–10. The king's treasury ran so low that he had to melt down the silver in his furniture, melt down his gold plates and even his throne! And since the nobles and the Church were exempt from taxes, venal offices were sold to tax collectors, who milked the commoners and the peasants of all they could give. Louis XIV's failure to provide France with an equitable financial and tax system was to plague his successors and contribute materially to the eventual downfall of the ancien régime.

What had begun as a popular and glorious reign ended in gloom and widespread disappointment. In a letter to the king that was never sent, Fénelon speaks of France as "a large, desolate hospital without supplies"; scarcity of goods led to uprisings; and La Bruyère describes the peasants as "ferocious animals, male and female, . . . black, livid, and burnt by the sun, living in dens, . . . eating black bread, water, and raisins."[1]

And so the Sun King (*le Roi Soleil*), after a reign of fifty-four years, died amidst general indifference, even relief, mourned only by his servants whom he had treated better than his people.

Having outlived his sons and grandsons, Louis XIV tried to rule France even from his grave. The new king, his great grandson, was only five years old when Louis XIV died, in 1715. The regent, the duc d'Orléans, was cultured and witty but rather immoral, so the old king had made a will that intended to restrict severely the powers of the regent. The duc d'Orléans, however, had that will annulled by the parlements, courts of justice whose function was to register the king's edicts and who had the right to remonstrate against measures they considered contrary to French tradition.

Whatever his private pleasures may have been, the fact remains that the regent was a liberal thinker who tried to ease the iron rule Louis XIV had imposed on France. The historian Michelet credits the Regency with the first attempt to set French minds free. Pleasure and relaxation returned to the country after the stern and somber mood that had prevailed during Louis XIV's late years. People dressed gaily, bantered, and made outings to Cythera to enjoy the *fêtes galantes* that inspired the painter Watteau and that Verlaine later celebrated in his poems.

Yet even with the best will the Regency government, unstable by its very nature, was unable to effect the reforms needed to cure the financial ills it had inherited. So when the regent met a Scotsman by the name of John Law, a godsend solution seemed to present itself. Law proposed the creation of credit by printing paper money, a revolutionary idea at the time. In 1716 he founded a private bank, which, in 1718, became the Royal Bank. Law had meanwhile obtained a trading monopoly with Louisiana, the West Indies, and Canada; and he was appointed French controller general of finances in 1720.

Exaggerated reports of wealth in Louisiana led to wild speculations in the stock of the trading company, which turned valets into millionaires and nobles into paupers. But soon the bubble burst and with it Law's system. He was forced to flee to London, thus putting an end to any hopes for financial reform.

In foreign policy, alliances changed according to circumstances. The regent's foreign minister, Abbé Dubois, arranged the betrothal of Louis XV to the young Spanish infanta after a short war against Philip V, during which France was allied with England. However, both the regent and Dubois, now a cardinal, died in 1723.

The new regent was the duc de Bourbon who, in 1725, broke Louis XV's betrothal and sent the five-year-old infanta back to Spain. Instead, he married the fifteen-year-old king to Marie Leczinska, the daughter of Stanislas, the deposed Polish king, who was then living in

France. While this marriage secured the succession in case Louis XV should die, the duc de Bourbon incurred the young king's disfavor by trying to dismiss Bishop Fleury, the king's tutor. Louis XV exiled the regent into the provinces and had Fleury installed as his chief minister in 1726.

Chronology

1672–1678:	War with Holland; Treaty of Nimwegen.
1684:	Louis XIV's secret marriage with Mme de Maintenon.
1685:	Revocation of the Edict of Nantes.
1688–1697:	War against the League of Augsburg; Treaty of Ryswick.
1701–1714:	War of Spanish Succession.
1709:	Destruction of Port-Royal, the Jansenist center.
1713:	Papal bull *Unigenitus*.
1715:	Death of Louis XIV; Philippe d'Orléans, regent.
1716:	Law sets up his financial system.
1717:	Creation of Mississippi Company.
1720:	Collapse of Law's system.
1721:	Montesquieu: *Les Lettres persanes*.
1722:	Dubois named chief minister.
1723:	Death of Dubois and of the regent; duc de Bourbon named regent.
1725:	Marriage of Louis XV and Marie Leczinska.
1726:	Louix XV exiles duc de Bourbon. Fleury in charge of government.

Montesquieu

How Can One Possibly Be a Persian?

If ever a book appeared at the right time, it was Montesquieu's *Les Lettres persanes* (1721). The subject, the tone, the criticisms expressed or implied—everything was right. Even though published anonymously in Holland, and by a fictitious publisher besides, the *Lettres persanes* turned out to be an immediate success. And when it became known that the author was in reality a thirty-two-year-old lawyer attached to the Parlement of Bordeaux, Montesquieu found the doors of the most fashionable salons open to him and soon achieved international fame.

Already in the last years of Louis XIV's reign, and obviously more so during the Regency, mockery of previously respected values and persons had become prevalent, not only in the irreverent salon of Ninon de Lenclos but at the court itself. "My aunt," the duchesse de Bourgogne is reported to have remarked to Mme de Maintenon, whom she called by that familial name, "people make fun of everything here." Moreover, the Orient had become a subject of interest in France due to travel books by Jean-Baptiste Tavernier, François Bernier, and Jean Chardin, among others, and oriental characters had appeared in literary works by Charles Dufresny and the Italian writer Giovanni Paolo Marana, translated into French.[2]

But Montesquieu's stroke of genius went far beyond the utilization of a success formula. He stretched its inherent possibilities to the limit by "publishing" the fictitious letters of Persian travelers who visit Europe, and particularly France, of course. The choice of educated and intelligent oriental letter writers placed at his disposal characters who are *ingénus* when relating naively what they see, yet at the same time mature and reasonable people when judging and comparing their observations against their own experiences.

Although Voltaire's *Candide* remains the model of the genre, Montesquieu presents us with a far more complex set of characters than the simpleminded and monolithic Candide. He not only wrote a true letter novel with all the accompanying requirements (plot, characterization, conflicts, a sense of time elapsed, etc.), but the views exposed by his characters are modified according to experience gained, and contain nuances and often profound reflections. The subjects he touches on constitute a virtual panorama of his time, and, finally, he goes beyond the minimal obligations of satire by offering constructive solutions to balance the negative criticism. Many of the ideas Montesquieu will express in his *L'Esprit des lois* (1748) can already be found in the *Lettres persanes*.

The novel is written in such a way that it can be read as a realistic narration, for no unlikely events take place in it. The harem story, which recounts a revolt in the harem and the vengeance of Usbek's favorite Roxane, although conventional, bears tragic overtones and gives rise to reflections and comparisons concerning the role of women in Eastern and Western cultures. What happens to the Persian travelers is unusual only in the way they recount it and in their reactions to it. This is why Montesquieu could "get away with it" at a time when open attacks on royal or religious authority risked severe punishment, and this is the secret of his art as an opposition writer.

Take some carefully chosen individual from one world and plunge him suddenly into another, make him keenly sensitive to all the absurdities we never notice, the strange customs, odd laws, peculiar manners, sentiments and beliefs . . . —such is the literary device. . . .
    To visit people for the purpose of upsetting their ideas and giving them the surprise of being surprised at what they do and what they think—which they had never imagined could be otherwise—is to bring out by means of feigned or real artlessness, all the relativity of civilization, of habitual confidence in the established order. . . . It is also to prophesy the return of a certain disorder—and even a little more than to prophesy it.[3]

Still, those Persians are not so different from the eighteenth-century Frenchmen as to seem bizarre. They share with them a belief in reason and justice, the two yardsticks of the recurring judgments emitted by the letter writers. In fact, the subtitle of Montesquieu's satiric work could have been: "How Persian travelers, endowed with reason and a sense of justice, see us." And whereas, later in the century, Voltaire will measure actions and events against "the best of all possible worlds," here Montesquieu's Persians hold up what they observe against the transparencies of reason and justice.
    Obviously, Montesquieu has grievances to express, the kind of grievances that the parlements were charged to bring to the king's attention and that rendered them so "hateful":

They approach kings only to tell them sad truths, and whereas a crowd of courtiers constantly tells them of a people that is happy under their government, these come to unmask that flattery, and depose at the foot of the throne the lament and the tears entrusted to them.

[Ces compagnies sont toujours odieuses: elles n'approchent des rois que pour leur dire de tristes vérités, et, pendant qu'une foule de courtisans leur représentent sans cesse un peuple heureux sous leur gouvernement, elles viennent démentir la flatterie, et apporter aux pieds du trône les gémissements et les larmes dont elles sont dépositaires. (Lettre 140, p. 221)[4]]

There are various ways of making people swallow criticism. In Anglo-Saxon countries, where morality carries weight, a serious and moralizing tone is called for. Morality is certainly not absent in Montesquieu's novel, nor is an occasional moralizing tone, but such letters, "Persian" in nature, counterbalance the predominant tone, as do the oriental stories. Most of the time Montesquieu resorts to the most effective weapon: wit, a bantering tone that makes people laugh with him. For this was the easiest way of getting his points across: have those who would put you in jail laugh with you and enjoy your wit. Was he making fun not only of the French in general but of himself when he had Rica remark, "The rage of most Frenchmen is to be witty, and the rage of those who want to be witty is to write a book"? [La fureur de la plupart des Français, c'est d'avoir de l'esprit, et la fureur de ceux qui veulent avoir de l'esprit, c'est de faire des livres (Lettre 66 p. 114).]

Milking Two Sacred Cows: Religion and Royalty

For, among other matters, Montesquieu was taking on two sacred cows which, even during the more relaxed Regency, retained the power that could crush any adversary at will: religious authority and royal government, even royalty itself. Prudently, the author takes pains in his preliminary remarks to explain that his Persians arrive in France filled with ignorance and prejudices, so that what might be taken as criticism of the Christian religion stems necessarily from a reaction of surprise and astonishment at observing matters that seem strange to them. On a literal level his explanation is valid, all the more so since the Persians do become rather more appreciative of French life as they spend more time in Paris. But if these oriental tourists had said out loud what is contained in their letters, which the author "translated," they would certainly not have spent nearly ten enjoyable years in Paris.

The pope is the first to receive his share. He is "an old idol that people pay homage to out of habit." [C'est une vieille idole qu'on encense par habitude (Lettre 29, p. 63).] He is a magician who makes the king believe "that three equals one, that the bread we eat is not bread, that the wine we drink is not wine, and a thousand other things of the sort." [que trois ne sont qu'un, que le pain qu'on mange n'est pas du pain, ou que le vin qu'on boit n'est pas du vin, et mille autres choses de cette espèce (Lettre 24, p. 56).] Next come the bishops whose principal function is to grant dispensations from fasting, marriage vows, and other duties imposed by Christian commands. And finally the priests.

These dervishes take three vows: obedience, poverty, and chastity. People say that the first is the one that is best kept; as for the second, I assure you that it is not kept; judge for yourself about the third. But, however rich these dervishes may be, they never give up the status of poverty. . . . They are right: for the label of being poor prevents them from being so.

[Ces dervis font trois voeux: d'obéissance, de pauvreté et de chasteté. On dit que le premier est le mieux observé de tous; quant au second, je te réponds qu'il ne l'est point; je te laisse juger du troisième. Mais, quelque riches que soient ces dervis, ils ne quittent jamais la qualité de pauvres. . . . Ils ont raison: car ce titre de pauvre les empêche de l'être. (Lettre 57, p. 101)]

The tone is not uniform here. While the remarks about the pope and the bishops may be attributed to the Persians' "complete ignorance as to the real connections between those dogmas and our other verities,"[5] the last observation bristles with personal indignation. The irony turns bitter and anticipates Usbek's later prediction that Catholicism cannot possibly last another five hundred years (Lettre 117, p. 188). Usbek, whose letters display the love of virtue, at times fails to observe even the kind of elementary courtesy one would expect of a cultured Parisian, and even more so of a visiting Persian. Such is the case when he meets an old, white-haired casuist who reveals to him the secrets of his trade, on whom he angrily slams the door (Lettre 57, p. 102).

Detached irony returns when the author deals with the Spanish Inquisition, in a passage that contains some of the best lines of candid reason and humorous exposure of contradictions, illustrating the fanaticism of Spanish inquisitors, while suggesting ulterior motives.

Other judges presume an accused to be innocent; these always presume him to be guilty. When in doubt, they follow the rule of leaning toward severity, apparently because they believe people to be bad. But, on the other hand, they have such a high opinion of them that they judge them incapable of lying, for they accept the testimony of their worst enemies, of women of ill repute, and of those who exercise abominable professions. When pronouncing their sentencing, they add a little compliment for those dressed in a brimstone shirt by telling them that they are sorry to see them so badly dressed, that they are gentle people, abhor shedding blood, and are distressed to have condemned them. But, to console themselves, they confiscate for their own benefit all the goods of these unfortunate victims.

[Les autres juges présument qu'un accusé est innocent; ceux-ci le présument toujours coupable: dans le doute, ils tiennent pour règle de se déterminer du côté de la rigueur; apparemment parce qu'ils croient les hommes mauvais. Mais, d'un autre côté, ils en ont si bonne opinion, qu'ils ne les jugent jamais capables de mentir: car ils reçoivent le témoignage des ennemis capitaux, des femmes de mauvaise vie, de ceux qui exercent une profession infâme. Ils font dans leur sentence un petit compliment à ceux qui sont revêtus de chemise de soufre, et leur disent qu'ils sont bien fâchés de les voir si mal habillés, qu'ils sont doux, qu'ils abhorrent le sang et sont au désespoir de les avoir condamnés. Mais, pour se consoler, ils confisquent tous les biens de ces malheureux à leur profit. (Lettre 29, pp. 64–65)]

Even when Usbek writes about his own country, his shafts are pointed in the direction of France. In Lettre 85 he relates the project formed by some of Shah Soliman's ministers to give the Armenians the choice of converting to Islam or being chased out of the kingdom. The parallel implied is obviously the treatment the French Huguenots received under Louis XIV when, in 1685, he abrogated the Edict of Nantes, which had granted religious tolerance, and forced them into exile.

By chasing the Armenians, they came close to destroying in one single day all the merchants and almost all the artisans of the kingdom. I am sure that the great Shah Abas would rather have had his arms cut off than to sign an order like that, which would have sent his most industrious subjects to the Mogul and the other kings of the Indies. It would have amounted to giving them half of his realm.

[En proscrivant les Arméniens, on pensa détruire en un seul jour tous les négociants et presque tous les artisans du royaume. Je suis sûr que le grand Chah Abas aurait mieux aimé se faire couper les deux bras que de signer un ordre pareil, et qu'en envoyant au Mogol et aux autres rois des Indes ses sujets les plus industrieux il aurait cru leur donner la moitié de ses états. (Lettre 85, p. 143)]

Usbek bears down even harder on religious intolerance in the form of proselytism, wherever it may appear. "Whoever wants to make me change my religion probably insists on it only because he would not change his, even under pressure of force; therefore he is surprised that I won't do something that he would perhaps not do for an empire." [Celui qui veut me faire changer de religion ne le fait sans doute que parce qu'il ne changerait pas la sienne, quand on voudrait l'y forcer; il trouve donc étrange que je ne fasse pas une chose qu'il ne ferait pas lui-même peut-être pour l'empire du monde (Lettre 85, p. 144).] The key word here is *therefore,* which ironically connects two contradictory statements.

He goes to the heart of the matter—namely, the monopoly enjoyed in France by Catholicism and the Jesuits in particular—by suggesting that religious pluralism benefits a state, because all religions contain precepts that are useful to society, and because their members are likely to behave well so as not to expose their sect to criticism and attacks from rival religious groups.

What Montesquieu actually favors amounts to a form of deism that produces virtuous people and good citizens. He cites the prayer of a pious man who, confused by all the religious quarrels, ceremonies, and rites, cries out to his god:

I cannot move my head without running the risk of offending you; yet I want to please you and dedicate to that purpose the life you gave me. Perhaps I am mistaken, but I believe the best way to do this is to live as a good citizen in the society where you had me born, and as a good father for the family you have given me.

[Je ne puis remuer la tête que je ne sois menacé de vous offenser; cependant je voudrais vous plaire et employer à cela la vie que je tiens de vous. Je ne sais si je me trompe; mais je crois que le meilleur moyen pour y parvenir est de vivre en bon citoyen dans la société où vous m'avez fait naître, et en bon père dans la famille que vous m'avez donnée. (Lettre 46, p. 83)]

Louis XIV and Absolute Monarchy

It may not be useful to beat a dead horse, but the same does not hold true of a dead king. Louis XIV, whose long reign is nearing its end when the Persians arrive in Paris in 1711, is described as a magician, very much like the pope. He makes his subjects believe that one *écu* is worth two, or that a piece of paper is the same as money when he needs funds to wage his wars. Another way of raising revenue is to charge money for bestowing titles of honor on his vain soldiers.

Criticism is transferred to the personal level in the brief but daring Lettre 37, where the king's errors of judgment and the contradictions in his appointments are derived from a common master faculty: his vanity, which makes him believe that "without examining whether the one he showers with distinctions is a person of merit, his choice will

make him so." Allusions become increasingly pointed and unmistakable, enabling us to add the persons referred to in parentheses.

He has a minister who is only eighteen years old (Louvois's son) and a mistress
of eighty (Mme de Maintenon); he loves his religion but cannot stand those
who tell him to observe it rigorously (the Jansenists); . . . he loves trophies
and victories but fears as much having good generals lead his armies as having
them lead those of an enemy. (The last reference is to several famous generals,
such as Catinat and Vendôme, whom Louis XIV unwisely replaced by men he
favored personally, or who lost his favor because they had criticized social
inequities, as in the case of Vauban.)

[sans examiner si celui qu'il comble de biens est homme de mérite, il croit que
son choix va le rendre tel. . . . Il a un ministre qui n'a que dix-huit ans, et une
maîtresse qui en a quatre-vingts; il aime sa religion, et il ne peut souffrir ceux
qui disent qu'il la faut observer à la rigueur; . . . il aime les trophées et les
victoires, mais il craint autant de voir un bon général à la tête des ses troupes,
qu'il aurait sujet de le craindre à la tête d'une armée ennemie. (Lettre 37, p. 73)]

Had Montesquieu limited his attacks to Louis XIV, he would have
had little to fear. The Sun King had been dead for six years, his subjects
had shed few tears at his death,[6] and the regent had no reason to rise to
the defense of a king whose last will was designed to deprive him of
most of his power. But Montesquieu does not stop there. Dispersed
among the letters and through subtle cross references, one discovers an
attitude that decries monarchy itself as a type of government.

Passing through Smyrna, Usbek describes the harmful effects of
violent Ottoman rule, which persecutes Christians and Jews alike,
leaving its towns in ruins, the countryside deserted, and commerce and
agriculture abandoned (Lettre 19); yet Louis XIV admits to a great
admiration of Turkish government (Lettre 37). The evolution of the
legendary Troglodytes from savagery to a golden age—owing to virtue
and the ideal size of the family group—and finally to decadence when
they decide they need a king (Lettre 14), underlines Montesquieu's
antipathy for absolute monarchies, which Usbek defines as

a violent state which always degenerates into despotism or a republic: power
can never be equitably divided between the people and the prince; the balance
is too difficult to maintain. Power has to diminish on one side while increasing
on the other. But the advantage is usually held by the prince who is at the head
of the army.

[C'est un état violent, qui dégénère toujours en despotisme ou en république;
la puissance ne peut jamais être également partagée entre le peuple et le prince;
l'équilibre est trop difficile à garder. Il faut que le pouvoir diminue d'un côté
pendant qu'il augmente de l'autre; mais l'avantage est ordinairement du côté
du prince, qui est à la tête des armées. (Lettre 102, p. 164)]

Although Usbek's criticism of Louis XIV is tempered by some praise
(the Invalides, the flourishing of commerce and industry), his preference clearly goes to the English system of government, where the
people, often stronger than their king, make their submission condi-
tional on the gratitude they owe him for the benefits they derive from
his government (Lettre 104). More subtly, the same judgment is invoked when Rica is shown a library of historical works in which England, Holland, and Switzerland, where gentle government encourages
commerce and trade, illustrate successful nations compared with absolute monarchies, such as France or Spain, founded by barbarians who
had destroyed the Roman Empire. "These people were not properly
speaking barbaric, since they were free; but they have become so since
most of them, being subjected to absolute power, lost that sweet
liberty so consistent with reason, humanity, and nature." [Ces peuples
n'étaient point proprement barbares, puisqu'ils étaient libres; mais ils
le sont devenus depuis que, soumis pour la plupart à une puissance
absolue, ils ont perdu cette douce liberté si conforme à la raison, à
l'humanité et à la nature (Lettre 136, p. 216).]

Here we encounter the key terms in the *Lettres persanes:* reason,
humanity, nature, conformity, contradiction. Well before Rousseau's
Contrat social (1762), Montesquieu could have exclaimed in a similar
vein, "Man is born free to live in conformity with reason, humanity,
and nature; yet everywhere he is in chains and his actions are a bundle
of contradictions." What went wrong? He supplies the answer in the
complaints of the wise Troglodyte, elected king by his countrymen.

I shall die of grief to have seen the Troglodytes free when I was born only to see
them subjected today. . . . I see indeed what has happened. . . . Your virtue
is beginning to turn into a burden for you. In your present state, having no
chief, you have to be virtuous in spite of yourselves. . . . But this seems too
heavy a burden for you; you prefer being ruled by a prince and obeying his
laws, less rigid than your customs. You know that henceforth you will be able
to satisfy your ambitions, acquire wealth, and languish in slothful voluptuousness; and that, so long as you manage not to commit great crimes, you will not
stand in need of virtue.

[Je mourrai de douleur d'avoir vu en naissant les Troglodytes libres et de les voir aujourd'hui assujettis. . . . Je vois bien ce que c'est, ô Troglodytes! votre vertu commence à vous peser. Dans l'état où vous êtes, n'ayant point de chef, il faut que vous soyez vertueux malgré vous. . . . Mais ce joug vous paraît trop dur; vous aimez mieux être soumis à un prince et obéir à ses lois, moins rigides que vos moeurs. Vous savez que, pour lors, vous pourrez contenter votre ambition, acquérir des richesses et languir dans une lâche volupté, et que, pourvu que vous évitiez de tomber dans les grands crimes, vous n'aurez pas besoin de la vertu. (Lettre 14, p. 44)]

At least the first king of the Troglodytes is a virtuous man, but he is an exception. Even as able a ruler as Louis XIV will soon be spoiled by absolute power; and with age and unlimited vanity, surrounded by flatterers, he will turn into a tyrant and a bigot, full of contradictions that will make his people sigh with relief at his death.

Law's System and the Nobility

But have matters improved since then? Hardly. Montesquieu does not directly attack the regent (in fact, in Lettre 138, p. 219 he praises the short-lived councils created by the regent); yet he heaps abuse on the regent's minister, Abbé Dubois, whom he accuses of wickedness and dishonesty (Lettres 127 and 146), and, of course, on Law and his system.

All those who were rich six months ago are at present poor, and those who had no bread to eat are wallowing in wealth. Never before did the two extremes come so close. The foreigner has turned the state inside out like a used clothes dealer does with a suit: he turns the inside out and the outside in. What unexpected fortunes, unbelievable even for those who made them! Even God cannot raise people more quickly out of nothingness. How many valets are served by their former colleagues and tomorrow perhaps by their masters!

[Tous ceux qui étaient riches il y a six mois sont à présent dans la pauvreté, et ceux qui n'avaient pas de pain regorgent de richesses. Jamais ces deux extrémités ne se sont touchées de si près. L'Etranger a tourné l'Etat comme un fripier tourne un habit: il fait paraître dessus ce qui était dessous; et, ce qui était dessus, il le met à l'envers. Quelles fortunes inespérées, incroyables même à ceux qui les ont faites! Dieu ne tire pas plus rapidement les hommes du néant. Que de valets servis par leurs camarades et peut-être demain par leurs maîtres! (Lettre 138, pp. 219–20).]

Not content to have already attacked religious authority and the king himself, Montesquieu next takes on the nobles, who have lost their usefulness and are reduced to begging favors of ministers. His biting definition of great nobles anticipates that by Beaumarchais in *Le Mariage de Figaro*.

A grandee is a man who sees the king, who talks to the ministers, who has noble ancestors, debts, and a pension. If, under these circumstances, he can hide his idleness under an air of being busy or a feigned fondness of pleasure, he deems himself the happiest of men.

[Un grand seigneur est un homme qui voit le roi, qui parle aux ministres, qui a des ancêtres, des dettes et des pensions. S'il peut, avec cela, cacher son oisiveté par un air empressé ou par un feint attachement pour les plaisirs, il croit être le plus heureux de tous les hommes. (Lettre 88, p. 147)]

But it takes money, enormous sums of money, to maintain the nobles in the state of idleness and uselessness to which they are accustomed—and that means heavy taxes on the bourgeois, the farmers, and the laborers. In an imaginary royal decree Montesquieu expresses his indignation in terms that recall Swift.

We recommend that every farm laborer having five children take away from them daily one-fifth of the bread he gives them. . . .
We command that all persons engaged in low and mechanical labor, who have never been present at the rising ceremony of Our Majesty, buy henceforth their clothes and those of their wives and children only every four years. . . .
And, since we have been advised that most of the bourgeois of our good towns are entirely devoted to providing for the marriage of their daughters, who have not been notable in our state except for their sad and boring modesty, we order that they delay marrying them off until, having reached the age limit prescribed in our ordinances, they are forced by them to do so. We forbid our magistrates to provide for the education of their children.

[Que tout laboureur ayant cinq enfants retranchera journellement la cinquième partie du pain qu'il leur donne. . . .
Ordonnons que toutes personnes qui s'exercent à des travaux vils et mécaniques, lesquelles n'ont jamais été au lever de Notre Majesté, n'achètent désormais d'habits à eux, à leurs femmes et à leurs enfants, que de quatre ans en quatre ans. . . .
Et, d'autant que nous demeurons avertis que la plupart des bourgeois de nos bonnes villes sont entièrement occupés à pourvoir à l'établissement de leurs

filles, lesquelles ne se sont rendues recommandables dans notre état que par
une triste et ennuyeuse modestie, nous ordonnons qu'ils attendront à les
marier jusqu'à ce qu'ayant atteint l'âge limité par les ordonnances elles
viennent à les y contraindre. Défendons à nos magistrat de pourvoir à
l'éducation de leurs enfants. (Lettre 124, p. 198)]

The Courts and Women

Montesquieu extends his criticism of conditions in France to the
judicial system, which he finds to be too complicated and cluttered
with Roman customs (Lettres 100 and 129); to judges who do not
bother to read the laws; and to punishments that exceed the crime. He
is concerned about the falling birthrate in Europe and recommends the
legalization of divorce, among other things (Lettre 16). He also attacks
slavery and the conquest of colonies.

But he does not go to the other extreme, which would have been to
set up Persia as a model to be imitated. That would have been a serious
error, because it would have deprived his critical travelers of credibility. More often than not the Orient comes out on the short end in
comparisons with Europe, and with France in particular. Usbek finds
the Christian religion less fanatic than his own; he approves the fact
that European monarchs punish opponents less cruelly than do the
Persian tyrants; and he applauds the greater liberty enjoyed by French
women, even though he is not happy about the use they make of it
(gambling, seeking to use their influence in politics, etc.). His views
on the conditions of women strike us as extremely modern.

The power we have over them is a veritable tyranny; they have let us take that
power only because they are endowed with more gentleness than we and
consequently, with more humanity and reason. These advantages, which
should have given them a status of superiority, if we had been reasonable, have
made them lose it, because we are not at all reasonable. . . . Why would we
enjoy this privilege? Because we are stronger? In that case it is a veritable
injustice. We use every means to discourage them; equal education would
result in equal strength. Let us test them in talents that have not been
weakened by education, and we shall see who is stronger.

[L'empire que nous avons sur elles est une véritable tyrannie; elles ne nous l'ont
laissé prendre que parce qu'elles ont plus de douceur que nous, et par conséquent, plus d'humanité et de raison. Ces avantages qui devaient sans doute
leur donner la supériorité, si nous avions été raisonnables, le leur ont fait
perdre, parce que nous ne le sommes point. . . . Pourquoi aurions-nous donc

un privilège? Est-ce parce que nous sommes les plus forts? Mais c'est une véritable injustice. Nous employons toutes sortes de moyens pour leur abattre le courage; les forces seraient égales si l'éducation l'était aussi. Eprouvons-les dans les talents que l'éducation n'a point affaiblis, et nous verrons si nous sommes si forts. (Lettre 38, pp. 74–75)]

Montesquieu's Wit

Had Montesquieu limited himself to the harem story and sociopolitical considerations, he would not have achieved the success enjoyed by the *Lettres persanes*. He knew very well how to capture the attention of his audience completely: by adding a humorous and satiric description of Parisian society, its types, its foibles, its ridiculous aspects. La Bruyère had already exposed the types of his times in *Les Caractères* (1688), but Montesquieu mixes satire and caricature in a broad depiction of French manners and of Paris drawing rooms, a subject that will engender future versions by Voltaire (*Candide*), Chateaubriand (*Attala*), and Taine (*Thomas Graindorge*), to mention only the most striking ones.

Today we still smile appreciatively at Montesquieu's bemused portrait of Parisians who cannot understand "how one can possibly be a Persian" [Comment peut-on être Persan? (Lettre 30 p. 66)], and who place vanity above virtue and prefer being complimented for their elegant clothes rather than their intelligence. Here the author frankly amuses himself as he views his countrymen and the inhabitants of the capital through the eyes of his Persians. Just a few of the many delightful pokes he takes at his compatriots:

They gladly admit that other nations are wiser, provided the latter agree in turn that they are better dressed. They are prepared to submit to the laws of a rival nation, provided the French wigmakers can legislate the shape of foreign wigs. . . .
With such noble advantages, what does it matter to them that good sense comes to them from elsewhere and that they have taken from their neighbors all that concerns their political and civil government?

[Ils avouent de bon coeur que les autres peuples sont plus sages, pourvu qu'on convienne qu'ils sont mieux vêtus. Ils veulent bien s'assujettir aux lois d'une nation rivale, pourvu que les perruquiers français décident en législateurs sur la forme des perruques étrangères. . . .
Avec ces nobles avantages, que leur importe que le bon sens leur vienne d'ailleurs et qu'ils aient pris de leurs voisins tout ce qui concerne le gouvernement politique et civil? (Lettre 100, p. 162)]

Frenchmen almost never speak of their wives; the reason is that they are afraid they may be talking of them to people who know them better than they do themselves.

[Les Français ne parlent presque jamais de leurs femmes; c'est qu'ils ont peur d'en parler devant des gens qui les connaissent mieux qu'eux. (Lettre 55, p. 98)]

There is a house here where mad people are locked up. On first view one would be led to believe that it is the largest house in town. Not so! The remedy is quite weak for the illness. Perhaps the French, who are held in low esteem by their neighbors, lock up a few madmen in a house to convince people that those outside are sane.

[Il y a ici une maison où l'on met les fous. On croirait d'abord qu'elle est la plus grande de la Ville. Non! Le remède est bien petit pour le mal. Sans doute que les Français, extrêmement décriés chez leurs voisins, enferment quelques fous dans une maison, pour persuader que ceux qui sont dehors ne le sont pas. (Lettre 78, p. 136)]

The variety of tone in the *Lettres persanes* is astonishing, ranging from oriental pompousness to moral indignation and serious philosophical reflections. In the satiric passages the key resides in contradiction: contradiction between words and action; between pretense and reality; between laws, institutions, customs, and reason, the ultimate judge in human affairs.

Montesquieu is a pioneer in the art of the philosophical tale. Like Voltaire, he does not want to overturn the system but only to subject it to reasonable examination. Nor does he feel in himself the call to become a martyr. Hence the tone: that of a cultured, witty writer who speaks the language of his readers. The formula is simple: have people laugh with you, and you will be read; pound the table, and you'll only hurt your fist.

So it was to be in the eighteenth century, at least until the French Revolution changed all that. But the government was not so ready to laugh as Montesquieu's readers. In two letters (24 and 101) the Persians refer to the Constitution, a term that is likely to puzzle the uninitiated. Crébillon fils will shed more light on this subject, in his own way.

Chapter Two
A Religious Loyalty Oath

The Reign of Louis XV, 1723–54: The Bull Unigenitus

When governments lose their vigor or are headed by leaders who are preoccupied by death rather than by the future, they commit the kind of stupid acts that come back to haunt them and their nation for decades. Such was the case of the papal bull *Unigenitus*.

In the latter half of the seventeenth century a dissident group of Catholics had become known as the Jansenists. Dissatisfied with the moral laxity they felt to be prevalent at the court and in France in general, and with the tolerant attitude of the Jesuits, they proposed a strict adherence to religious doctrines, based on the precept that only the grace of God can save those who have been elected by predestination. They established their own schools at Port-Royal with excellent teachers and lived irreproachable lives. Among those educated by the Jansenists were Pascal and Racine.

Viewing the Jansenists as potential rivals, the all-powerful Jesuits obtained papal orders condemning the Jansenist group, which was dissolved in 1709; Port-Royal was destroyed in 1710. But decrees and acts of destruction do not kill beliefs, and Jansenism continued to have its adherents, particularly in the lower clergy and among many members of the parlements.

A pious book entitled *Réflexions morales sur le Nouveau Testament,* written by Pasquier Quesnel in 1671 and approved by Cardinal de Noailles, was used by the Jesuits to obtain the papal bull *Unigenitus* in 1713 from Clement XI, condemning 101 propositions in Father Quesnel's treatise. This bull, referred to also as the Constitution, led not only to quarrels about religious doctrines but raised at the same time the issue of Gallicanism, a declaration proclaimed in 1682 by the French clergy that accepted the pope's authority in matters of faith but did not consider his pronouncements irrevocable until accepted by consent of the Church.

To circumvent this requirement, Louis XIV presented the bull to a carefully selected group of church dignitaries who, according to the pastoral instructions of Cardinal de Rohan, accepted the condemnation of Quesnel's book, with Cardinal de Noailles and seven bishops dissenting. De Noailles was ordered to leave the court and the dissenting bishops were exiled to their dioceses. To become law, the bull now had to be registered by the parlement, which seized on this opportunity to regain some of its lost power. After great pressure from Louis XIV, the parlement finally registered the bull, but with restrictions. Finally, the Faculty of Theology voted 128 to 9 to accept the bull. Of the dissenters, four were exiled from Paris and five excluded from the assembly.

During the Regency the parlement gained in strength and raised the subject again. A compromise, signed both by de Rohan and de Noailles, produced an illusion of unity. Clement XI died in 1721, the regent in 1723. Noailles wrote to the new pope, Benedict XIII, offering to submit to the bull with certain conditions. Receiving no reply, he submitted unconditionally but retracted near the end of his life, in 1729. In 1727, Bishop Jean Sonan issued a pastoral letter in opposition to the bull. Cardinal Tencin thereupon called together a provincial council to condemn the bishop, who was suspended from his functions until he would withdraw his pastoral letter.

The dispute might have ended there, but in 1730 Louis XV revived it with a declaration forcing all clergy to accept the bull *Unigenitus* without modification and then pressured the parlement to accept his stand, even though the majority opposed it. For their part, the Jesuits demonstrated equal blindness and intolerance by forcing the faithful to present an attestation signed by an approved priest in order to obtain the sacraments. Furthermore, these *billets de confession* were to be issued only to those who had formally adhered to the bull *Unigenitus*.

These measures unleashed unprecedented indignation. Entire towns were abandoned by their priests, so that even burials could not be performed. Now the parlements again entered the quarrel by ordering the clergy to grant Communion to those who requested it or else face confiscation of their property or imprisonment. Matters became so heated that once again Louis XV had to intercede. On 13 December 1754 he issued an order proclaiming the bull the law of church and state. But nothing would quell the opposition, and gradually the scales tipped the other way. In 1762 the Jesuits paid for this and other errors by being chased out of France in their turn.

This blunder, begun by Louis XIV and emphatically continued by his successor, ranks in importance with such divisive issues as the

Dreyfus affair in France or the Vietnam War in the United States, for it left deep scars. Not only did the bull *Unigenitus* lead to dissensions in France for some fifty years (1713–62) but it created resistance to both religious and royal authority, thus contributing to the French Revolution, to an extent that has not yet been properly evaluated. If the Jesuits stood to gain advantages by the bull, at least in the short run, the two kings involved could only lose in their stubborn efforts: for Gallicanism guaranteed their right to appoint cardinals, for all practical purposes, and it was not in their best interest to weaken that doctrine by insisting on adherence to an unpopular papal bull.

The affair of the bull *Unigenitus* should be compulsory reading for all statesmen: it teaches a historical lesson warning them to reflect long and hard before taking on matters that, though not purely political, are yet highly divisive. It is also very instructive on the risks to political leaders (or judges, for that matter) who align themselves with religious groups or who attempt to force their personal moral convictions, whatever the merits and no matter how sincerely held, on the people as a whole.

Religious dogma was apparently a lesser preoccupation of the various parties involved in the dispute. The ultramontane Jesuits were interested in strengthening their position, the parlement in gaining power, the kings in imposing their will. Only the lower clergy and dissenting church leaders demonstrated their faith by the risks they took.

The liberal philosophes, about whom we shall learn more in the next chapter, watched this power struggle with bemused indignation. If they denounced the bull and its defenders, it was because they saw in it an act of intolerance, and because it provided them with an ideal opportunity to cast discredit on both royal and religious authority. A certain tenor in their writings seems to suggest that they were more sympathetic to the Jansenists than to the Jesuits,[1] but in reality they only used the Jansenist issue to embarrass the more powerful Jesuits. D'Alembert's letters to Voltaire around the time the Jesuits were banished leave little doubt about their feelings. "Believe me, no human weakness. Let the Jansenist and Parlement rabble get rid of the Jesuit rabble for us, and don't prevent the spiders from devouring each other" (25 September 1762). And later: "If you want to know my scale of values: for me, a philosopher ranks above a king, a king above a minister, a minister above an intendant, an intendant above a counselor, a counselor above a Jesuit, and a Jesuit above a Jansenist" (12 January 1763).

As for Crébillon fils, who did not, properly speaking, belong to the philosophes, what seems to have galled him particularly was the loyalty oath that was being exacted of the French people. Loyalty oaths do not sit well with independent thinkers, regardless of whether they are imposed in eighteenth-century France or during the McCarthy era in the United States. And Crébillon seized on that aspect of the bull *Unigenitus* dispute to express his own indignation.

Chronology

1723:	Louis XV assumes reign of government.
1726–1743:	Ministry of Cardinal Fleury.
1727:	Pastoral Letter by Bishop Sonan against bull.
1730:	Louis XV orders all clergy to accept the bull *Unigenitus*.
1733:	Beginning of War of Polish Succession.
1734:	Crébillon fils: *L'Ecumoire*.
1738:	Treaty of Vienna: Lorraine awarded to Stanislas and, on his death, to France.
1741–1748:	War of Austrian Succession.
1745–1764:	Mme de Pompadour mistress of Louis XV.
1751:	First volume of *Encyclopédie* published.
1754:	Order by Louis XV making bull *Unigenitus* the law of church and state.

Crébillon fils: *L'Ecumoire*

Oh! Those Mad Japanese!

Just what made Crébillon fils write *L'Ecumoire; ou, Tanzaï et Néadarné. Histoire japonaise* (1734) will probably never be known. But then Crébillon is full of surprises, especially for those who, without having read a single line of his, relegated him for some two centuries to the position of second rank as a writer of light and licentious novels.[2] On closer examination one discovers, beneath the bantering and elegant tone of his novels, a biting social critic but little, if any, political commentary. When learning that Crébillon was appointed censor in 1759, we are even more at a loss to explain why he would have taken it upon himself to write so subversive a work as *L'Ecumoire.*

Perhaps it will help to recall that the young Crébillon had been president of le Caveau at the rue de Bussi in Paris, where, between 1733 and 1740, writers and artists gathered to drink, judge new plays, and talk irreverently about everything. Nor should it be forgotten that the young writer, living in the shadow of his famous father, the playwright, was obviously looking for ways to make a name for himself. Did he perhaps write *L'Ecumoire* because he hoped to create a scandal and benefit from it? If so, he had calculated correctly. The book turned out to be his best-seller. Between 1734 and 1789, 32 editions were printed. If one compares this with the number of editions produced during the same period of the two record holders, Voltaire's *Candide* (55) and Rousseau's *La Nouvelle Héloïse* (35), it is easy to gauge the popular success of Crébillon's Japanese tale.

On the other hand, Crébillon was no doubt sincerely outraged at the way the bull *Unigenitus* was being forced on the French clergy and people. For that indignation he took a grave risk: *L'Ecumoire* appeared on 5 December 1734; on 8 December he was imprisoned in the donjon of Vincennes. On the intercession of influential persons, particularly the Princesse de Conti, he was released on 13 December.[3] Had it not been for his good relations at the court, Crébillon might well have become a political martyr and perhaps even an inhabitant of the Bastille.

Yet, he had taken quite a few precautions. The first edition had appeared anonymously in Amsterdam, with these dates of publication: "At Peking: Lou-Chou-Chu-La, Sole Printer of His Chinese Majesty for Foreign Languages. 1734." And in the preface, the author had taken care to present a highly confusing account of the fate of this tale, attributed to Confucius but actually written by a certain Kiloho-éé ten centuries earlier. The "translator" had dug up a Venetian version and produced the present work, which he had especially prepared for French readers by omitting oriental mannerisms and embellishing it with suitable reflections.

Crébillon here uses the customary preface of self-protection where the author poses as a translator (Montesquieu had employed the same device) or as the simple editor of letters he claims to have found. But the tone of the preface is so obviously tongue-in-cheek that one cannot possibly take it seriously. Perhaps Choderlos de Laclos profited from

Crébillon's misadventures by assuming a more serious tone in his preface of *Les Liaisons dangereuses* (1782), where he claims a moral purpose for his novel.

Crébillon's Japanese tale primarily serves, of course, as a pretext for satirizing and chastising the ruthless power play of royalty and the Jesuits in enforcing the bull *Unigenitus*. Nevertheless, it has a charm of its own, due especially to the mixture of pseudo–oriental language in the telling of the story, French sophistication in the author's reflections, and unexpected biting seriousness in certain speeches. In this respect Crébillon's *L'Ecumoire* occupies a medial position between Montesquieu's *Lettres persanes*, where the author supposedly never intervenes, and Voltaire's *Candide*, where the tone is almost uniformly satiric.

Formally, *L'Ecumoire* is a parody of the oriental tale. It maintains the exterior form of the genre but changes the content in such a way that a comical tension between subject and narrative manner is produced. At the same time the exotic and erotic character of the tale provides a protective pretext intended to shield the anonymous narrator against censors who might sense the allusions to contemporary situations.

The plot of *L'Ecumoire* is basically simple: two young people in love cannot consummate their marriage until each has been initiated by someone else. Crébillon envelops this licentious material in a mist of complicated and fantastic circumstances, no doubt intentionally so, in order to confuse and mislead the censors.

The hero, Prince Hiaouf-Zélès-Tanzaï (Rival of the Sun), although "knowing everything without ever having learned anything" (compliments of Molière), is a perfectly nice young man, who is protected by the fairy Barbacela. Since the characters are subject to power struggles among the powerful fairies, Crébillon takes a swipe at the corruption inherent in absolute power, in an indirect allusion to the French monarchy.

In those times the fairies governed the universe. It is well known that these spirits, relying more on whims than reason, were bound to conduct their functions rather badly. It is rare that unlimited power is not abused, and whoever can do whatever he pleases does not always consult justice when carrying out his will. That was true of the fairies.

[En ce temps-là les fées gouvernaient l'univers. On n'ignore pas que ces intelligences, consultant plus le caprice que la raison, en devaient assez mal régler la conduite. Il est rare qu'on n'abuse pas d'un pouvoir sans bornes et quiconque peut faire tout ce qui lui plaît, ne détermine pas toujours ses volontés sur la justice. C'est ce qui arrivait aux fées. (p. 12)][4]

Crébillon's language is very cautious. He uses moderating terms, such as "it is rare" or "not always" to indicate that there are exceptions to these rules, which, along with the distant period referred to ("in those times"), leaves room to exempt Louis XV from this criticism.

Compounding the confusion by making Céphaès (Happiness of the People; read: le Bien Aimé-Louis XV) the father of Tanzaï (Rival of the Sun; read: le Roi Soleil-Louis XIV), Crébillon depicts the ruler of Chéchian as a kindly king, who leaves the choice of a wife up to his son. The trouble is that the fairy Barbacela has warned Tanzaï not to marry until he has reached the age of twenty, for otherwise a great misfortune will befall him. But at a court where love affairs are the principal preoccupation, a young and sensitive man finds it impossible to wait that long and Tanzaï decides to get married, regardless of the consequences.

Reminiscent of Louis XV's marriage, twelve princesses arrive at the court (in the case of Louis XV, a list of seventeen eligible candidates had been drawn up) and Tanzaï is to spend a week with each of them. But he immediately falls in love with the beautiful and gracious Néadarné and decides to marry her despite Barbacela's entreaties for delay. As a means of counteracting the fate that awaits him, the fairy gives him a golden skimmer, three feet long with a round handle three inches in diameter and pierced so that a string of jewelled beads can be inserted.

Thereupon the following discussion ensues among the fairy, the king, and Tanzaï. It is a fine sample of Crébillon's tone, which succeeds in making horrible matters sound naive and humorous:

The day of your nuptials, you will meet, at a little distance from the temple, with a little old woman. Seize her; and tho' she struggle ever so hard, and use ever so many entreaties, cram the handle of this skimmer, without the least pity or remorse, into her mouth. — But, aetherial highness, says the prince, where shall I find a mouth to fit that skimmer? — You are not to trouble yourself about that, replied the fairy; nor do I myself tell you that the old woman won't let you cram it in. But this is not all. The instant you have drawn the handle out of this venerable dame's mouth, you must fly with it to the high priest, and make the same experience on him. — The high priest! cried the king; he surely will never suffer Tanzaï to do that: How! swallow the handle of a skimmer! —I can't say, says the prince, what he will do; but that I know, that were I in his place, no power in the universe should cram me in that manner. — This, however, continued the fairy, must be attempted, not by force but by persuasion, and all the soothing arts you can think of. — Persuasion, however, continued Tanzaï, would probably succeed better than any other method you hint at. . . . But pray, tell me, cries Tanzaï, do you think that a man, to whom so whimsical a proposal should be made, would be so silly as to acquiesce with it? This handle is of so monstrous a size, that no mouth, be it ever so wide, will be capacious enough to take it in.

[— Le jour de vos noces, vous trouverez auprès du temple une petite vieille. Saisissez-vous-en et quelque résistance qu'elle vous fasse, de quelque prière qu'elle use, enfoncez-lui sans pitié le manche de cette écumoire dans la bouche.

—Mais, Altesse éthérée, dit le prince, où trouverai-je une bouche à qui ce manche puisse convenir?

—Cette inquiétude n'est pas faite pour vous, reprit la fée, aussi ne vous dis-je pas que la vieille ne souffre pas à soutenir cette opération. Ce n'est pas tout. Dans l'instant que vous aurez retiré le manche de la bouche de cette vieille, vous irez le porter au grand-prêtre, à qui vous ferez la même chose.

—Le grand prêtre! s'écria le roi. Il n'y consentira jamais: avaler le manche d'une écumoire!

—Je ne sais, reprit le prince, ce qu'il fera, mais à sa place, aucune puissance ne m'y forcerait.

—C'est cependant ce qu'il faut tâcher qu'il fasse, dit la fée, non par la violence, mais par la persuasion et les moyens les plus doux que vous pourrez employer.

—Elle serait pourtant plus sûre, reprit Tanzaï, que tout ce que vous dites. . . .

—Mais, de bonne foi, dit Tanzaï, croyez-vous qu'un homme à qui l'on fera une pareille proposition, puisse l'accepter? Ce manche est d'une grosseur si monstrueuse, qu'il n'y a point de bouche si énorme où il ne trouvât encore à fendre. (*L'Ecumoire,* pp. 36–37)]

Tanzaï succeeds with the old woman, who turns out to be Concombre (Cucumber), the fairy nurse of one of the ladies he had rejected, but the high priest Saugrénutio staunchly refuses to have the skimmer stuck into his mouth, and Tanzaï, anxious to get married, promises to leave him in peace.

At the wedding night Tanzaï discovers to his horror that the indispensable organ for that occasion has disappeared. He rubs the spot with the skimmer, which sticks to it. In this dilemma the Royal Council decides to consult the Great Monkey, the local oracle, which replies through the voice of Concombre, "He must set out, he must travel over, he must lie down, he must return." [Qu'il aille, qu'il parcoure, qu'il couche, qu'il revienne. (*L'Ecumoire*, p. 80)]

So Tanzaï sets out. He comes upon an old woman who is brewing something and needs a skimmer. He offers his, which now comes loose. The woman, who is of course a fairy, tells him she cannot help him, but that he must go to the Island of the Wasps and spend the night with the beauty who rules there. That "beauty" is of course Concombre, who informs him that he must lie with her thirteen times, and she cheats him at that. Tanzaï obeys with such obvious displeasure that Concombre swears further vengeance.

Crébillon very cleverly entitles chapter 18, where the allusions to the bull *Unigenitus* are too obvious, "The Least Diverting in the Whole Book" (Le moins amusant du livre). Meanwhile, back home in Chéchian, the king has been joined by the patriarch, who threatens the high priest with punishment if he does not lick the skimmer. Everybody is now aligned against Saugrénutio: the king, the patriarch, the nobility, the people, even the clergy; but the latter change alliances when it appears that they too will have to lick the skimmer. They form a secret society and spread the rumor that everybody, including the king, will eventually be forced to go through that ordeal.

This rumor makes the king feel uneasy, and an assembly is called at which Saugrénutio again refuses the patriarch's demand to obey. He answers with a speech in which he berates the pusillanimity of the people and the decadence of the nobility.

When Tanzaï returns to the court, he finds that a misfortune similar to his has befallen Néadarné. Her oracle states, "The Princess will never be restored to her former state till the Great Genius Chawmole shall have treated her agreeable to his sacred pleasure." [La Princesse ne se reverra dans son premier état, que le Grand Génie Mange-Taupe n'en ait disposé selon sa sainte volonté. (*L'Ecumoire*, p 144)]

They set out together and meet Moustache, who has been transformed into a mole and whose lover Cormoran has been condemned by the genie Jonquille to dance at his court. After listening to Moustache's story, told in a pastiche of Marivaux's style, Néadarné, after much resistance, is "cured" by the gallant Jonquille. Moustache reveals to her the secret of restoring her virginity and then takes Cormoran back with her by means of a magic slipper that renders them invisible.

Tanzaï is surprised by Néadarné's recovery but prefers not to ask too many questions. They return to Chéchian, where Saugrénutio has promised to lick the skimmer, so that he can take over the succession of the deceased patriarch—and all ends well.

Keys to the Characters

Crébillon's characters do not always neatly correspond to historical persons and seem at times to be a combination of several people holding similar or even opposite views. Although Louis XIV (Tanzaï) and Louis XV (Céphaès, Tanzaï's father) are interchanged, Tanzaï is obviously modeled on Louis XV. He displays the religious devotion and premarital problems reminiscent of Louis XV. The reference is all the more direct, since on 9 June 1733, only eighteen months before *L'Ecumoire* appeared, a Jansenist woman had created a scandal by publicly accusing Louis XV of being impotent. Néadarné consequently represents the queen, Marie Leczinska, except for physical differences.

A number of different models have been suggested for the high priest Saugrénutio. They include, besides the obvious bull resisters Cardinal de Noailles and Bishop Sonan, Cardinal Dubois and Bishop Gui de Guérarpin, abbé de Vauréal. Some critics even point to Cardinal de Rohan who, although a vigorous defender of the bull, bears some resemblance to Saugrénutio.[5] The patriarch, in his insistence on obedience to the bull, obviously recalls Cardinals de Rohan and Tencin. He may also represent Cardinal Fleury or even Pope Clement XI; in turn, the latter can be perceived in the fairy Barbacela, who persuades the king and Tanzaï to force people to lick the skimmer.

From these examples we can see how Crébillon combined sometimes contradictory references to characters and opinions to confuse the censors and amuse those who tried to play the game of finding the keys to the characters he depicts.

On closer examination, matters do indeed turn out to be more complicated than they appear at first view, for Crébillon created a satiric web in which the "good guys" are in reality the villains and vice versa. If we read *L'Ecumoire* sympathetically (and Crébillon inclines the reader to do just that), we align ourselves with the young couple, hoping that they will overcome all obstacles in the way of their union and live happily ever after. But if we read the novel from the political point of view, it soon dawns on us that Tanzaï, willingly or unwillingly (unwillingly at first, willingly thereafter), plays the role of a Japanese Joe McCarthy, insisting at all cost that Saugrénutio lick the skimmer. And that very Saugrénutio is the villain of the story, the kill-joy whose refusal to submit causes all the problems the young lovers have to contend with. Thus the forewarned reader has to interpret Crébillon's novel on several levels, that do not correspond as in an orchestral score, since the political line has to be read counter to the straight story line.

Political and Erotic Symbols

The skimmer, around which all the events revolve, was a stroke of genius on the part of the author, because the object not only symbolizes to perfection the act to be attacked but joins the two principal aspects of *L'Ecumoire:* the political and the erotic.

The skimmer as an object suggests a multiform symbol, both in its description and in its function. On the political level it obviously represents the bull *Unigenitus,* with its oversized handle, which the French king and the ultramontane Jesuits want to force into the mouth and literally cram down the throat of clergy and believers alike.[6] Its material function, which is to separate what is to be kept from what is to be thrown away, or what is more precious from what is less valuable, enables Crébillon to comment on reactions to the bull without having to express his views in words, for the skimmer divides the French into two sorts of people: the cream who reject the bull, and the scum who accept it.[7]

On the erotic level the handle of the skimmer is obviously a phallic symbol,[8] and licking the skimmer suggests fellatio, a gratuitous act in this instance, designed for the pleasure of royal and religious authorities, placing those who accept the bull in a subservient and servile position. Like all of Crébillon's novels, *L'Ecumoire* contains erotic elements, which are cleverly woven into the political fabric of the work. Both Tanzaï and Néadarné have to go through an amorous experience with a third party before they can be happily united, and the author treats these relations not as acts of adultery but as a rite of initiation, for Néadarné's virginity is miraculously restored and both, despite some doubts, choose not to pursue the matter too far.

Crébillon was too skillful a writer to risk boring his readers with a didactically "committed" novel. Although contemporary critics condemned the licentious and satiric parts of the work, he knew that his readers (and critics as well, for that matter) would pore over them with unavowed pleasure. The greatest asset of *L'Ecumoire,* however, is its comic, lighthearted tone, interspersed with reflections on amorous, literary, and political matters.[9] Crébillon maintains the elegant, sophisticated tone that makes for the charm of the best eighteenth-century novels. And many a reader no doubt forgot all about the grave questions concerning papal bulls and forced-down skimmers while being entertained by such intriguing matters as how a woman should act in love if she wants to keep her man, or how a noble or society lady always knows full well what she is doing when she puts herself into a compromising situation, observations that can take their place alongside Crébillon's often-quoted remarks in *La Nuit et le moment* on eighteenth-century relations between the sexes. [10]

Criticism of Church and Nobility

The tone changes when the subject turns to politics, not so much the tone of the author, who never drops his detached manner of story telling, as the one assumed by his characters, particularly in formal speeches or in the rendering of their thoughts and apprehensions. On these occasions the religious, social, and political ills that beset France are brought to light: the power of the Church, the corruption of the priests, their dependence on the pope, and the latter's attempts to curtail the privileges of the French kings.

Especially daring are the passages that deal with the impotence of the aristocracy, the reasons for the alliance between throne and church, and Saugrénutio's appeal to the people to resist the forced acceptance of the bull *Unigenitus*. Addressing the nobles, Saugrénutio chastises them for their degenerate state, which leaves them entirely dependent on royal favors, and he shames them with the example of their ancestors.

Behold then those haughty Chechianians, whose reputation filled every corner of the universe! Behold this so famous people! A vile skimmer now makes this race of heroes tremble! Pristine defenders of the state, pursued he, addressing himself to the nobility, it is not of you that I implore relief: the abject condition wherein I behold you, sufficiently informs me of your meanness of spirit. Bend you under the yoke of tyranny, you are not worthy of enjoying liberty: but burn these celebrated records, which have transmitted down to you the glorious actions of your ancestors. I exhort you not to set before your eyes their glorious examples. . . . They who don't blush at submitting to slavery, deserve not to know that ever men were free.

[Les voilà donc ces fiers Chéchianiens, qui remplissaient le monde entier de leur gloire! Voilà ce peuple si fameux! Une vile écumoire fait trembler ces augustes mortels! Anciens défenseurs de l'Etat, ajouta-t-il, en adressant la parole à la noblesse, ce n'est pas à vous que je demande des secours: l'avilissement où je vous vois m'instruit de votre faiblesse. Pliez donc sous le joug de la tyrannie, vous n'êtes pas dignes de jouir de la liberté: mais brûlez ces fastes célèbres qui vous ont conservé les faits glorieux de vos ancêtres. Je ne vous encourage point à y puiser des exemples de vertu. . . . Qui ne rougit point de sa servitude, ne mérite pas de savoir qu'il y a eu des hommes libres. (pp. 123–24)]

Over two hundred years before Jean-Paul Sartre attacked the alliance between absolute rulers and the Church in *Les Mouches,* Crébillon took the risk of exposing the reasons that make a king enter into this association.

He [Céphaès] was incensed at seeing the patriarchs owe their dignity to kings, and yet continually to be wanting in their respect to them. But superstition rendered them venerable. Besides, he thought it concerned him, not to destroy absolutely an authority, which, accustoming his subjects to obey, rendered them more subservient to his commands, and faithful to their oaths.

A people without religion will soon be without obedience. If they neither acknowledge, or stand in favor of any gods, human laws are no longer any restraint upon them, they become their own legislators; their caprice is the only rule they go by; they only set up, in order to have the pleasure of tearing down. Continually disgusted with their own handy work, fond of novelty, they run perpetually from project to project: fearless of what may happen, they either absolutely destroy the remembrance of the gods, or look upon their anger as something so distant from them that they hardly think it is to be dreaded.

But a people who are governed by other maxims, submissive to their kings, look upon them as a present from the deity, and never imagine they have liberty to judge them, or even to examine the nature of their authority, or prescribe any limits to it. But, on the other hand, when more superstitious than religious, more timorous than enlightened, a mistaken notion of religion will carry them a great way. More struck with the external worship, than with the existence of the deity; more obedient to his ministers than to himself, they imagine them wronged when they have but justice done them; and the king, being the victim of the prejudices of his subjects, dares not deliver himself from slavery, for fear of exciting troubles wherein his person and dignity would be equally exposed.

[Il était indigné de voir les patriarches devoir leur place aux rois, et sans cesse leur manquer: mais la superstition les rendait vénérables. Il avait cru d'ailleurs qu'il lui importait de ne pas anéantir absolument une autorité qui accoutumant les sujets à obéir, les rendait plus dociles à ses volontés, et plus fidèles à leurs serments. Un peuple sans religion est bientôt sans obéissance. S'il ne connaît point de dieux, s'il n'en craint pas, les lois humaines ne sont plus rien devant lui. Il devient son législateur, son caprice seul fait sa règle; il n'élève que pour abattre. Incessamment révolté contre son propre ouvrage, son génie en proie aux nouveautés le fait courir sans cesse de projets en projets: sans crainte pour l'avenir, ou il anéantit absolument le souvenir des dieux, ou il envisage de si loin leur colère, qu'à peine pense-t-il qu'elle soit à craindre. Un peuple qui se conduit par d'autres maximes, tranquille à l'égard des rois, les regarde comme un présent de la divinité, et n'imagine pas qu'il lui soit réservé de les juger, ou de discuter seulement la nature de leur autorité, et d'y donner des limites. Mais aussi, plus superstitieux que religieux, moins vertueux que timide, plus crédule qu'éclairé, une idée mal entendue de la religion le mène loin: plus frappé du culte extérieur, que de l'existence de la divinité, plus soumis à ses ministres qu'à elle-même, il les croit lésés où on leur fait justice et le roi, victime des préjugés des sujets, n'ose sortir d'esclavage, dans la crainte d'exciter des troubles où sa personne et sa dignité seraient également compromises. (pp. 116–17)]

A Call to Revolution

The precautionary remark on superstition being worse than religious belief should not distract us from being amazed at the boldness of this speech. Taking on at the same time the king, the church, and the pope required unusual courage. But more is yet to come. New, previously unheard of accents, a literal call to revolution (we are in 1734!) pervade Saugrénutio's appeal to the nobles, to the recalcitrant clergy, and to the people to resist the forced acceptance of the bull *Unigenitus*.

Let us die, if need be, but let us die as citizens; useful to our country until our last breath, let us at least show how to rid oneself of servitude. . . . Call on all your courage. Smash the shackles that have been put on you; they will disappear when you no longer kiss them. People only humble those whom they believe capable of remaining in that state. . . . Let us cast off this odious yoke under which we have cowered so long! Let the people, after witnessing our indignities, finally watch our vengeance! We shall be feared as soon as we want to be. Let us obliterate those offensive decrees dictated by enmity and injustice, and I guarantee that we shall succeed. Nothing is impossible for men who fight for their gods and for their liberty.[11]

[Mourons, s'il le faut, mais mourons en citoyens; utiles à notre patrie jusque dans nos derniers instants, montrons-lui du moins comme on sait se délivrer de la servitude. . . . Rappelez votre courage. Brisez les fers qu'on vous impose, ils disparaîtront quand vous ne les baiserez plus. On ne jette dans l'abaissement que ceux qu'on croit capables d'y rester. . . . Secouons ce joug odieux, sous lequel nous avons si longtemps fléchi! Que le peuple, témoin de nos affronts, le soit enfin de notre vengeance! Nous serons craints dès que nous voudrons l'être. Effaçons ces décrets offensants qu'ont dictés l'inimitié et l'injustice, je vous réponds du succès. De quoi ne sont pas capables des hommes qui combattent pour leurs Dieux et pour leur liberté? (pp. 124, 127–28)]

And so an apparently innocent Japanese fairy tale, invented by Crébillon fils, turned into a violent attack on the abuse of power by narrow-minded Jesuits and a stubborn absolute monarchy, both incapable of realizing that loyalty oaths to papal bulls was one sure way of teaching the French how to resist religious and royal decrees. And who would have thought that a writer who would be considered for well over two centuries as a minor author of libertine novels would be the one to risk his freedom and his career, perhaps even his life, to express the indignation of his countrymen?

While *L'Ecumoire* does not figure among Crébillon's best works, in the realm of eighteenth-century opposition literature it deserves a special place because of its originality. It is neither a satire nor a *conte philosophique*. The former, as a rule, contains no serious passages, and the latter attempts to convey a message or a lesson (this is not the best of all possible worlds; we should not exaggerate our importance in the universe, etc.). By contrast, *L'Ecumoire* is a Japanese commedia dell'arte where the love problems of the young couple serve as a pretext for the plot, where the older stereotyped characters (king, patriarch, high priest) conduct the action, and where Tanzaï wields a Harlequin's stick that is used, not to beat the bottoms of other characters, but to shove it down their throats.

And while Montesquieu's *Lettres persanes* and Voltaire's *contes philosophiques* flail at many ills, Crébillon, in *L'Ecumoire,* points his pen at a single issue, thus achieving a unity of purpose that is very rarely found in similar works of the eighteenth century.

Chapter Three
A Philosophical Gardener
The Reign of Louis XV, 1755–74

The abbé, and later cardinal, Fleury turned out to be a capable minister who surrounded himself with competent men. He felt that, after Louis XIV's costly wars, what France needed most was peace. Despite a strong war party, headed by Chauvelin, Fleury managed to keep France out of hostilities until 1733, when Stanislas, having been restored to the Polish throne, was toppled by the Russian army. Fleury had no choice but to defend Louis XV's father-in-law, but he kept the conflict with Russia and Austria to a minimum. Lorraine was occupied by the French and some territory taken in the Milan region. Stanislas was made king of Lorraine and peace was restored by 1736. Chauvelin was fired from his office and exiled.

With peace and a stable government, economic conditions improved, especially benefiting financiers, merchants, and traders, who profited from overseas and colonial trade as well as from rising prices. But industry developed far more slowly than in England, due to a strong conservatism that opposed new methods; to rigid state regulations; and to the restrictive practices of the guilds. Contrary to Montesquieu's fear of depopulation, France had grown from a nation of some 17 million in 1715 to nearly 22 million by 1750. But with little modernization of agriculture, many rural inhabitants had to turn to domestic jobs or work for low wages in the towns.

When Fleury died in 1743, Louis XV decided he would henceforth have no prime minister but run the government himself. The French king was certainly more concerned with the welfare of his subjects than one would gather from the saying attributed to him, "Après moi, le déluge." But he simply did not possess the firmness of character and the patience to deal continuously with matters of state, to devise policies and stick to them, and to ward off the intrigues of ambitious people around him. His only passion was hunting, and his congenital boredom was barely assuaged by mistresses. Mme de Pompadour and Mme du Barry were the most notable among the number of women who assumed that function. Mme de Pompadour, although involved in court intrigues, favored the arts and gathered writers around her.

Under these circumstances it was, of course, impossible to solve the ancien régime's most pressing problem: finances. Louis XIV, lavishing money on his court and on expensive wars, had left the French treasury in a sorry state. After the failure of Law's system during the Regency, several reforms were attempted so as to have the burden of taxes more equitably distributed. But all efforts ran afoul on the opposition of those who refused to give up their tax-exempt status: the nobles and the Church, aided by the parlements, which eagerly seized on every opportunity to oppose the will of the government. Consequently, taxes continued to be collected by *fermiers généraux* who bought their charges and then proceeded to squeeze all they could out of the taxpayers. Most of the French actually loved their king (Louis XV was called "le Bien-Aimé"), but they must have had second thoughts on the matter when taxes took such ugly forms as the *gabelle,* the odious salt tax, or the *taille,* a tax imposed on land.

After the death of peace-loving Fleury, France participated in the game of shifting alliances that were the rule during the eighteenth century. Now allied with Frederick II, a most unreliable friend, now with Austria against Frederick, French policy was made by ambitious but self-seeking and mediocre ministers. To make matters still worse, Louis XV pursued his own secret plans, which were frequently at odds with official policy. As a result of this confused conduct of foreign affairs, by 1756 France found itself involved in the Seven Years' War. Allied with Austria, Russia, Sweden, and Saxony, the French were fighting Prussia and England. After some initial successes, Frederick drove the French back in Europe, while England succeeded in dismantling French overseas possessions. Placed in charge of foreign affairs in 1758, the duc de Choiseul managed to have Spain join the war in 1761. Still, the 1763 Treaty of Paris with England deprived France of Canada, Senegal, a number of West Indian islands, and of Indian possessions, while Louisiana was ceded to Spain.

After that disastrous war Choiseul managed to rebuild some of France's lost power by reforming and improving its military and naval organizations. In 1766, when Stanislas died, Lorraine was made part of France. In addition, Corsica was purchased from the Republic of Genoa for two million livres. Faithful to his policy of alliances with Spain and Austria, Choiseul arranged the marriage between Marie-Antoinette of Austria and the future Louis XVI. But he lost his favor with the king when he urged military support of Spain in a dispute with England over the Falkland Islands. Power now fell into the hands of Maupeou and Abbé Terray, who desperately tried to introduce once again needed financial and judicial reforms. The opposition of the parlements was crushed by exiling them to far-off places. A number of important reforms were actually put into operation, but Louis XV's death in 1774 left their implementation in a state of uncertainty.

More important, in the long run, than the opposition of the parlements to established authority was that of the intellectuals, who formed a loose group variously known as the philosophes or the *encyclopédistes*. While not necessarily agreeing on all issues and, in fact, quarreling lustily among themselves (e.g., Rousseau against almost everybody), they thought essentially alike on basic questions, such as the application of reason (not always uniformly defined) to human and social affairs, tolerance in religion, the abuses of aristocratic privileges, the insanity and inhumanity of wars. Hence the philosophes were not metaphysical philosophers, like Plato, Aristotle, or Descartes, but primarily social philosophers living, and deeply interested, in their own society and its problems.

The *Encyclopédie* contained the arsenal of weapons that were to be fired at existing conditions. Its editor was Denis Diderot, seconded by d'Alembert. Among its contributors the most eminent were Montesquieu, Voltaire, Rousseau, Helvétius, Condillac, and d'Holbach. Utilizing a method already applied by Pierre Bayle in his *Dictionnaire historique et critique* (1697), the *Encyclopédie* (1751–80) is, in large part, a subversive enterprise. Underneath the veil of a traditional encyclopedia filled with conventional-looking articles, a system of cross references, footnotes, and apparently academic remarks creates a network of attacks against government, religion, and superstition, which are judged against enlightened, rational, and scientific standards. The general tone is one of optimism engendered by the hope that the Age of Enlightenment would result in almost linear progress. As time progressed, Voltaire was forced to modify this attitude in the light of facts and events.

Chronology

1756–1763:   Seven Years' War against Prussia and England.

1759:   Voltaire: *Candide*.

1760: Rousseau: *La Nouvelle Héloïse.*

1762: Jesuit order chased from France.

1763: Treaty of Paris; France loses Canada and other overseas possessions.

1766: Lorraine becomes part of France.

1770: Marriage of future Louis XVI and Marie-Antoinette.

1771: Maupeou introduces financial and judicial reforms; parlements exiled.

1774: Death of Louis XV.

Voltaire

In his *Pensées,* Pascal writes, "If Cleopatra's nose had been shorter, the entire face of the world would have been changed." One can play this game with many other hypotheses. If Voltaire had not been beaten up by the lackeys of the chevalier de Rohan and if Beaumarchais had been accorded honors by Louis XVI's government, France might still be a monarchy. But Voltaire *was* beaten up by a nobleman's valets, and rarely was revenge sweeter, longer, and more effective. A propaganda machine went into motion that shook the ground loose from under one of the most solidly established regimes in history.

Theater

Voltaire believed quite rightly that the theater was the most suitable place to create an immediate effect. Considered, along with Crébillon père, the greatest playwright of his age, Voltaire inserted verses in his tragedies that spoke directly to the audience of the day. Obviously, this very relevance prevents his theater from being relevant today, but he cared far more about influencing his own times than about the immortality of his plays.

While he was far from alone in expressing daring opinions in the theater,[1] Voltaire illustrates better than any other dramatic author of his age the issues raised and the method employed. By treating classical or historical themes, he was able to make oblique but readily identifiable references to kings, clergy, nobility, wars, and current events.

Since reason rejects supernatural dogma in religion, the philosophes could hardly be expected to accept the idea of the divine right of kings,

a doctrine that endowed the reigning monarch with divine approval as
the representative of God on earth. Hence they suggested that kings are
human beings like everybody else and that the origin of their exalted
status can be found in an act of usurpation of power.

> The first one to be king was a happy soldier. . . .
> But in this common danger, a king is but a man. . . .
> To die for his country is the duty of a king.

> [Le premier qui fut roi fut un soldat heureux. . . . (*La Mort de César*)
> Mais un roi n'est qu'un homme en ce commun danger. . . .
> Mourir pour son pays, c'est le devoir d'un roi.
>
> (*Oedipe*, 1718: 1.3; 2.4)]

And, addressing Octavius and Anthony, Voltaire casts a gauntlet at the
rulers. "To what masters, great gods, you abandon the universe!" [A
quels maîtres, grands dieux, livrez-vous l'univers!] (*Le Triumvirat*,
1.1).

Still bolder are the verses in *Brutus* (1730), Voltaire's most obviously
antiroyalist play, where the king is reminded that there exists a social
contract between him and his subjects and that they are free to rebel if
he breaks his part of the contract.

> Remember that in this very place, at this august altar,
> Before these same gods, he swore to be just;
> This was the link between him and his people:
> He relieves us of our oaths when he breaks his;
> And, once he dares be unfaithful to Roman laws,
> Rome no longer is his subject, and he alone a rebel.

> [Songez qu'en ce lieu même, à cet autel auguste,
> Devant ces mêmes dieux, il jura d'être juste;
> De son peuple et de lui tel était le lien:
> Il nous rend nos serments lorsqu'il trahit le sien;
> Et dès qu'aux lois de Rome il ose être infidèle,
> Rome n'est plus sujette, et lui seul est rebelle.
>
> (*Brutus*, 1.2)]

In *Mahomet*, first performed in 1741, Voltaire deals religion a serious
blow. He is not the least concerned with historical veracity in his

depiction of the prophet as a power-hungry tyrant, who uses religious ideology to subject masses of people by creating a mystique that enables him to "stifle any critical thought, to raise the young in blind obedience, to terrorize the people, to impose an equality which implies neither liberty nor respect of human rights."[2] To achieve his goal, any means are good, including murder and incitement to parricide and incest. Voltaire cleverly combines what he perceives as the clergy's lust for power with his criticism of the divine right of kings.

> The people, blind, weak, are born for great men;
> To admire, to believe, and to obey us. . . .
> Whoever does more than he should does not serve me well.
> I obey my god; as for you, obey me.
>
> [Le peuple, aveugle, faible, est né pour les grands hommes;
> Pour admirer, pour croire, et pour nous obéir. . . .
> Qui fait plus qu'il ne doit ne sait point me servir.
> J'obéis à mon dieu; vous, sachez m'obéir.
> *(Mahomet,* 1.3; 2.4).]

Not very poetical, perhaps, but the point is driven home. "He criticizes divine right and defends freedom of conscience and political morality, which takes into account the rights of the individual and the happiness of the people. He dreads above all political 'fanaticism.' . . . His ideal is an enlightened despotism by a gentle and merciful king, who is strong enough to suppress injustices and to counteract the power of the priests and of ambitious men."[3]

Priests, he warns, are likely to be impostors, like Mohammed.

> Our priests are only what unsuspecting people think,
> Our gullibility makes up all their learning. . . .
> Let us trust only in ourselves, trust only our eyes;
> They are our trivets, our oracles, our gods.
>
> [Nos prêtres ne sont ce qu'un vain peuple pense,
> Notre crédulité fait toute leur science. . . .
> Ne nous fions qu'à nous: voyons tout par nos yeux;
> Ce sont là nos trépieds, nos oracles, nos dieux
> *(Oedipe,* 4.1; 2.5)]

Although not a staunch pacifist, Voltaire expressed his horror of war in these verses in *Mahomet*, 3.8:

> Exterminate, great God, from the earth we live on,
> Whoever takes pleasure in shedding the blood of man.
>
> [Exterminez, grand Dieu! de la terre où nous sommes,
> Quiconque avec plaisir répand le sang des hommes.]

But perhaps the greatest personal satisfaction Voltaire enjoyed stemmed from the thunderous applause that greeted verses he purposely added to plays in order to comment on a burning question of the day. After the battle of Rossbach (1757), the capable Maréchal de Broglie, who had not been responsible for the defeat (incurred by Pompadour's favorite, M. de Soubise), was recalled and exiled. Two days later Voltaire's *Tancrède* was performed at the Théâtre Français, and the audience widly applauded these verses:

> Tancredi is stripped of his rank, exiled, insulted;
> It is the fate of heroes to be persecuted. . . .
> Hate and self-interest are too strongly aimed at him.
> All his supporters keep silent: who will take his side?
>
> [On dépouille Tancrède, on l'exile, on l'outrage,
> C'est le sort d'un héros d'être persécuté. . . .
> $$(Tancrède, 1.6)$$
> La haine et l'intérêt s'arment trop contre lui.
> Tout son parti se tait: qui sera son appui?
> $$(Tancrède, 2.1)]$$

The play was indeed the thing in Voltaire's time, yet by their very nature tragedies must not roam too far: they are most effective when they deal with one problem. Many of Voltaire's issues, cast in their time frame, no longer move us. The divine right of kings, the spiritual and political power of the Jesuits, the privileges of the nobility, the demotion of a worthy general, belong to history and may even bore us if presented in a devious manner. But take all these issues, and several more, raise them to a general level, incorporate them in an adventurous satire that mocks superstition, irrationality, fashions, and even makes fun of the young hero; and you have the success formula that Voltaire employed in the greatest of his *contes philosophiques*.

An Idea Never Disproved Except by the Facts: Candide

Voltaire did not lack courage; his defense of victims of injustice attests to that. But he did not in the least aspire to the status of martyrdom and he took every precaution to avoid persecution or imprisonment for his writings. His attitude in this respect is summarized in the phrase, "Strike and hide your hand," contained in a letter of 7 May 1761 to d'Alembert. Thus he never hesitated to deny authorship: "As soon as the slightest danger signs appear, I beg of you, for heaven's sake, let me know, so that I can disavow the work in all published papers with my usual candor and innocence" (Letter to d'Alembert, 19 September 1764). If one takes seriously the Abbé Galiani's somewhat facetious definition of perfect, or sublime, style as "the art of saying everything without being put into the Bastille,"[4] then indeed Voltaire has few rivals.

Candide appeared anonymously, published in 1759 in Geneva by Cramer. The book was condemned both in Geneva and Paris, and the police confiscated whatever copies it could lay its hands on. Suspected of being the author, Voltaire indignantly denied any connection with the work. "Who are those idlers who charge me with being the author. . . . of that schoolboy's joke I have received from Paris? I assure you I have other things to do. . . . God forbid that I should have the least thing to do with that book." (Letter to Formey and Thieriot, March 1759)

At the same time Voltaire does not hesitate to encourage his readers to look beneath and beyond the simple story line: "A work that has more to say than it seems to say. I beg of you: read it and judge it." (Epistle Dedicatory to *Zadig*) Or even more broadly, "I would like, above all, that, underneath the veil of the story, trained eyes would glimpse some subtle truth that escapes ordinary people" (*Le Taureau blanc*).

In *Candide,* Voltaire remained true to these two principles: deception of authorities and hints to those who can read between the lines. The trick is achieved by deviousness. As his central theme he chose a metaphysical question, which he first reduced to simple and banal terms and subsequently carried ad absurdum. No doubt he was concerned about and irritated by philosophical optimism. Still, the stand he took was likely to offend few of his readers; the majority would laugh along with him. But while laughing, they would also swallow more bitter pills on a subject closer to home—Voltaire's biting criticism of existing condi-

tions—without raising too many objections. The façade of a philosophical quarrel likewise tends to reduce the vigilance of the censors, for the
evils described can be camouflaged as a satiric counterattack that exaggerates reality in order to ridicule abstract optimism.

Candide's many-faceted satire pervades the very narrative: it is a
parody of the epic-heroic genre and of the picaresque adventure tales.
Young Candide is a tongue-in-cheek mixture of Lesage's Gil Blas,
going from adventure to adventure; and of Cervantes's Don Quixote,
chasing after, saving, and protecting an increasingly ugly Dulcinea-
Cunégonde. In fact, the breathtaking rhythm of this philosophical tale
constitutes one of its many merits. It takes us across a good part of the
world, and Voltaire knows exactly when to quit a scene: just after the
height of action and before exhausting its possibilities. The only exception, perhaps, can be found in the Paris episode, but that is inevitable,
given the interest Paris has for the reader.

Fortunately, Voltaire utilizes this allegro rhythm, because the story
line in itself it fraught with monotony: Candide gains fortunes and loses
them, he finds Cunégonde and loses her, he believes Pangloss, Cunégonde, and her brother to be dead and rediscovers them alive—in
brief, the mechanical ups and downs of fortune and the losing and
finding of friends and beloved. But *Candide* is, of course, not a tale to be
read for its story content alone—although one can enjoy it innocently in
that way—but for its attack on a metaphysical point of view and its
satiric description of the follies and injustices of rulers and ruled alike.

The philosophical view attacked is the one held by Leibnitz and his
disciple Wolff: that this is the best of all possible worlds.[5] It matters
little for our purposes, and those of the tale, that the philosophical
argument is arrived at after a series of deductions and that it is more
complex than stated by Voltaire. Satires do not, and do not pretend to,
present fairly and squarely the matters they hold up to our laughter.
What is admirable is Voltaire's splendid synthesis of philosophical
optimism, at least for his purposes, and his method of arriving at a
reductio ad absurdum.

Pangloss (All-Tongue, i.e., Windbag), the tutor at the castle of
Baron Thunder-ten-tronckh in Westphalia, represents philosophical
optimism at the same level as the provincial damsels represent Parisian
preciousness in Molière's farce *Les Précieuses ridicules*.

Pangloss taught metaphysico-theologo-cosmolonigology. He proved admi-
rably that there is no effect without cause and that, in the best of all possible

worlds, Monseigneur le Baron's castle was the most beautiful one and Madame la Baronne the best of all possible baronesses.

"It has been proven," he said, "that things cannot be otherwise; for, since everything has been made for an end, everything is necessarily for the best end. You will notice that noses have been made to wear glasses, and so we have glasses. Legs have visibly been meant to be covered with knee breeches, and so we have knee breeches. Stones have been formed to be cut and build castles with, and so Monseigneur has a very beautiful castle; the greatest baron in the province should have the best lodging; and since pigs have been made to be eaten, we eat pork all year long. Consequently, those who have maintained that all is well have spoken nonsense—they should have said that all is for the best."

[Pangloss enseignait la métaphysico-théologo-cosmolonigologie. Il prouvait admirablement qu'il n'y a point d'effet sans cause, et que, dans ce meilleur des mondes possibles, le château de monseigneur le baron était le plus beau des châteaux et madame la meilleure des baronnes possibles.

"Il est démontré, disait-il, que les choses ne peuvent être autrement: car, tout étant fait pour une fin, tout est nécessairement pour la meilleure fin. Remarquez bien que les nez ont été faits pour porter des lunettes, aussi avons-nous des lunettes. Les jambes sont visiblement instituées pour être chaussées, et nous avons des chausses. Les pierres ont été formées pour être taillées, et pour en faire des châteaux, aussi monseigneur a un très beau château; le plus grand baron de la province doit être le mieux logé; et, les cochons étant faits pour être mangés, nous mangeons du porc toute l'année: par conséquent, ceux qui ont avancé que tout est bien ont dit une sottise; il fallait dire que tout est au mieux." (Chap. 1, p. 138)][6]

Young Candide (Pure, Innocent, Naive), who is a servant in the castle, avidly drinks in all these lessons, all the more so since he is in love with the baron's daughter Cunégonde. Alas, the two young people are surprised in an embrace by the baron, and Candide is chased from the castle. From then on one disaster after another befalls the once-happy group. The castle is invaded by the Bulgarians, and the baron and his wife killed. Cunégonde is raped and carried off to be sold to a Jew in Portugal, who shares her with the Grand Inquisitor; she later becomes the mistress of the governor of Buenos Aires and is finally reunited with Candide. Unfortunately, by that time she has become quite ugly. Pangloss contracts syphilis, is hanged by the Inquisitor but does not die, then is sold into slavery, and finally freed by Candide. As for our young hero, he is forcibly enlisted into the Bulgarian army, whipped until he nearly dies, arrested by the Inquisition; he kills the

Portuguese Jew and the Grand Inquisitor and runs a sword through Cunégonde's brother, who has become a Jesuit officer in Paraguay. The gold he is given in the utopian country of Eldorado, much of which he loses through disaster or theft, enables him to buy the freedom of those in slavery, and the remaining members of the group finally set themselves up on a small farm near Constantinople, where everybody contributes by working according to the best of his or her capacity in a modest but fruitful enterprise.

Throughout this accumulation of disasters and sufferings Voltaire has Pangloss steadfastly maintain that all is for the best, even when he runs out of cause-and-effect arguments.

"Well, my dear Pangloss," Candide said to him, "when you were hanged, dissected, beaten to a pulp, and when you were a galley slave, did you still think that all was for the best in the world?"

"I still hold to my first view," Pangloss replied, "for, after all, I am a philosopher: it is unsuitable for me to gainsay myself, being that Leibnitz cannot be wrong and preestablished harmony being, moreover, the most beautiful thing in the world along with the plenum and subtle matter."

[— Eh bien, mon cher Pangloss, lui dit Candide, quand vous avez été pendu, disséqué, roué de coups, et que vous avez ramé aux galères, avez-vous toujours pensé que tout allait le mieux du monde? — Je suis toujours de mon premier sentiment, répondit Panglosss, car enfin je suis philosophe: il ne me convient pas de me dédire, Leibnitz ne pouvant pas avoir tort, et l'harmonie préétablie étant d'ailleurs la plus belle chose du monde, aussi bien que le plein et la matière subtile." (Chap. 28, p. 228)]

However much Voltaire mistreats this "consistent" philosopher, he does not fall into the trap of refutation by argument, which would be deadly to his satire. Instead, "nobody answers Pangloss back, nor is there any need to contradict him; he is his own undoing, and, by an extraordinary comical device, no interlocutor tells him he is wrong, even though this is evident. On the contrary, he continues to appear for a long time as an oracle. By emphasizing thus the blunders of the character, Voltaire convinces us—more forcefully than he could have done by a dialogue in which Pangloss would always have come off on the short end—that optimism is a simple construct of the mind, a game for subtle metaphysicians that takes no account of reality."[7]

Indeed, no one needs to contradict Pangloss. One can say of his philosophy what Voltaire says of a moral precept in his tale *La Princesse de Babylone,* that it has never been disproved except by the facts.[8] And he very skillfully juxtaposes Pangloss's most farfetched reasoning and one of the greatest natural calamities of the eighteenth century, the 1755 Lisbon earthquake.

"All that was indispensable," replied the one-eyed doctor, "and individual misfortunes bring about general well-being, so that the more individual misfortunes there are, the more all is well." While he was thus reasoning, the air darkened, the winds were blowing from the four corners of the earth, and the boat was shaken by a most horrible tempest as the port of Lisbon came into view.

[—Tout cela était indispensable, répliquait le docteur borgne, et les malheurs particuliers font le bien général, de sorte que plus il y a de malheurs particuliers, et plus tout est bien." Tandis qu'il raisonnait, l'air s'obscurcit, les vents soufflèrent des quatre coins du monde, et le vaisseau fut assailli de la plus horrible tempête à la vue du port de Lisbonne. (Chap. 4, p. 147)]

There is really no model character in *Candide.* A foil to Pangloss, Martin is a Manichaean, who believes that the world is ruled by two principles: good and evil. Although, in theory, these two tend to balance each other, Martin leans very heavily toward assigning greatest power to evil, which is understandable in view of his past sufferings and the experiences he goes through in Candide's company. Although probably closer than any one else to the worldview Voltaire exposes in his tale, Martin fails to qualify as a reasonable spokesman for the author because his pessimism is as extreme as Pangloss's optimism.

If any of the characters arrives at a balanced and realistic view, it is Candide, for, to the extent one can consider Voltaire's satire in terms of novelistic techniques, *Candide* is an *Erziehungsroman,* a novel in which a young person learns about life through experience and education. Only—and this is, of course, intentional—Candide is an excruciatingly slow learner whose inculcated optimism is being kept alive by the hopes of finding, and being united with, his beloved Cunégonde. In fact, it takes him about two-thirds of the story to express his first doubts about Pangloss's infallibility. It happens in Surinam when he and his servant Cacambo encounter a slave, who had been sold by his parents and maimed by his master. At this pitiful sight Candide finally exclaims, " 'Oh Pangloss, you had not even dreamed of this abomination; this is too much, I finally have to renounce your optimism.' 'What is optimism?' Cacambo asked. 'Alas,' said Candide, 'it is the mania of maintaining that all is well when all is bad.' " [— O Pangloss! s'écria Candide, tu n'avais pas deviné cette abomination; c'en est fait, il faudra qu'à la fin je renonce à ton optimisme. — Qu'est-ce qu'optimisme? disait Cacambo. — Hélas! dit Candide, c'est la rage de soutenir que tout est bien quand on est mal (Chap. 19, p. 190).]

But Candide has not finished his education yet. That stage he reaches only at the very end when, content to till the soil on a small farm, he replies to Pangloss's chain of metaphysical reasoning with the famous phrase, "That is well said, but we must cultivate our garden." [—Cela est bien dit, répondit Candide, mais il faut cultiver notre jardin" (Chap. 30, p. 234).]

What Voltaire Attacked.   Of course, things are not at all for the best in Voltaire's time. There are wars and there is slavery; governments are irrational, run by arrogant, selfish rulers, and are based on a social system in which only birth and titles count, and even these are subject to the caprices of the rulers. Natural law is flouted everywhere and judges and police are corrupt. Religion has turned either into fanaticism or bigotry or serves as a shield for the enjoyment of personal gain or political power. And everywhere people are at each other's throat. Martin, in his somber description of the state of affairs, is not so far from reality, even though his pessimism is meant to serve as an antidote to Pangloss's rosy picture of life.

I have scarcely seen a town that did not wish for the ruin of the next town, no family that did not want to exterminate another one. Everywhere the weak execrate the powerful before whom they grovel, and the powerful treat them like cattle whose wool and flesh is to be sold. A million regimented assassins roam all over Europe, murdering and robbing with discipline to earn their bread, because they don't have a more decent occupation.

[Je n'ai guère vu de ville qui ne désirât la ruine de la ville voisine, point de famille qui ne voulût exterminer quelque autre famille. Partout les faibles ont en exécration les puissants devant lesquels ils rampent, et les puissants les traitent comme des troupeaux dont on vend la laine et la chair. Un million d'assassins enrégimentés, courant d'un bout de l'Europe à l'autre, exerce le meurtre et le brigandage avec discipline pour gagner son pain, parce qu'il n'a pas de métier plus honnête (Chap. 20, p. 194).]

Religion comes off worst in *Candide*. Fanaticism of every color is condemned, whether practiced by Protestant zealots in Holland or by Portuguese officers of the Inquisition who burn supposed heretics, because after the earthquake which had destroyed three-fourths of Lisbon, the wise men of that country had not found a more efficacious means of avoiding total ruin than to offer their people a nice auto-da-fé; it was decided by the University of Coïmbra that the spectacle of several persons being slowly burned, in a grand ceremony, is an infallible secret for preventing the earth from quaking.

[Après le tremblement de terre qui avait détruit les trois quarts de Lisbonne, les sages du pays n'avaient pas trouvé un moyen plus efficace pour prévenir une ruine totale que de donner au peuple un bel auto-da-fé; il était décidé par l'université de Coimbre que le spectacle de quelques personnes brûlées à petit feu, en grande cérémonie, est un secret infaillible pour empêcher la terre de trembler. (Chap. 6, p. 150)]

Voltaire's greatest contempt is reserved for theocracy, such as the one the Jesuits had established in Paraguay in the early seventeenth century, and which lasted until 1768. "Los Padres have everything, and the people nothing; it's a masterpiece of reason and justice." [Los Padres y ont tout, et les peuples rien: c'est le chef-d'oeuvre de la raison et de la justice (Chap. 14, p. 171).] After having severely wounded Cunégonde's Jesuit brother, Candide and Cacambo are taken prisoners by the Oreillon Indians, whom the Jesuits had come to convert. Since Candide has donned the garb of the baron for their escape, the Indians are delighted at the thought of having a Jesuit for dinner, but when they learn the truth, they free their prisoners and treat them generously.

On an individual level, priests are depicted as lascivious, greedy, and dishonest: the Grand Inquisitor shares Cunégonde with a Jew; the old woman who accompanies Candide and Cunégonde on their flight from Portugal is the bastard daughter of a pope; a Franciscan monk steals their money and diamonds; the abbé from Périgord, who shows him around Paris, sets a trap to have Candide arrested so that he can obtain his money. The only one who comes off moderately well is Brother Giroflée, but then he detests his state, has a prostitute for a mistress, and, above all, is a natural human being forced to wear a priest's frock.

Wars are presented as being fought by soldiers conscripted against their will for no particular purpose other than the self-glorification of rulers. The Bulgarians destroy the towns of the Avars and vice versa,[9] the French and the English are at war over "a few acres of snow" in Canada. In a masterful stroke Voltaire exposes the combined absurdities of wars and of Pangloss's philosophical dogma.

Nothing could be so beautiful, so smart, or well ordered as the two armies. The trumpets, the fifes, the oboes, the drums, the cannons produced a harmony such as was never heard in hell. First, the cannons brought down about six thousand men on each side; next, the musketry removed from the best of worlds some nine or ten thousand scoundrels who infected its surface. The bayonets were also the sufficient reason for the death of several thousand men. The total was probably close to some thirty thousand souls. Candide, who trembled like a philosopher, hid as best he could during this heroic slaughter.

[Rien n'était si beau, si leste, si brillant, si bien ordonné que les deux armées. Les trompettes, les fifres, les hautbois, les tambours, les canons, formaient une harmonie telle qu'il n'y en eut jamais en enfer. Les canons renversèrent d'abord à peu près six mille hommes de chaque côté; ensuite la mousqueterie ôta du meilleur des mondes environ neuf à dix mille coquins qui en infectaient la surface. La baïonnette fut aussi la raison suffisante de la mort de quelques milliers d'hommes. Le tout pouvait bien se monter à une trentaine de mille âmes. Candide, qui tremblait comme un philosophe, se cacha du mieux qu'il put pendant cette boucherie héroïque. (Chap. 3, p. 142)]

Not only is this slaughter senseless, but the rulers responsible for it show little gratitude to those who risk their lives for them; in fact, defeat leads to disgrace. In the scene depicting the execution of the English admiral Byng, Voltaire also recalled the fate of Maréchal de Broglie after the battle of Rossbach (1757).

"What is this all about?" Candide said, "and what sort of demon is imposing his power everywhere?" He asked who was that stout man who had just been ceremoniously killed. "An admiral," was the reply. "And why was that admiral killed?" "Because," he was told, "he did not have enough people killed; he engaged in battle with a French admiral, and it was felt that he did not move close enough." "But," said Candide, "the French admiral was just as far from the English admiral as the English from the French." "That is incontrovertible," was the answer; "but in this country it is considered a good idea to kill an admiral once in a while so as to encourage the others."

[— Qu'est-ce donc que tout ceci? dit Candide, et quel démon exerce partout son empire?" Il demanda qui était ce gros homme qu'on venait de tuer en cérémonie. — C'est un amiral, lui répondit-on. — Et pourquoi tuer cet amiral? — C'est, lui dit-on, parce qu'il n'a pas fait tuer assez de monde; il a livré un combat à un amiral français, et on a trouvé qu'il n'était pas assez près de lui. — Mais, dit Candide, l'amiral français était aussi loin de l'amiral anglais que celui-ci l'était de l'autre! — Cela est incontestable, lui répliqua-t-on; mais dans ce pays-ci il est bon de tuer de temps en temps un amiral pour encourager les autres." (Chap. 23, pp. 208–9)]

If admirals do not always fare well, nobles enjoy privileges, power, and wealth. A typical example of the aristocratic arrogance that Voltaire had come to detest is displayed by the governor of Buenos Aires, Don Fernando d'Ibaraa, y Figueroa, y Mascarenes, y Lampourdos, y Souza.

This nobleman had a pride befitting a man who bore so many names. He spoke to people with the noblest disdain, lifting his nose so high, raising his voice so mercilessly, assuming such an imposing tone, affecting such haughty bearing that all those who bowed to him were tempted to beat him up.

[Ce seigneur avait une fierté convenable à un homme qui portait tant de noms. Il parlait aux hommes avec le dédain le plus noble, portant le nez si haut, élevant si impitoyablement la voix, prenant un ton si imposant, affectant une démarche si altière, que tous ceux qui le saluaient étaient tentés de le battre. (Chap. 13, p. 168)]

Voltaire goes even further in exposing the blindness of nobles who disregard the most obvious realities once it is a question of rank. Cunégonde's brother, who has received Candide with open arms in Jesuit-ruled Paraguay, goes into a tantrum on learning that his former servant intends to marry his sister, who, despite her ancient nobility, has by then passed through quite a few hands. Having rescued the baron later on from a slave galley, Candide suffers the same refusal of his projected marriage with Cunégonde, who by then has even lost her beauty. In the face of such stupid stubbornness Candide decides to return the baron to the slave galley owner. It is worth noting that the baron is the only one closely associated with Candide after he leaves the castle—if one excepts the Anabaptist Jacques, victim of a natural disaster—who does not end up in the "garden," for in this tale, where cannons, swords, and sticks wreak havoc, the principal characters miraculously escape death and are finally reunited.

The most daring episode in *Candide* can be found in chapter 26, where Candide and Martin dine in Venice with six deposed rulers: a sultan, a Russian emperor, a king of England, two Polish kings, and a former king of Corsica. From their stories the message emerges that such exalted rulers are subject to the same vicissitudes of fate as ordinary human beings and that their reigns last only as long as they manage to hold at bay those who lust after their position, rivals who are often brothers or other members of their family.

When Candide expresses his astonishment at these strange dinner stories, Martin replies: "That is no more extraordinary than most of the things that have happened to us. It is quite common for kings to be dethroned; and what you call the honor we have had of eating supper with them is a trifling matter that does not deserve our attention." [Cela n'est pas plus extraordinaire, dit Martin, que la plupart des choses qui nous sont arrivées. Il est très commun que des rois soient détrônés; et à l'égard de l'honneur que nous avons eu de souper avec eux, c'est une bagatelle qui ne mérite pas notre attention (Chap. 27, p. 223).] It is easy to understand why the censors had the book seized. One may perhaps trifle with the behavior of German or Spanish nobles, but the divine right of kings must not be placed in doubt.

Voltaire's boldness in this episode can be fully appreciated only by keeping in mind the historical consciousness of the French in the mid-eighteenth century. In the memory of the people France had always been ruled by kings and only very few could even so much as conceive of another kind of government. Someone like Montesquieu or some disgruntled philosophe might suggest reforms within a monarchy, but in the minds of the vast majority of the French, who knew little about other countries, kings succeeded each other. Some might be better, others worse; but they could neither be deposed nor the monarchy abolished.

Such is the power of the protesting pen. It can suggest the inconceivable, laying the seeds that dispose the mind to accustom itself, however gradually, to options that previously could not have entered it.

Yet not even Voltaire, in his wildest dreams, could have imagined that only thirty-four years later, in 1793, a French king would be deposed in a manner such that he could not have attended a dinner in Venice or any other place, for that matter.

Voltaire's Satirical Devices.   A writer may have all of Voltaire's criticisms to express and yet not succeed in making himself read or heard. The art of conveying these views to the reader—and even more so to an eighteenth-century French reader—or at least of rendering him sympathetic to them, lies in the manner in which they are presented. The most effective way turned out to be, not shouting them from rooftops or proclaiming them indignantly in leaflets, but embodying them in satire, one of the most difficult of the arts, because the writer is constantly walking a tightrope. The tone is so important that the slightest false note threatens to destroy the entire fabric. It is like saying things with tongue in cheek while keeping a poker face all the while.

The predominant tone in satire is irony, defined variously as a figure of speech in which one says the contrary of what one wants the reader to understand, or a pretense of asserting one thing in order to let the contrary be more forcefully understood. According to David Worcester, the satirist must maintain a balance between appearing amiable to his audience and hostile to his enemies, while keeping an attitude of detachment, so as to give the reader a sense of being independent and of not being forcibly fed ideas. Not least, a successful satire gives the reader a feeling of belonging to a special group. "The distinction between the world of uninitiated, common souls and the select few who share some special knowledge underlies every form of irony. . . . The sense of belonging to a privileged minority arises from verbal irony in solving the puzzle of inversion or understatement."[10]

Voltaire meets all these requirements for the simple reason that the definitions of satire have been primarily established on examples drawn from his writings; for, although he is neither the first nor the only writer to have produced satires, he carries the form to its perfection. In *Candide,* his principal devices are contrast, contradiction, and absurdity: contrast between the horror of a situation and the light tone used to describe it, contradiction between philosophical pronouncements and the reality that disproves them, and absurdity of reasoning and conclusions arrived at.

To begin with the last, Voltaire considers the Leibnitzian worldview absurd, and he arouses laughter by carrying philosophical optimism to both its logical and absurd conclusions. We have already had occasion to note Pangloss's exposition of these ideas and the conclusions he arrives at concerning the wearing of glasses and knee breeches. Pangloss continues this type of reasoning throughout the tale. His disciple Candide and women as well will resort to absurd reasoning, especially when it suits their purpose. Thus Candide, after listening to Pococuranté's disparaging judgments of great literary works, exclaims admiringly: "Oh, what a superior man! . . . What a great genius this Pococuranté is! Nothing can please him." [Oh, quel homme supérieur! . . . quel grand génie que ce Pococuranté! rien ne peut lui plaire (Chap. 25 p. 218).] And the old woman advises Cunégonde to become the mistress of the governor of Buenos Aires, "who has a very beautiful mustache" (Chap. 13, p. 169).

We have also had occasion to appreciate the contrast between a horrible event and the light tone in which it is reported in the narration of the battle in which Candide takes part. At another place, the old woman concludes the description of a savage battle by stating: "Everybody was killed, and I remained half dead on a heap of dying people. Similar scenes took place . . . all over an area of three hundred leagues, without anybody failing to observe the five daily prayers prescribed by Mohammed." [Tout fut tué, et je demeurai mourante sur un tas de morts. Des scènes pareilles se passaient . . . dans l'étendue de plus de trois cents lieues, sans qu'on manquât aux cinq prières par jour ordonnées par Mahomet (Chap. 11, p. 163).]

Contradiction between philosophical statement and event can be noted in Pangloss's absurd insistence that the greater individual misfortunes are the more all is well, at the very moment the boat is rocked by a terrible storm due to the earthquake of Lisbon. In a general way, most of *Candide* illustrates this kind of contradiction.

Even though Voltaire deploys his entire arsenal of satiric devices, his efforts would have been in vain if he had failed to maintain his detachment and the good-humored tone of amusement at philosophical and human folly. The very "villain" of the story benefits from this attitude. Beaten, injured, one-eyed, hung, sold into slavery, Pangloss remains alive and ends up in Candide's garden.

Taine underlines the gaiety of Voltaire and reveals the reasons for his universal appeal.

What can be gayer than an evening with Voltaire? He makes fun of things, but do you detect any vicious intent in his jests? He flares up, but do you detect any natural and wicked hatred in his anger? In him everything is pleasant. In one single instant, for need of activity, he strikes, caresses, changes his tone, his face a hundred times with abrupt movements, impetuous sallies, sometimes childish, but always a man of the world, of taste, and of conversation. . . . If I were with him and he made fun of me, I would not get angry, I would adopt his tone, laugh at myself, I would feel that his only desire is to spend a pleasant hour, that he is not angry with me, that he treats me as his equal and his guest, that he comes out with cracks like a wintry fire breaks into sparks, and that he is no less pleasing for it, nor less salutary or charitable.[11]

The Positive Aspects of *Candide*.   Satire, by its very nature, is essentially negative. It uses ridicule, irony, exaggeration, and caricature to attack the vices or wrongs the author intends to hold up to our view. Criticizing such a work for not providing solutions is tantamount to missing the point of the whole thing, and so is expecting a fair exposure of arguments or a faithful psychological portrayal of characters or of reality.[12] A satirist who attempts to propose solutions to the problems he evokes takes a considerable risk, because in so doing he may fall into a serious, pompous, or didactic tone, which would be fatal to satire.

Voltaire steers his ship of fools, foolishness, and folly with consummate skill past the reefs of positive reforms and model heroes. Nevertheless, he offers us glimpses of a better life, illustrated in the experiences that shape Candide's slow evolution from an openmouthed admirer of false philosophical principles to a sober and realistic leader of a group of diverse characters.

Viewed from this perspective, Candide encounters three gardens: the first is illusional, due to his inexperience of the world; the second is utopian; and the third is real.

The first is the castle in Westphalia, which impresses the young servant as the most perfect place imaginable. Voltaire presents it as a parody of the biblical Garden of Eden, for Candide is expelled from this "paradise" for having tasted the fruit of the knowledge offered by a woman (Cunégonde).

Next he comes to Eldorado, that never-never land, a country whose inaccessible mountains and wealth of resources have protected it from greed, selfishness, vanity, and political and religious conflicts. The secret of Eldorado's perfection is simplicity and good sense, i.e., reason. Its inhabitants worship God by offering him their thanks. There are no priests, no law courts, no prisons, but an impressive Palace of Science. And in this happy land, which the Incas have foolishly left for ill-fated conquests, there are no humiliating ceremonies to satisfy the vanity of noble rulers.

Before being presented to the king, Cacambo asks how one salutes His Majesty,

whether they were to throw themselves down on their knees or flat on their bellies, whether they should put their hands on their heads or their behinds, whether they should lick the dust on the floor,—in short, what the ceremony was. "The custom," the Great Officer said, "is to embrace the king and kiss him on both cheeks."

[Cacambo demanda à un grand officier comment il fallait s'y prendre pour saluer Sa Majesté; si on se jetait à genoux ou ventre à terre; si on mettait les

mains sur la tête ou sur le derrière; si on léchait la poussière de la salle; en un
mot, quelle était la cérémonie. "L'usage, dit le grand officer, est d'embrasser le
roi et de le baiser des deux côtés." (Chap. 18, pp. 185–86)]

Why then does Candide not remain in Eldorado? For one thing, he is
not philosophically ready for such perfection, but, more important
still, Eldorado is a utopian country, isolated from outside influences by
nature and by a law that prohibits its inhabitants from leaving the
country. A walled-in country that does not permit its citizens to leave
has never been popular with freedom-loving people, regardless of
whether they live in the eighteenth century or in the twentieth. In all
likelihood people in Eldorado lead a far happier life than those on the
outside, but theirs is a stagnant happiness that promotes a natural
acceptance of the status quo; and that was not the ideal Voltaire was
eager to propose to his contemporaries.

The third garden is the small farm Candide acquires where his little
group settles down to a productive life in which everybody contributes
to the general well-being of the community. It is there that, in conclusion, Candide replies to Pangloss's philosophical reasoning with a
compliment—but adds the famous phrase that "we must cultivate our
garden."

Voltaire's final comment has led to much interpretation, both pro
and con. It has been both denigrated as a bourgeois stay-at-home
attitude and elevated to a grand vision of an earthly paradise made up of
innumerable fertile gardens. It is somewhat surprising that a short
passage at the end of *Candide,* and a remark that may merely have been
a pirouette before closing the curtain on this adventurous tale, should
have led to so much discussion.

If we are to take this remark seriously, then it must be viewed in the
larger perspective—not only of Voltaire's intentions but of the general
tendencies perceptible in the writings of the philosophes.

Voltaire's attack on philosophical optimism cannot be said to have
been solely induced by his historical research and some personal experiences, including financial setbacks. Nor is it correct to claim that
Candide represents a change in Voltaire from youthful optimism to
mature pessimism. In attacking the Leibnitzian worldview, Voltaire
remains true to the principle of the philosophes who want to improve
the state of affairs by social, political, and economic change. To insist
that this is the best of all possible worlds and that whatever happens is a
part of the inevitable divine scheme amounts to saying that all is well as

is. Such an attitude encourages inactivity and a passive acceptance of the status quo and, hence, of what is evil in the world. This static view is not at all the optimism of the philosophes, who believed in a better future through action and progress. If things are bad now, all will be better and perhaps eventually well, but these improvements will not be God-willed or God-given but the result of continuous human effort.

Voltaire's optimism was not that of a starry-eyed Rousseau, who believed that human nature is intrinsically good and that it would suffice to change institutions, customs, and attitudes to recapture a mythical golden age. Martin is not far off in characterizing Voltaire's concept of human nature.

"Do you believe," Candide said, "that men have always massacred each other as they do today? That they have always been liars, knaves, traitors, ingrates, brigands, weak, fickle, cowardly, envious, gluttons, drunkards, stingy, ambitious, bloodthirsty, slanderous, lecherous, fanatical, hypocritical, and foolish?"

"Do you believe," Martin said, "that hawks have always eaten pigeons when they found them?"

"Yes, no doubt," Candide said.

"Well then," Martin said, "if hawks have always had the same character, why do you expect men to have changed theirs?"

[— Croyez-vous, dit Candide, que les hommes se soient toujours mutuelle-ment massacrés comme ils font aujourd'hui? qu'ils aient toujours été men-teurs, fourbes, perfides, ingrats, brigands, faibles, volages, lâches, envieux, gourmands, ivrognes, avares, ambitieux, sanguinaires, calomniateurs, dé-bauchés, fanatiques, hypocrites et sots? — Croyez-vous, dit Martin, que les éperviers aient toujours mangé des pigeons quand ils en ont trouvé? — Oui, sans doute, dit Candide. — Eh bien! dit Martin, si les éperviers ont toujours eu le même caractère, pourquoi voulez-vous que les hommes aient changé le leur? (Chap. 21, p. 197)]

From such vicious beings one cannot expect too much, and, not surprisingly, Voltaire was a conservative in politics. The best he believed possible was government by an enlightened despot, a philosopher-king, if such a species were to exist, one who would keep his subjects in line, not for his own sake but for theirs. Yet among all the offensive epithets heaped on man you will not find one that denies his ability to work and create.

For if man's nature cannot be changed, the conditions of his existence can. If he can do nothing about natural disasters, he can improve social, political, and economic conditions. But to do so, he must get down to the immediate tasks before him and not waste his energies on futile metaphysical speculations.

The question of improvement and regeneration was inevitably linked to the social preoccupations of the philosophes, and one discovers a general view shared by even those who disagree on most other matters: namely, that improvement, or the road to an ideal state of affairs, starts with a small, homogeneous group, be it the family or individuals who are united in a common effort. A close reading of Jean-Jacques Rousseau reveals that he places the golden age of humanity not—as is too often erroneously claimed —at the period of the cave man but at the moment when a small number of families create a self-sufficient state of economy. [13]

Candide's statement that we must cultivate our garden must be considered in this larger perspective. While Voltaire's solution is by no means as explicit as Montesquieu's, it implies at least a first step toward improvement. What distinguishes the two authors, moreover, is that whereas Montesquieu's virtuous duo teaches that "individual interests are always contained in the general interest" (Lettre 12), Voltaire seems to feel that individual interests add up to the general interest. But both writers attempt to motivate individual effort by appealing to the practical benefits that result from it rather than to some purely abstract principle.

Voltaire's conclusion is both pessimistic and optimistic. It is pessimistic in the implication that we shall never be able to know the answers to such metaphysical questions as: Among which options did God choose when he created the world? What was the purpose of that creation? What is the meaning and purpose of our existence? It is optimistic in the hope of better things to come. Voltaire's garden is not the biblical Garden of Eden; it is the Garden of Man. It may become an *earthly* paradise, but only if we work at its cultivation rather than sit under its trees, speculating about things we cannot know.

One must, however, not interpret Voltaire's conclusion of *Candide* too literally. His long-range vision does not advocate cultivating garden after garden in the hope that an earthly paradise of self-sufficiency will result, for Voltaire was not so naive as to imagine the possibility of an economic system based on cumulative agriculture. Rather, the example of Candide and his garden group contains two important lessons: first, that we should concentrate our efforts on matters that concern us directly and on which we can exert an influence; second, that everyone should concentrate on what he or she is best qualified to do and that work well done constitutes sufficient gratification in itself. Everything else is gravy, so to speak. Better conditions are likely to follow, but improvement begins at home, because two of the three greatest evils to be overcome are personal: boredom and vice; and work will take care of the third one, need.[14]

The appeal of Voltaire's conclusion lies in its simplicity. It is basically personal and concrete, and that is in keeping with the thesis that has been communicated to the ideal reader throughout *Candide*. Voltaire answers the question, What can we, you and I, ordinary people, do to survive in an irrational world, or perhaps even to improve it? Instead of offering sweeping solutions designed to cure political, social, and economic ills; instead of proposing abstract philosophical arguments to explain the unknowable, he tells us to mind our own business—and to mind it well.

Voltaire's Personal Commitment

In his actions Voltaire was a mighty gardener, indeed. Constantly active and indefatigable, he was a righter of wrongs, not of imaginary ones like Don Quixote but of real ones. Among his many efforts, three stand out: his defenses of the Calas family, of the Sirven family, and of the chevalier de la Barre.

Jean Calas, a Protestant, was accused of having killed his son who supposedly had planned to convert to Catholicism. In 1762 Calas was executed after having first been practically whipped to death. Voltaire attacked the judgment of the court of Toulouse, which was reversed in 1764 and the following year Calas was exonerated. A similar result was obtained by Voltaire in 1771 for Paul Sirven, a Calvinist, who had been accused of having killed his daughter for similar reasons. The case of the chevalier de la Barre moved Voltaire to extreme indignation. Accused of having shown disrespect at a religious procession, of having damaged a cross, and of having used impious language in speaking of the Virgin, the young chevalier was condemned to be tortured, beheaded, and burnt. The execution took place on 1 July 1766.

No doubt, Voltaire was doubly incensed because these monstrous judgments were confirmed by Jansenist-dominated parlements, which he intensely disliked on account of their systematic opposition to proposed governmental reforms. But that fact does not authorize liberal

critics, such as Emile Faguet, to claim that Voltaire's actions on behalf
of the accused owed more to his campaign against the parlements than
to his conviction that Calas, Sirven, and the chevalier de la Barre were
the victims of enormous injustices. [15]

Voltaire's effect on French thought of the eighteenth century can
hardly be exaggerated. No other writer was as widely read, and *Candide*
retains the record for the number of editions of a book printed in the
century (55). It is a commonplace to assert that his popularization of
ideas greatly contributed to directing French minds toward the Revolution. Although he advocated changes, his vision of a future France was
at least as far removed from the realities of the Revolution as were
Madame Bovary's romantic dreams from the realities into which they
were eventually transformed. But then Voltaire is not the only thinker
who would have shuddered with horror if he had lived long enough to
meet his disciples and to see what they had done with and to his ideas.

That is probably the reason Voltaire does not enjoy the favor he
would otherwise deserve from modern liberal thinkers, who find him
too bourgeois and even too conservative for their taste. Indeed, he
would never have given up his privileges of wealth the way the French
nobles did on the night of 4 August 1789—he had worked much too
hard and long for them. And being neither a guillotine-happy radical
nor a light-headed noble, he might very well have ended up on the
guillotine in the company of André Chénier. It is a good thing for both
Voltaire and the French Revolution that he died before 1789.

In a brilliant and penetrating essay, Roland Barthes calls Voltaire the
last of the happy writers. Evoking the difficulty of satirizing crimes like
the annihilation of six million Jews by the German Nazis as compared
to the *relatively* few victims of the Spanish Inquisition, Barthes attempts to demonstrate that a modern writer cannot deal as lightly and
ironically with horrors that exceed our imagination as Voltaire did with
readily defined crimes and fanaticism. "It was indeed an exceptional
stroke of fortune to have to fight in a world where power and stupidity
were continuously allied: a privileged situation for a witty writer. He
was on the same side as history, all the more happily as he looked upon
it as a crowning achievement, and not as something beyond him that
might have carried him with it." [16]

Had he lived in the twentieth century, Voltaire might have surprised
us all. He probably would have hurled satire at concentration camps,
gulags, and atomic bombs. But then, indeed, he was on the same side as
history—he had left the court of Frederick the Great after a short stay,

and he would not have worshipped Stalin, Mao Tse-tung, and Ho Chi Minh. A satirist, like every other critic of society, needs credibility. Yes and alas, Voltaire was the last happy writer, one who was able to smile openly, without afterthoughts, without complexes. Critics usually refer to Voltaire's smile as a sneer. This is just another of the many dubious legends that have grown up around the great satirist. This one was probably far more inspired by his bust at the Comédie Française (do you expect an old man living in the eighteenth century to open his mouth wide when he wanted to smile?) and by Alfred de Musset's self-pitying reference to him[17] than by a sympathetic reading of his texts. Irony is the elegant smile, with a wink to those who understand, a wink at human folly and injustice; and in Voltaire it is not accompanied by cheap vengeance on the villains of his stories. It is time to put the teeth back into Voltaire's smile and to read him the way he wrote.

But toward the end of the eighteenth century, the clear, candylike colors of Boucher and Fragonard, which illustrated editions of *Candide,* were darkened by approaching clouds, and gay laughter began to give way to an underlying melancholy. Beaumarchais's Figaro laughs indeed at everything, but he hastens to laugh for fear of having to weep.

Chapter Four

Of Servants and Masters

The Reign of Louis XVI, 1774–89

Louis XVI, grandson of Louis XV, was only twenty years old when he assumed the reins of France. Well-meaning and of a kindly disposition, he possessed none of the attributes needed by a king in times of crisis. Of all his defects, an inability to make decisions was certainly the most fateful. The queen, Marie-Antoinette, daughter of the Austrian ruler, was no doubt more intelligent. But court life encouraged a natural tendency in her toward frivolity, and she withdrew to the Little Trianon at Versailles, where she enjoyed herself in a small and select company.

Largely cut off from the nobility outside the court, and even more so from the people, the royal couple thus indulged themselves in hunting or in playing at the game of dressing as shepherds and shepherdesses à la Rousseau, while ministers succeeded each other in a tragic race toward catastrophe. Louis XVI dismissed Maupeou and, on the advice of an aunt, appointed the aged Maurepas as head of the government. With the parlements back in action and supported in turn by the privileged orders in opposition to any financial reforms, there was little hope that France's most pressing problem would be solved. Turgot introduced some reforms, but when he submitted edicts abolishing the guilds (which controlled work in the industries) and the corvée (forced labor on roads by the surrounding population), he was dismissed, as opposition mounted.

Nevertheless, the French armed forces were rendered far more effective by an increase in regular troops, the modernization of the artillery, and a buildup of the navy. Thus, when France came to the support of the American colonists in the War of Independence, Great Britain was facing a far more serious opponent than it had some twenty years earlier during the Seven Years' War. But despite the success of the French intervention, the cost of the war placed finances under an enormous strain.

At that point Necker, a banker from Geneva, was called on to accomplish the miracle none of his predecessors had been able to perform. From 1776 to 1781 Necker managed the Treasury by using his credit with financiers in order to borrow money. This enabled him to finance the French aid of the American rebels without imposing new taxes. But in 1783 Necker was dismissed and replaced by Calonne, who continued his predecessor's borrowing policy until the vein ran dry in 1786. Thereupon Calonne proposed a general land tax, which met the usual combined opposition of the parlements, clergy, and nobles—and Calonne went the way of Necker.

To succeed him Louis XVI appointed the archbishop of Toulouse, Loménie de Brienne, who, in 1787, was promoted to the status of prime minister, the first one since Fleury. After first opposing the policies of his predecessors, Brienne soon put forth the same proposals. After the Notables rejected them, he decided to submit them to the parlements. The latter not only rejected them but demanded that the States General be called into session. The parlements were exiled to Troyes, but eventually a compromise of sorts was reached: the edicts were withdrawn and the parlements agreed to ratify further royal loans on condition that the States General would be called together, an event that had last occurred in 1614!

But the parlements continued to harass the government and were suspended in May 1788. This did not stop their agitation, nor were they the only ones to render the political situation difficult. The clergy joined them while refusing to offer a voluntary contribution; so did the nobles, especially the poorer provincial ones. Even the duc d'Orléans, the pretender to the throne after the Bourbon line, took up the defense of the parlements and had to be exiled to a country castle.

Besieged on all sides and betrayed by his natural allies, by August 1788 Louis XVI felt he had no choice but to summon the States General to meet on 1 May 1789. Brienne resigned and Necker was recalled. But this time he proved unequal to the situation, as the third estate, the commoners, obtained the concessions of double representation and, later on, individual vote instead of vote by order. This decision immensely increased Louis XVI's popularity, and he could have not only saved his head—in the literal sense—but even increased his power by aligning himself with the people. But, more hesitant than ever, he made concessions to the nobles and lost his last chance to preserve the throne. To make matters worse, the poor 1788 harvest led to serious riots due to a shortage of bread in the summer of 1789. An

economic depression brought great numbers of unemployed farm workers into urban centers, while brigands and disorganized bands ravaged
the countryside.

When the session of the States General opened on 4 May 1789,
Necker merely pleaded with the clergy and nobles to give up their
exemption from taxes but had little else to offer. Impatient and disappointed, the third estate declared itself the National Assembly on 17
June and was soon joined by dissident clergymen and liberal nobles.
Although the king still maintained considerable popularity, the arrival
of large contingents of troops around Paris and Versailles and the
dismissal of Necker on 11 July created fears of a military coup. As the
duc d'Orléans was plotting against the king and as mobs were roving
around Paris in a feverish atmosphere, the fateful day of 14 July 1789
arrived.

Chronology

1774:	Maurepas in charge of government.
1774–1776:	Turgot minister of finances and navy.
1777–1781:	Necker in charge of finances.
1778–1783:	Alliance with American revolutionaries.
1783–1787:	Calonne minister of finances.
1784:	Beaumarchais: *Le Mariage de Figaro*.
1787:	Loménie de Brienne in charge of government; edict of tolerance of Protestants; conflict with Parlement of Paris.
1788:	Necker recalled to manage finances.
1789 (May):	Meeting of States General.

Beaumarchais: *Le Mariage de Figaro*

Of Servants and Masters

Only twenty-five years separate Voltaire's Candide from Beaumarchais's Figaro, and yet what a difference of tone! Both are servants of
noblemen, but whereas Candide stands in awe before "one of the most

powerful lords in Westphalia," Figaro sees in his master "a quite ordinary man. " In reality, Voltaire had no greater respect for nobles than
had Beaumarchais, but—aside from the literary necessity that required
a naive and innocent character—he could not have gotten away with
the language Beaumarchais would hurl at his audience in 1784.

Servants, especially valets of noblemen, have a long tradition in the
theater. In most cases their role is a subservient or ridiculous one: they
help carry out their masters' plans, perhaps grudgingly or with moral
indignation; or else, in comedies, they evoke laughter by awkwardly
aping the elegant manners of their masters. The French theater inherited this tradition from the Spanish gracioso (Corneille's *Le Menteur*, for
example), but Molière adopted the model of the Italian commedia dell'-
arte, the theater of masks and improvisation, where the servant assumes
the major role, under various names (Harlequin, Mascarille, Sganarelle,
Scapin), and often proves to be superior to his master in intelligence
and ingenuity. There was, of course, a technical reason for this. Comedy was essentially limited to characters from the common classes and a
nobleman could therefore not be portrayed in a major role. But in one
of Molière's early plays, *L'Etourdi* (1651), the plot centers around the
feats of cleverness the servant has to perform in order to overcome the
blunders of his master, whose conceitedness is equalled only by his
ineptness.

Molière can hardly be called a revolutionary; nevertheless, he established a tradition that usually raised the valet to a higher status than
that of a simple and humble servant: even Sganarelle, the least courageous of them, dares contradict his terrible master Dom Juan and takes
his meals at the same table. Marivaux generally preserved this attitude
in his comedies, where valets play important roles. Although reverting
at times to the type of servant who comically exposes his lack of
manners when exchanging clothes with his master (Arlequin, in *Le Jeu
de l'amour et du hasard*, 1830), Marivaux's servants are bright and are
frequently the less fortunate companions of their young masters rather
than their inferiors. The comic device of having servant and master
exchange roles can be viewed, if not yet as a reversal of status, at least as
a first indication that merit should not be measured by the splendor of
one's attire but by one's personal qualities. And the way in which the
servants berate their masters during the exchange demonstrates that the
rigid wall of social separation was beginning to crumble.

So it is not surprising that Beaumarchais should use a valet to carry
the burden of denouncing the ills and injustices of his time.[1] As a

barber, Figaro had already shown his cleverness in Beaumarchais's earlier play *Le Barbier de Seville* (1775), where he arranged the marriage
between Count Almaviva and Rosine despite the plotting of her greedy
tutor Doctor Bartholo. But there his role was principally that of the
"fixer." Now the valet of the count, in *Le Mariage de Figaro* the ex-
barber uses his razor-sharp tongue to cut away the sham that lies hidden
behind mechanical good manners, at the same time accomplishing the
feat of making the nobles laugh—all the way to the guillotine!

Censorship, Prohibition, and Performance

Few episodes illustrate the irresolution of Louis XVI, the disarray of
his government, and the suicidal lightheartedness and lightheadedness
of the nobility of the time better than the battle surrounding Beaumarchais's *Le Mariage de Figaro*. For how was it possible that such an
explosive play could be performed, against the king's will, under an
absolute monarchy that had at its disposal every means of suppressing
dangerous and subversive works and throwing their authors into jail?

Beaumarchais probably wrote *Le Mariage de Figaro* between 1776 and
1778. It was accepted by the Comédie Française for performance in
1781. The first censor, Coquelay de Chaussepierre, raised only minor
objections. But Louis XVI had heard about the play and had it read to
him and the queen by Mme Campan, a lady in waiting, who recorded
this memorable occasion.

I began reading; the king interrupted me often with remarks of praise or
blame. Most of the time he exclaimed: "That is in bad taste; that man
continually drags on stage Italian *concetti*." During Figaro's monologue, where
he attacks various administrative agencies, but especially during the tirade
against state prisons, the king rose with vivacity and said: "That is detestable,
it will never be played. We would have to destroy the Bastille, so that the
performance of that play would not be a dangerous inconsistency. That man
snaps his fingers at everything that is to be respected in a government." "So it
will not be played," the queen said. "Certainly not," Louis replied, "you can be
sure of that."[2]

This reply deserves a place of honor among famous last words, for
Beaumarchais continued his efforts to have the play performed by reading it in aristocratic circles, including that of the king's brother, the
comte d'Artois, who was won over. He was probably responsible for
having the king change his mind, for a performance of the play was

scheduled on 13 June 1783 for the court. A select and excited crowd filled the royal Théâtre des Menus Plaisirs, but at the last moment orders arrived to cancel the performance. By now many aristocrats were getting annoyed at what they considered royal caprice, and curiosity to see this mysterious play increased. A private performance was given at the theater of the comte de Vaudreuil at the Château de Gennevilliers, on 27 September 1783, in the presence of the comte d'Artois. The play was submitted to several censors, Beaumarchais made some changes, talked his critics out of others, and permission was finally granted to perform the play publicly.

The premiere, on 27 April 1784, was a historic event at the Comédie Française. Nobles sent their valets hours ahead of time, schemed to obtain tickets, brought along their food, and ate standing up. Finally the gate was crashed and people threw money on the tables as they entered the theater. Beaumarchais himself watched the scene from behind an iron-fenced loge in the company of two abbés, "in order to receive very spiritual [the word has a double sense in French, meaning both spiritual and witty] last sacraments in case of death." He did not need to fear, for the receipts beat all previous records of the Comédie Française, and *Le Mariage de Figaro* was performed sixty-eight times in a row, an unheard-of success when compared to previous long runs of the eighteenth century: La Motte's *Inès de Castro* (32), and Voltaire's plays *Zaïre* (30) and *Mérope* (28). Three years later Mozart presented his opera *Le Nozze di Figaro* based on a libretto by Da Ponte.

The Plot

What caused all this uproar? A witty and entertaining play, vibrant with action, which, from a technical point of view, one could at most criticize for being a bit long and at times too complicated. The brief summary Beaumarchais himself provided in 1778 sounds no more subversive than the plot of any other well-conceived comedy of the time.

Figaro, the concierge of the Château d'Aguas Frescas, has borrowed ten thousand francs from Marceline, the housekeeper at the same castle, and written her a promissory note to repay the sum in due time or else to marry her. Very much in love with Suzanne, however, the maid of countess Almaviva, he intends to marry her, for the count, taken himself with young Suzanne, has encouraged their marriage in the hopes that a dowry he has promised the bride will obtain for him secretly the opportunity to exercise his "seignorial right" (*le droit du seigneur*), a privilege he renounced before his vassals upon his own marriage. This little domestic intrigue is conducted for the count by the unscrupulous Bazile, the music master of the castle. But young and decent, Suzanne feels obliged to inform her mistress and her bridegroom of the gallant intentions of the count. Thus the countess, Suzanne, and Figaro join to thwart the count's scheme. A little page, loved by everybody in the castle but mischievous and fiery like all bright children of thirteen or fourteen, escaping gaily from his master, causes by his giddiness some amusing incidents in which he and the count get into each other's way. Realizing that he has been tricked without knowing how, the count decides to avenge himself by supporting Marceline's claim: if he cannot have the young one as his mistress, he will make Figaro marry the old one. But the very moment he thinks he has taken vengeance by his judgment as first magistrate of Andalusia, condemning Figaro to marry Marceline that very day or pay her back the ten thousand francs (which Figaro cannot do), it turns out that Marceline is actually Figaro's mother, which destroys all the projects of the count, who cannot pretend to be happy or avenged.

Meanwhile the countess, who has not given up hopes of regaining her unfaithful husband by surprising him in flagrante delicto, has made Suzanne agree to feign to grant him a rendezvous in the garden, where he will find a wife instead of a mistress. But an unforeseen circumstance informs Figaro of the rendezvous his bride has granted. Angry because he thinks he has been deceived, he hides at the place of the rendezvous in order to surprise the count and Suzanne. At the height of his rage he is pleasantly surprised to learn that the whole thing is but a game between the countess and her maid to deceive the count, and he willingly agrees to take part in the practical joke. Proven by his wife to be unfaithful, the count, on bended knees, begs her to forgive him, which she does laughingly, and Figaro marries Suzanne.[3]

There is little in this plot that would rob a censor of his sleep. Almaviva may not be a model nobleman, but others, far more sinister than he, had paraded across the French stage. Compared to Molière's "great lord but wicked man" Dom Juan, Almaviva is but a pleasant skirt chaser, who neither beats his valet nor offends God and the statue of a man he has killed in a duel.[4] The "seignorial right," which supposedly granted the lord the first night with any maiden of his domain who was to be married, had long been abandoned (if it was ever practiced in fact), and, besides, the count had publicly given up this privilege. Furthermore, in the action of the play Beaumarchais never forgets the respect that is due the count.

But what about a valet who dares measure himself with his master over a woman? This too must be brought into focus. Bridegrooms have always defended their brides against the seductions of noblemen. In

Molière's *Dom Juan*, the peasant Pierrot does not hesitate to stand up against Dom Juan, who is about to deprive him of his bride. It is true that he takes a beating in the process, but times have changed since 1665 when *Dom Juan* was performed. Not only do masters and servants exchange clothes in amorous pursuit, they can even become rivals.[5] What is new, however, in the evolution that leads from Pierrot to Crispin and then to Figaro, is that in the rivalry between master and servant, the latter wins out, not because circumstances aid him, but because he is the smarter of the two.

Themes and Attacks

While it is true that, in public, the count is always treated with the respect due a great noble, the same cannot be said of the occasions when Figaro reveals his real opinions in monologues. "Because you are a great lord, you think you are a great genius! . . . Nobility, wealth, rank, offices, all that makes one proud! What have you done to deserve so much? You took the trouble to be born, and nothing more; aside from that, a quite ordinary man." [Parce que vous êtes un grand seigneur, vous vous croyez un grand génie! . . . Noblesse, fortune, un rang, des places, tout cela rend si fier! Qu'avez-vous fait pour tant de biens? Vous vous êtes donné la peine de naître, et rien de plus; du reste, homme assez ordinaire (*Le Mariage*, 5.3).] Courtesans fare no better. "Receiving, taking, and requesting: that is the secret in three words." [Recevoir, prendre et demander: voilà le secret en trois mots. (*Le Mariage*, 2.2).] Even the gentle countess is not spared. Having had to make up a hasty explanation to deceive her husband, she receives this dubious compliment from Suzanne: "And in this I have seen how much frequentation of high society makes it easy for respectable ladies to lie without batting an eyelash." [et c'est là que j'ai vu combien l'usage du grand monde donne d'aisance aux dames comme il faut, pour mentir sans qu'il y paraisse (*Le Mariage*, 2.24).]

The count is about to be appointed Spanish ambassador to Great Britain, but Figaro shows as little respect for his master's future function as for his person.

Pretending not to know what one knows, to know what one does not know, to understand what one does not comprehend, not to hear what one hears, especially to be capable of doing things beyond one's capacities; often to shroud in great secrecy the fact that there isn't a secret, to lock oneself into one's office to sharpen pens and appear to be a profound thinker when one is, as the saying goes, but hollow and empty; acting a role, well or badly, sending out spies and paying off traitors, dissolving the wax that seals letters, intercepting correspondence, and trying to dignify the baseness of the means by pointing to the importance of the end—that, upon my life, is all there is to politics!

[Feindre ignorer ce qu'on sait, de savoir ce qu'on ignore, d'entendre ce qu'on ne comprend pas, de ne point ouïr ce qu'on entend, surtout de pouvoir au-delà de ses forces; avoir souvent pour grand secret de cacher qu'il n'y en a point, s'enfermer pour tailler des plumes et paraître profound quand on n'est, comme on dit, que vide et creux; jouer bien ou mal un personnage, répandre des espions et pensionner des traîtres; amollir des cachets, intercepter des lettres, et tâcher d'ennoblir la pauvreté des moyens par l'importance des objets: voilà toute la politique, ou je meure! (*Le Mariage*, 3.5)]

Beaumarchais draws on his own experiences and grievances in Figaro's attacks on censorship and justice. We have already seen that *Le Mariage de Figaro* had to get past seven or eight censors before it could be performed. One of these, Suard, had declared himself completely opposed to permitting performance of the play. This leads Figaro to explain how severe censors conceive of freedom of the press.

Provided that in my writings I discuss neither authority, nor religion, nor politics, nor morality, nor people in high places, nor respectable assemblies, nor the opera, nor other spectacles, nor any people who are concerned about anything, I can freely print anything—after inspection by two or three censors.

[Pourvu que je ne parle en mes écrits ni de l'autorité, ni du culte, ni de la politique, ni de la morale, ni des gens en place, ni des corps en crédit, ni de l'Opéra, ni des autres spectacles, ni de personne qui tienne à quelque chose, je puis tout imprimer librement, sous l'inspection de deux ou trois censeurs. (*Le Mariage*, 5.3)]

The tone of the play becomes harsh and the characters turn into caricatures when it comes to the shortcomings of justice: "indulgent toward the great, tough with the little people." [Indulgente aux grands, dure aux petits. (3.5)] From 1770 until 1778 Beaumarchais had been involved in a law suit concerning certain clauses favorable to him in the last will of the powerful financier Pâris-Duverney, which his heir, the comte de La Blache, refused to recognize. In 1773 Judge Goëzman was put in charge of the case. Beaumarchais, imprisoned at the time for a fistfight with the duc de Chaulnes over a woman, obtained permission to present his case to the judge, whom he offered 100 louis, plus 15 louis for the secretary, and a precious watch. The judge returned the 100 louis and the watch, and shortly thereafter Beaumarchais lost his case, was condemned to pay 56,300 livres, and his possessions were seized. Thereupon he published four memoranda revealing the behavior and actions of the judge. A new trial was held in 1774, which condemned Judge Goëzman but Beaumarchais as well, who was stripped of his civil rights, which he recovered only in 1776 after he had organized a fleet to help the American revolutionaries. Finally, in 1778, Beaumarchais won his suit against the comte de La Blache.

The author did little to hide his references, for he calls the president of the tribunal Don Guzman Brid'oison. Stuttering, stupid, pretending to know what he does not understand, this venerable representative of justice is assisted by his clerk Double-Main (Double-Hand, Double-Dealer), who reads the charges in a legal jargon which has been a constant source of French farce from *La Farce du Maître Pathelin* (about 1470) to Courteline's popular sketches. Beaumarchais also attacks the practice of selling judgeships, "a great abuse," Marceline remarks. "Yes," Brid'oison replies, "they would do better by giving them to us for nothing." [— C'est un grand abus que de les vendre! — Oui, l'on ferait mieux de nous les donner pour rien (*Le Mariage*, 3.12).] Both parties fear the corruption of justice: "The head judge has been bribed, he bribes the other judge, and I lose my case," Marceline complains. [On a corrompu le grand juge, il corrompt l'autre, et je perds mon procès (*Le Mariage*, 3.15).] Yet, the judgment the count renders seems perfectly fair: since Figaro cannot pay the sum he borrowed, he has to marry Marceline.[6] Fortunately for him, she turns out to be his mother.

In his long monologue (*Le Mariage*, 5.3), Figaro launches a terrible indictment against the government and the abuses of power and privileges. He attacks the nobility, religious bigotry, the brutality and injustices of the authorities, the incompetence of bureaucrats, the evil and pettiness of censorship, and the dishonesty of gambling establishments. La Harpe, a conservative literary critic, describes his reactions on watching this scene.

I shall never forget my amazement on hearing this monologue which lasts at least a quarter of an hour. But this amazement soon changed in kind, for the tirade was extraordinary in more than one way. More than half of it was but a satire of the government; I knew it well, having heard it before. But I had never even imagined that the government would permit insults of that sort to be hurled in its face in a sold-out theater. The more the applause mounted, the more I was dumbfounded and bemused. I finally concluded that, as far as I was concerned, it was not the author who was to blame. Yes, the tirade, in view of where it had been inserted, was an incomprehensible absurdity, but the tolerance of the government, which let itself be debased to such an extent was a far greater one; and that, after all, Beaumarchais was right to speak that way in the theater, regardless of where in the play, because it was considered all right to let him do so.[7]

It must be remembered that this applause, which amazed La Harpe so much, was produced by hands that were mostly noble. In her *Mémoires,* the baronesse d'Oberkirch condemns her fellow aristocrats. "The great lords," she observes, "showed a lack of tact and measure by their applause; they slapped their own cheeks; they laughed at their own expense and, worse still, made the others laugh. They will regret it later."[8]

Beaumarchais is not afraid to take on other causes as well. He vigorously advocates that illegitimate children should not be discriminated against, and he exposes and defends the position of the "fallen" poor girl and condemns the treatment of women in general.

"More than ungrateful men," Marceline exclaims, "who cover with contempt the playthings of your passions, your victims! You are the ones who should be punished for the errors of our youth, you and your magistrates, so frivolous in your right to judge us, and who let us be deprived, by their guilty negligence, of all decent means of subsistence. . . . Even ladies of rank only obtain a perfunctory consideration: beneath a semblance of respect, they are kept in actual servitude, treated as minors so far as our wealth is concerned, punished as adults for our faults! Ah! from every point of view, your behavior with us inspires horror or pity."

[Hommes plus qu'ingrats, qui flétrissez par le mépris les jouets de vos passions, vos victimes! c'est vous qu'il faut punir des erreurs de notre jeunesse; vous et vos magistrats, si vains du droit de nous juger, et qui nous laissent enlever, par leur coupable négligence, tout honnête moyen de subsister. . . .
Dans les rangs même les plus élevés, les femmes n'obtiennent de vous qu'une considération dérisoire: leurrées de respects apparents, dans une servitude réelle, traitées en mineures pour nos biens, punies en majeures pour nos fautes! Ah, sous tous les aspects, votre conduite avec nous fait horreur ou pitié.
(*Le Mariage,* 3.16)]

On the Road to Revolution

"Unable to degrade wit, they take vengeance by mistreating it." [Ne pouvant avilir l'esprit, on se venge en le maltraitant (*Le Mariage*, 5.3).] This complaint by Figaro in his monologue summarizes Beaumarchais's most important grievance.

> Indeed, he desires neither the destruction of the nobility, to which he aspired, nor the taking over of power by the lower classes. . . . All he asks for is a place for the aristocracy of mind and talent. . . . He especially feels that an enterprising and resolute man, such as Figaro and Beaumarchais himself, should be able to procure glory and advantages for himself. And as obstacles, suspicions, and prejudices hold him back and threaten to render him powerless, he becomes exasperated and uses persiflage. Beneath an appearance of gaiety, the tone reveals far more rancor and personal animosity than generous and profound liberalism.[9]

Persiflage and insolence toward one's superiors—those are the keynotes in Beaumarchais's *Le Mariage de Figaro*. The play demonstrates the increasing boldness of writers who criticized the social and political inequities in France during the eighteenth century. Not that Montesquieu, Crébillon fils, and Voltaire had lacked courage. Montesquieu refers to the pope as "an old idol," but this observation is made by a Persian; Crébillon expressed contempt of an impotent aristocracy, but it takes place in the exotic atmosphere of a Japanese fairy tale; Voltaire declares that it is a common occurrence for kings to be dethroned, but those referred to are foreign kings and *Candide* can hardly be called a realistic story.

But in *Le Mariage de Figaro* there can be no mistake about the place and characters: they are French, regardless of the names Beaumarchais gives them.[10] His references are clear to every one and deal with current practices and situations (except for the "seignorial right"); he inserts into the play his personal grievances (Judge Goëzman); and, despite the imbroglios and recognition scenes, the action is both essentially realistic and contemporary.

There is obviously a connection between the changed tone and the reaction of the authorities. *Les Lettres persanes* was published anonymously, Crébillon fils was imprisoned for his *L'Ecumoire,* Voltaire's *Candide* was seized and prohibited, while *Le Mariage de Figaro* was performed publicly, with the author both known and present, before an enthusiastic audience, the majority of which was aristocratic. The weakness of the government is proportionate to the boldness of the authors.

Five years after *Le Mariage de Figaro* was first performed, the French Revolution broke out. Did the play contribute in any way to it? Opinions differ considerably about this. According to Victor Hallays-Dabot, "*Le Mariage de Figaro* did not advance the hour of the Revolution by one minute; but it explains and makes us understand more clearly to what extent the catastrophe was imminent and inevitable."[11]

The famous critic Sainte-Beuve, although admitting that Beaumarchais did not consciously attempt to call his contemporaries to action, feels that he hastened the course of events. "A play of the sort . . . where everything is attacked and turned upside down: marriage, motherhood, the magistrates, nobility, everything concerning the state; where the master-lackey holds the floor from beginning to end, and where license is the handmaiden of politics, became an obvious signal to revolution."[12]

Yet the most fervent historian of the French Revolution, Jules Michelet, shows little sympathy for this supposed precursor of 1789.

I have little liking for *Figaro*. I do not detect in it the spirit of the Revolution. Sterile, completely negative, the play is a hundred leagues from the great revolutionary heart. That character is not at all the man of the people. He is a bold lackey, the insolent bastard of some great lord (and not at all of Bartholo).

The play misses its target. The great nobleman is a fool all right. But who would want Figaro to be in power? He is worse than those he attacks. One senses in him all the vices of the great and the small. If that rascal were to climb to the top, what kind of a world would we have? What can we expect of someone who laughs at nature, makes fun of maternity, and who debases the very altar, *his mother*.[13]

Michelet is quite right. Figaro is not a revolutionary. He is neither prepared to risk his life for an ideal nor does he possess the "great revolutionary heart" of those who paraded around with the heads of their enemies atop pikes. Nor does he aspire to dispossessing his master and taking his place. He is a *débrouillard,* one who manages to steer his course *around* obstacles—not through them. The slogans of the Revolution would have had little meaning for him: he cares more for liberty than for fraternity and equality—but most of all, for the pursuit of happiness, an enterprise that tends to crown the efforts of the cleverest and the most resourceful people.

And yet, Figaro is more revolutionary than his creator, more revolutionary than Montesquieu, Crébillon fils, and Voltaire, primarily because he has less to lose. But did he hasten the Revolution? We have no tools to measure precisely the forces or the momentum of history. Was the Revolution inevitable? Could Louis XVI have prevented it by aligning himself with the people? Would it have happened even if there had been no philosophes, no Voltaire, no Beaumarchais? In short, is history a series of accidents? Or is it determined by great men, by important groups and their capacities or errors? Or does it run on rails along a predestined course?

But even if we assume the last of these hypotheses, the trains have to be steered by engineers who have an idea of where they are heading. And this brings us back to *Le Mariage de Figaro* and the other works of opposition of the eighteenth century. Their authors were undeniably responsible for bringing about a change in mentality that made the French realize that what they had not even imagined before was possible: that injustices could be fought, that abuses could be corrected, that kings could be dethroned; briefly, that change was possible. And by succeeding to have *Le Mariage de Figaro* performed contrary to royal will, Beaumarchais had conquered that part of the Bastille where rebellious ideas had been kept prisoner by censorship.

What makes the eighteenth-century writers we have discussed so effective is that they represented the most capable group in France, the middle class, which was on the rise and could not be denied its rightful place. They were not caught in the dilemma of present-day leftist intellectuals, who claim to fight for a class of which they are not a part and which they do not always understand. If someone had called Beaumarchais a bourgeois, he might have been offended, but only because his ambitions led him upward—into the aristocracy. It is this enlightened and representative self-interest that gives power to their writings and an echo to their message.

But now the dawn breaks on 14 July 1789. *La commedia è finita.* The laughter of Montesquieu, of Crébillon fils, of Voltaire, and of Beaumarchais will never be heard again in France.

Part 2

From the Revolution to the Second Empire

Chapter Five
Martyrs, Poets, and a Superwoman

The Revolution and Napoleon, 1789–1814

Every country has one or more sacred cows in its history. In the United States it is not considered good manners to speak ill of George Washington or the Founding Fathers; in Great Britain one had better leave the royal family alone. France has two established sacred cows: the Revolution and Napoleon; and a more recent one that shows every promise of eventually joining the other two: Charles de Gaulle.

Not surprisingly, most histories of the Revolution have been favorable, and the few authors who dared attack it outright have had to pay a heavy price for their audacity. To this day the liberal French intelligentsia has not forgiven Hippolyte Taine for his condemnation of the Revolution (and of Napoleon too, for that matter).[1] Nevertheless, one cannot begin to acquire even a general conception of that enormous event without reading both Taine and Jules Michelet,[2] its greatest detractor and its most enthusiastic supporter. The truth does not lie somewhere between these two extremes, as one might be prudently tempted to suggest—both are right, for the Revolution brought out the best and also the worst in the French people of the late eighteenth and early nineteenth centuries.

Even now, two hundred years after these events, it is impossible to write objectively about the French Revolution, not only because political interests continue to be tied to its reputation, but because one cannot calmly dispense praise or blame on people living and acting during a frantic period full of angels and devils, people of good will and monsters. It would require a master of antithesis, a sort of historically objective Victor Hugo, to do justice to the task.

On the one hand, the Revolution accomplished the unimaginable, the undreamed of: the overthrow of a monarchy that had reigned for centuries; an attempt to set up a government in which the people were to be supreme; the resistance by popular heroism of surrounding hostile powers and their eventual defeat. On the other hand, there were savage killings, an inability to establish any sort of stable government, followed by a Terror that resulted in a senseless and merciless march to the guillotine.

American readers should not give in to the temptation of comparing the French and the American revolutionaries. The latter came from a country that had a long constitutional tradition, which had enabled them to acquire political knowledge and experience; the former enjoyed no such advantages. The French had never known anything other than monarchy, more or less absolute, and their revolutionaries had no practical experience whatsoever in government. Besides, the Revolution was not the result of long years of planning, which would have given its leaders the opportunity to prepare themselves to govern—it was thrust on them in a short time and to everybody's surprise, including their own.

So much happened in the decade between 1789 and 1799 that one would have to draw up a daily account of events to describe the constantly changing situation. A feverish atmosphere; rumors of royal plots and of invasion by émigré armies; hungry peasants roaming the countryside; the Great Fear, mobs of people being used by various factions to terrorize their opponents into submission; attempts by Louis XVI to flee and his humiliation; hunger; inflation; inexperienced armies suffering defeats; uprisings in Brittany and Vendée; anarchy and short-lived efforts to establish a workable governing system; conspiracies to seize power; exile; executions; death by guillotine of victims and soon thereafter of those who had sent them there—this was the breathtaking pace of the Revolution during a time when no one could feel secure.

The 14 July 1789 taking of the Bastille, which contained only seven prisoners at the time, was but a symbolic action by the Paris crowd. What it demonstrated was that royal authority had lost control of the situation. Revolutionary committees sprang up all over France and often simply took over from the authorities in place. A National Guard was formed with La Fayette in command in Paris. Gradually the Revolution, which had been carried out mostly by the lower classes, was taken over by the middle classes: professional people, merchants, and property owners.[3] A National Assembly was formed to give France a new constitution; the property owned by the Church was nationalized and sold to avoid bankruptcy threatened by the government's inability to collect taxes; a Declaration of Rights was adopted and religious tolerance proclaimed. The Constitution was finally completed in 1791, but the members of the Assembly foolishly voted to disqualify themselves from being candidates for the Legislative Assembly, thus depriving the country of some of its most experienced minds.

In the newly elected body the left wing consisted of the Jacobin party and its less radical splinter group, the Feuillants. A struggle for leadership took place between Brissot and Robespierre; it was temporarily won by the former, who called for war against Austria, a proposal accepted by Louis XVI, who hoped that a French defeat would restore him to his former position of power. The campaign began indeed with French defeats. To divert attention from their failures, the Brissotins decided to arouse popular feelings against the king, whom they accused of plotting with foreign powers. Unrest broke out all over France. On 20 June 1792 an armed crowd invaded the Assembly and then went on to the Tuileries, where they forced Louis XVI to put on a red bonnet (the symbol of the Revolution) and to drink wine with them. On 8 July, National Guard troops were called to Paris from the provinces, but instead of protecting the royal family, they mingled with the excited crowds. On 10 August, the Tuileries were invaded again. While the royal family fled to the Assembly, fighting broke out that resulted in more than one thousand deaths.

The Legislative Assembly, incapable of handling the situation, was now replaced by a National Convention, elected by universal suffrage. By September, France's war fortunes improved with a victory in the battle of Valmy, after which French forces advanced to Brussels following their defeat of the Austrians at Jemappes. The Convention abolished the monarchy and, as of 22 September 1792, changed the calendar to reflect year one of the Republic. Next it voted the death sentence for Louis XVI, who was executed on 21 January 1793. "As a king," Rivarol wrote, "he deserved his misfortune, because he was unable to do his job."[4]

The Convention was dominated by the Brissot faction and the three great names of the Revolution: Marat, Danton, and Robespierre, who had been the instigators of the various popular uprisings. But the Convention did not constitute an effective government. After declaring war on England and Holland, France suffered severe setbacks, causing General Dumouriez, the hero of Valmy, to defect to the Austrians, as La Fayette had done before him. Faced with renewed unrest and food riots, the Convention set up a Revolutionary Tribunal to deal with traitors, and passed a law that permitted summary execution of rebels caught in an act of treason. The scene was set for a takeover by the Jacobins. An uprising on 31 May 1793 was followed by a march on the Convention and the demand for the arrest of Brissot, which was granted.

With the election of the Committee of Public Safety began the year of Terror, which lasted from July 1793 to July 1794. Certainly, Robespierre was not the only one responsible for governing. He was surrounded by bloodthirsty men, such as Billaud-Varenne and Collot d'Herbois, and by cold-blooded dogmatists, such as Saint-Just. Nor were all his political enemies pure and innocent. But it would take a better excuse than the sincerity of a political puritan (if such was indeed the case) to make of him anything but a dogmatic butcher. Robespierre's reputation matters less to us today than the lesson his example offers; namely, that sincerity bestows neither wisdom nor intelligence nor moral superiority on those who act or pretend to act in its name. The stabbing of Marat by Charlotte Corday on 13 July 1793 set off mass arrests, and for one year suicides and the guillotine removed from the best of all possible revolutions Brissot and thirty of his followers, the philosopher Condorcet, the duc d'Orléans (Philippe Egalité), Queen Marie-Antoinette, the king's sister Elisabeth, Mme du Barry, Danton, Lavoisier, France's greatest scientist of the time, and André Chénier, France's greatest poet of the time. In Paris alone, the guillotine cut off 2,627 heads between March 1793 and 27 July 1794. On 10 thermidor (29 July 1794) 17 heads rolled. This time Robespierre's was among them.

The most (and perhaps the only) creditable action of the Committee of Public Safety had been the raising of a large army, often by unscrupulous means. Led by young generals, French armies advanced and recaptured Belgium. Among the new military leaders, Bonaparte was at first in disgrace with the Thermidoreans, who soon had to call on him for help to protect the Convention. On 5 October 1795 he moved in troops and cannons, firing on an uprising, causing several hundred casualties. A Directory of five men was set up, which faced opposition from both Jacobins and royalists yet continued war with Austria after Prussia, Holland, and Spain had agreed to French peace terms. The Austrians were defeated at Arcola in 1796 and at Rivoli in 1797 and signed peace with France at Campo-Formio. Bonaparte departed on his Egyptian campaign in 1798, but a new coalition united Great Britain, Russia, Turkey, and later Austria. Bonaparte returned to France and established the Consulate by a coup d'état on 18 brumaire (9–10 November 1799) with himself as first consul.

The Revolution had now come full circle. Beginning with the overthrow of an absolute monarchy, it had passed through the Terror and ended up with a consul who was to become an emperor more absolute than any king since Louis XIV. "In this vaunted Revolution," a hostile Rivarol judged, "everything has been bad: the royal princes, the military men, the deputies, the people, even the assassins."[5]

In surgical terms one can say of the French Revolution that the operation was a success, but the patient kept ailing for eighty-two years, for that is how long it took to rid France of a series of kings and emperors before a lasting republic could be established.

Can one be more enthusiastic about Napoleon? Yes, if one esteems the skill of warfare and the glory of temporary victories; no, if one judges by ultimate results. Named consul for life in 1802 and crowned emperor on 2 December 1804, Napoleon I set out on the conquest of Europe. If General de Gaulle consoled his compatriots after the fall of France in 1940 by telling them that they had lost a battle but not the war, the opposite holds true of Napoleon: he won almost all the battles but lost the war. Paris is an everlasting monument to his glory—the two arches of triumph, the obelisque at the Place de la Concorde, the Place Vendôme, the streets that bear the names of his victories: Ulm, Iéna, Eylau, Friedland, Wagram. But you will not find any street named Beresina, Trafalgar, or Waterloo. The first is the river that the French army crossed on its pathetic retreat from the Russian campaign. Napoleon had set out with over five hundred thousand troops in June of 1812, but only some forty thousand made it back alive by November of that year; the second is the place where Nelson destroyed the French fleet, thus giving Great Britain control of the seas; the third, a battle that put an end to what there was left of Napoleon's hopes of returning to power. During his reign, the map of France could be likened to a man who had overeaten, gotten enormously fat, and finally returned to his original size—that of 1790.

Not all of Napoleon's career can be characterized so simply. He gave France a civil code, readable, clear, and unfavorable to women. He set up a rigid system of control over France from Paris, a system that has reduced the provinces to near impotence ever since. He reestablished religious authority by a concordat with the Vatican; in the long run, however, this proved more favorable to Rome than had the Gallicanism of the ancien régime. He set up an effective system of education and placed the government and finances on a more solid basis than had his predecessors. Administratively, present-day France still operates largely under the organization that was intended for the rule of a dictator. Taine hardly exaggerates when he concludes that Napoleon imprisoned the French in philosophical and administrative barracks.

In the long run, Napoleon's greatest achievement was the example he set, which proved that a merit system could accomplish splendid results. Following the precedent already established during the Revolution, he promoted young military and administrative talents who made France the first—and the most feared—power in the world, at least until he began distributing noble titles, and wooing to his court those of the old aristocracy who would agree to serve him. Still, it was his talent for recognizing and rewarding ability—enhanced by a poetic legend—that made Napoleon the idol of ambitious young men like Stendhal's Julien Sorel.

The more lasting, and far more damaging, heritage Napoleon has left us is the dream of world conquest, which has fascinated and encouraged pseudo-Napoleons, with or without mustache. No amount of ridicule, whether in Stendhal's novel *La Chartreuse de Parme* or in Charles Chaplin's film *The Great Dictator,* can discourage these scourges of modern times, nor can derision daunt the adoration they enjoy during their short and immensely destructive existence.

That Napoleon was a great man no one can deny, but military and political leaders must strictly be measured by final scores. In this respect, Napoleon resembles those marvelous dribblers in soccer who, receiving the ball from a defender, maneuver brilliantly past opponent after opponent, bringing the crowd to its feet in openmouthed admiration. The only trouble is that our virtuoso has been moving laterally across the field and when finally, hemmed in by too many opponents, he passes the ball back in panic to the defender from whom he received it, his team is far worse off than when he started his solo run. In soccer, only a game is lost, but in war hundreds of thousands (over 850,000 in Napoleon's case), perhaps millions, die. It does seem an exorbitant price to pay for a solo run, no matter how brilliant.

On 24 April 1814, Louis XVIII, "by the grace of God, king of France and Navarre," arrived at Boulogne. Despite the Hundred Days, during which Napoleon attempted an abortive comeback, the Restoration was installed, while Napoleon wrote his memoirs at Saint Helena. France returned to its borders of 1790 and the Bourbon kings were back.

Montesquieu

Crébillon fils

Voltaire.
Bust in terra-cotta by Houdon.

Beaumarchais.
Engraving by
A. de Saint-Aubin,
after Cochin.

André Chénier.
Engraving by Dupont,
1838, after J. B. Savée.

Mme de Staël.
Lithograph by Delpech.

Chateaubriand

Pierre-Jean Béranger.
Lithograph by Maurin.

Stendhal.
Reproduction of a painting.

Victor Hugo

Louis XIV.
Engraving by Edelinck,
after J. de la Haye.

Louis XV.
Engraving by François.

Louis XVI

Napoleon I.
Engraving by Marchand, after Chabord.

Louis XVIII.
By Potrelle.

Charles X

Louis-Philippe I

Napoléon III.
Lithograph by Noël,
after a photo by
Pierson.

Chronology

1789:   Meeting of the States General, which becomes National Assembly; (20 June): tennis-court oath of Assembly never to separate until their aims had been achieved; (14 July): taking of Bastille; (4 August): liberal nobles renounce their privileges.

1790:   Civil constitution of the clergy; Necker resigns.

1791:   Flight of Louis XVI to Varennes.

1791–1792:   Legislative Assembly.

1792:   War with Austria; king taken prisoner; victory over Prussia at Valmy.

1792–1795:   National Convention.

1793:   Louis XVI executed; Marat stabbed by Charlotte Corday.

1793–1794:   Reign of Terror.

1794:   André Chénier: *Iambes;* Chénier guillotined; Robespierre guillotined.

1794–1795:   Thermidorian reaction.

1795:   Treaties of Basel with Prussia and Spain.

1795–1799:   Directory.

1796:   French victories at Arcola and Rivoli.

1798–1799:   Bonaparte in Egypt and Syria.

1798–1802:   War of Second Coalition (Russia, Great Britain, Austria).

1799:   Bonaparte returns to France; (9–10 November): coup d'état of 18 brumaire; Bonaparte first consul.

1800:   Victory at Marengo.

1801:   Treaty with Austria at Luneville.

1801–1802:   Concordat with Vatican.

1802:   Treaty of Amiens with Great Britain; sale of Louisiana to United States.

1803:   Mme de Staël: *Delphine;* renewal of war with Great Britain.

1804:   First Empire; execution of duc d'Enghien.

1805:   French fleet defeated by Nelson at Trafalgar.

1805–1806: Victories over Austria at Ulm, over Prussia at Jena, over Russia at Austerlitz, Eylau, and Friedland.

1807:   Treaty with Russia at Tilsit; Mme de Staël: *Corinne.*

1808–1814: Spanish War. War with Austria; victory over Austria at Wagram.

1809:   Peace of Schönbrunn; Chateaubriand: *Les Martyrs.*

1810:   Napoleon divorces Josephine and marries Marie-Louise.

1811:   Birth of Napoleon's son, the duc de Reichstadt.

1811–1812: Russian campaign; retreat at Beresina.

1812:   Campaign of Germany.

1813:   Béranger: *Le Roi d'Yvetot.*

1814:   Allies enter France; Napoleon abdicates and is imprisoned at Elba.

Censorship

It is one of the ironies of history that the few writers who dared criticize two of the greatest steamrollers in French history turned out to be people usually considered weak: poets and a woman. True enough, they wrote during a barren literary period, when censorship had reached heights that made earlier censors, such as Malesherbes and the two Crébillons, appear like civil and tolerant editors with a delicate red pencil.

Actually, censorship had been officially abolished, but the revolutionaries managed to impose it on any work they considered contrary to their best interests. At first, all plays that had previously been prohibited were encouraged, especially those by Voltaire: *Brutus, La Mort de César,* and *Mahomet.* But by the end of 1793, two verses in *Mahomet,* which we encountered before, had to be cut.

> Exterminate, great God, from the earth we live on
> Whoever takes pleasure in shedding the blood of men.
>
> [Exterminez, grand Dieu! de la terre où nous sommes,
> Quiconque avec plaisir répand le sang des hommes.
> *(Mahomet,* 3, 8)]

Any play featuring nobles or containing references that could be interpreted as unfavorable to the revolutionary government was kept off the stage by Joly, the censor.

Instead the theater was inundated with patriotic plays or others that attacked religious intolerance or monastery life. As happens in periods of great upheaval and hysterical behavior, public and government alike demanded relevance, and relevance they got—a flood of plays that were didactic and usually sincere, but uninspired, unpoetic, unreadable, unvisible, and unbearable.[6]

Under Napoleon, censorship returned in full force. Plays about Brutus were definitely out, and, worse still, any criticism of the emperor or his government was considered a hostile and punishable act. "Tell the newspaper editors," he wrote to Fouché, "that I shall hold them responsible not for their criticism, but for their failure to praise."[7]

Among the plays that enjoyed a certain vogue was that of Marie-Joseph Chénier, *Charles IX; ou, L'Ecole des rois,* first performed on 4 November 1789. It depicts a weak king dominated by Catherine de Médicis, who is plotting the St. Bartholomew massacre of Protestant leaders (1572). His hesitations are overcome by rumors, spread by Catherine, that Admiral Coligny is planning to assassinate him. Confronted by Henri de Navarre after the massacre, Charles IX repents, but it is obviously too late. The play, full of verses that flattered popular feelings at the time, was frequently performed, but by the time the Terror had arrived, *Charles IX* fell into disfavor with the new rulers, who showed little appreciation for the many references to tyrants and bloodshed.

How to Kill Your Best Poet: André Chénier's Iambes

Regardless of the fate of his play, no one denied that Marie-Joseph Chénier was a *bon citoyen.* An enthusiastic partisan of the Revolution, he had never wavered in its support.

The same cannot be said of his older brother, André Chénier. After his education at the excellent Collège de Navarre, André eventually obtained a position as private secretary of the French ambassador to Great Britain, but when the Revolution broke out, he returned to Paris. There he threw himself into political journalism, joining his former schoolmates, the wealthy Trudaine brothers and François de Pange, in the moderate Feuillants party.

But there was no place for moderates in the French Revolution. Soon the *Journal de Paris,* where he had published articles, was suspended, and Chénier had to lead the life of a suspect. He went to Rouen for a while but returned to Paris, stayed in Versailles, and was arrested in Passy, where he had accompanied the marquise de Pastoret, the wife of a man imprisoned as a traitor and conspirator. He was guillotined on 25 July 1794, at the age of thirty-one. The Revolution had killed the greatest poet France had produced in the 130 years that had passed since La Fontaine had written his fables.

Chénier's fame is in great part due to his lyric and bucolic works, which revived the poetic vein in France. As a "committed" poet he holds a position midway between the seventeenth century Huguenot poet Agrippa d'Aubigné (*Les Tragiques,* 1616), who heaped his anger on the persecutors of the reformed faith, and Victor Hugo, whose vituperations were directed against Napoleon III. Although his production is much smaller than theirs, Chénier exhibits a great variety of tone, ranging from Olympian satire and irony to lyric and tragic outbursts.

The same variety can be found in the forms he used: the hymn, the ode, and the iambic meter. It is the latter that lends itself best to lashing out at injustice. Its originator was Archilochus, who hurled his verses at his fiancée's father, who had broken his word. In Greek poetry, the iambic meter, with its couplets of a long verse followed by a shorter one, came close to sounding like prose, but Chénier adheres more closely to classical French verse, which avoids enjambment (over-flow of verse into the next line). In his *Iambes,* too, he introduced a new note into French poetry by preserving classical forms while at the same time diminishing none of the sting of his attacks.

Not all of Chénier's political poems are in the iambic meter. His *Ode to Marie-Anne-Charlotte Corday* is constructed on the theme of opposi-tion. The revolutionaries are singing infamous hymns to Marat— Chénier will write an ode to the woman who killed Marat in his bath on 13 July 1793. For Marat he cannot find epithets insulting enough.

> The black serpent, leaving his filthy cave,
> Has finally suffered by your hand so sure and brave
> The end of its venomous existence so despised!
> From the tiger's guts, from his homicidal teeth
> You came and drew what he'd devoured from beneath:
> The blood and livid members of his victims sacrificed.

[Le noir serpent, sorti de sa caverne impure,
A donc vu rompre enfin sous ta main ferme et sûre
Le venimeux tissu de ses jours abhorrés!
Aux entrailles du tigre, à ses dents homicides,
Tu vins demander et les membres livides
Et le sang des humains qu'il avait dévorés!]

Opposition between an ideal civilization and perverted ideals. In ancient Greece, Charlotte Corday would have been honored. "But in France your head is cut off by the ax." [Mais la France à la hache abandonne ta tête.] Opposition, finally, between the slogan of the Revolution (Liberty, Equality, Fraternity)—which was a mockery at the time—and Truth, which remains silent, Justice, which is rendered by sinister judges, and Virtue, in the sense of moral and courageous qualities.

Virtue alone is free. Honor of our history,
Our immortal shame will live beside your glory.
Only you were a man, your knife did vengeance wreak;
And we, vile eunuchs, cowardly and soul-less cattle.
We can at best complain like women prattle,
But to wield a sword our hands would be too weak.
. . . .
In that mud crawls one scoundrel less.
Hear, lovely heroine, hear Virtue bless,
Hear the august voice of its virile praise.
Oh Virtue, the dagger that hope will raise,
Is your sacred arm, when Heaven holds its thunder
And lets crime rule, while laws are cut asunder.

[La vertu seule est libre. Honneur de notre histoire,
Notre immortel opprobre y vit avec ta gloire.
Seule tu fus un homme, et vengea les humains.
Et nous, eunuques vils, troupeau lâche et sans âme,
Nous savons répéter quelques plaintes de femme,
Mais le fer pèserait à nos débiles mains.
. . . .
Un scélérat de moins rampe dans cette fange.
La Vertu t'applaudit. De sa mâle louange
Entends, belle héroïne, entends l'auguste voix.
O Vertu, le poignard, seul espoir de la terre,
Est ton arme sacrée, alors que le tonnerre
Laisse régner le crime, et te vend à ses lois.
(*Oeuvres*, 179–80)][8]

Throughout the *Ode to Marie-Anne-Charlotte Corday* there rings a tone
of bitterness and, at times, shameful resignation. By using the pronoun
nous, Chénier includes himself among those who stand by, impotent
and cowardly, while injustice rewards crime.

A stronger tone of accusation appears in "Iambe VI," which describes
the drowning of prisoners at Nantes by the infamous Carrier and his
acolytes. Chénier dwells on the contrast between these atrocities and
the pleasure-filled life of the barbarians who get drunk on expensive
wine and satisfy their lust with cheap women.

Long before Victor Hugo and the romantic poets, André Chénier
defines the role of the poet as the conscience of the people. In "Iambe
V," referring to the bloodthirsty tyrants, he exclaims:

> Yet they live and their victims' throttled cries
> Do not rise up to your exalted heights.
> It is a poor poet, oh majestic god of the armies,
> Who, alone, in prison, as death he fights,
> Gluing to his verses the flaming wings
> Of your thunder that no longer stings,
> Of virtue exiled taking the defense,
> Denounces to the judges of all hells
> Those judges, those juries that strike innocence,
> Creating a hecatomb at their tribunals.
> Just let me stay alive, and that filthy breed
> Will feel the power of my pen.
> They cannot hide behind their dirty deed:
> I see them, I rush in, I have them.

> [Ils vivent cependant et de tant de victimes
> Les cris ne montent point vers toi.
> C'est un pauvre poète, ô grand Dieu des armées,
> Qui seul, captif, près de la mort,
> Attachant à ses vers des ailes enflammées
> De ton tonnerre qui s'endort,
> De la vertu proscrite embrassant la défense,
> Dénonce aux juges infernaux
> Ces juges, ces jurés qui frappent l'innocence,
> Hécatombe à leurs tribunaux.
> Eh bien, fais-moi donc vivre, et cette horde impure
> Sentira quels traits sont les miens.
> Ils ne sont point cachés dans leur bassesse impure;
> Je les vois, j'accours, je les tiens.
> ("Iambe V," *Oeuvres*, p. 190)]

Chénier reveals himself as a master of irony, worthy of Voltaire, in his *Hymne aux Suisses de Chateauvieux.* The Swiss mercenaries in the Chateauvieux regiment had revolted in August 1790. They held their officers for ransom, looted the funds of the regiment, and engaged in combat with the National Guard. Désille, a young officer, tried to avoid bloodshed and was killed by the Swiss. The rebels were tried: twenty-three were executed and forty-one sent to forced labor on the galleys. In December 1791 the galley prisoners were granted amnesty, and in February 1792 they were set free, whereupon they marched on Paris. The Jacobins felt they could turn the Swiss rebels to political advantage and, led by Collot d'Herbois, the painter David, and Chénier's brother Marie-Joseph, they arranged for a triumphal reception of the released prisoners.

On that day, 15 April 1792, André Chénier wrote his "hymn." The unsuspecting reader may be misled by the opening.

> Hail, divine Triumph! enter into our walls!
>   Welcome back those warriors honored
> For the blood shed of Désille and the funerals
>   Of so many Frenchmen massacred.
> Never before your gates saw anything so fine.
>   Not even when the shade of Mirabeau
> Of yore was carried to the sacred shrine,
>   A tomb that only glory can bestow.
> Nor when Voltaire's ashes, refused a calm retreat,
>   To Paris came back for repose,
> And fanaticism and calumny in full defeat
>   Prostrate lay before his prose.

> [Salut, divin Triomphe! entre dans nos murailles!
>   Rends-nous ces guerriers illustrés
> Par le sang de Désille, et par les funérailles
>   De tant de Français massacrés.
> Jamais rien de si grand n'embellit ton entrée,
>   Ni quand l'ombre de Mirabeau
> S'achemina jadis vers la voûte sacrée
>   Où la gloire donne un tombeau,
> Ni quand Voltaire mort, et sa cendre bannie
>   Rentrèrent aux murs de Paris,
> Vainqueurs du fanatisme et de la calomnie,
>   Prosternés devant ses écrits.]

Only the unexpected references to Désille (unknown to all but contemporaries or specialized historians) and the massacred Frenchmen (not identified in any other way) introduce a sense of ambiguity into what otherwise sounds like a traditional hymn.

But soon Chénier removes all ambiguity about the real meaning of his "song of praise." He begins with another oblique slap at the sight of civic leaders, who—honored by La Rapée, a restaurant where the Jacobin chiefs were suspected of indulging in orgies—

> Place on a radiant chariot
> These heroes, who previously on a galley bench
>   Were put by an outrageous sentence,
> And who strangled but very few of our brothers
>   And stole but little gold from others.
>
> [De voir des échevins, que la Rapée honore,
>   Asseoir sur un char radieux
> Ces héros, que jadis sur les bancs des galères
>   Assit un arrêt outrageant,
> Et qui n'ont égorgé que très peu de nos frères,
>   Et volé que très peu d'argent.]

In his conclusion Chénier rises to new heights of irony. Comparing the freed galley prisoners to illustrious conquerors of the sea, he chants:

> Let Night emboss their names in its veil,
>   And the Pilot, when he goes amiss,
> Invoke in their Galley, as the stars they trail,
>   Collot-d'Herbois's glorious Swiss.
>
> [Que la Nuit de leurs noms embelisse ses voiles,
>   Et que le nocher aux abois
> Invoque en leur Galère, ornement des étoiles,
>   Les Suisses de Collot-d'Herbois.
>   (Oeuvres, pp. 164–66)]

The word *Nuit* here has a double meaning: Night and Oblivion. And the final irony of transforming the former galley slaves into superseamen invoked by lost pilots constitutes a parting shot, not so much at the Swiss rebels as at those who had turned them into heroic martyrs.

In prison, Chénier matures. He opens his heart to the sufferings of others. His most famous ode, *La Jeune Captive*, celebrates a young woman who actually was not so pure as he imagined and whose life was spared. The historical person matters less here than the sentiment. In his last *Iambes*, the modern reader is struck by an existential note that anticipates by some 150 years Jean-Paul Sartre's *Mort sans sépulture*. The horror of mass butchery pervades "Iambe VII" and "Iambe VIII":

> When the somber slaughterhouse lets the bleating sheep
> Into its dark and deadly gate,
> Shepherds, dogs, and sheep, all of them keep
> Their thoughts on any but their fate. . . .

> . . . Who will be the prey
> On whom the ax will fall today?
> Everybody shivers, listens, and is relieved to see
> That the one called out is not yet he.
> It will be you tomorrow, unfeeling fool.

> [Quand au mouton bêlant la sombre boucherie
> Ouvre ses cavernes de mort,
> Pâtres, chiens et moutons, toute la bergerie
> Ne s'informe plus de son sort. . . .
> ("Iambe VII" *Oeuvres*, p. 192)

> . . . Quelle sera la proie
> Que la hache appelle aujourd'hui?
> Chacun frissonne, écoute; et chacun avec joie
> Voit que ce n'est pas encor lui:
> Ce sera toi demain, insensible imbécile.
> ("Iambe VIII" *Oeuvres*, p. 193)]

Chénier's last "Iambe" sums up his themes: a tenderness toward life, the defense of virtue, justice, and truth, the poet's role as witness of his times and of history, and a last shout of defiance.

> Like a last ray of light, like a last summer breeze
> Color the end of a beautiful day,
> At the foot of the gallows once more my lyre I seize.
> Perhaps I'll soon be on my way.
> . . . .

My life is Virtu⸱'s concern.
A decent man, whom outrage has fed,
    In prison, awaiting his turn,
Lifts higher his speech and higher his head.

    .   .   .   .

Addressing Justice and Truth, he cries out:

Save me. Preserve an arm
To hurl your thunderbolts, a lover to avenge you.
    .   .   .   .
Oh my pen! poison, gall, horror, God of my life,
    Through you alone I carry on my strife.
    .   .   .   .
No one would remain and move history to record
    About so many just people massacred?
To console their memory, their widows, their sons,
    So that abhorrent highway brigands
Will tremble at their black portraits in paint?
    To descend into hell, like a saint,
To tie the trifold whip, by vengeance praised,
    Already on those perverts raised?
To spit on their names, to see their sentence carved?
    Come now, stifle your cry;
Suffer, heart full of hate, for justice starved.
    And you, Virtue, weep if I die.

[Comme un dernier rayon, comme un dernier zéphyre
    Animent la fin d'un beau jour,
Au pied de l'échafaud j'essaye encor ma lyre.
    Peut-être est-ce bientôt mon tour.

    .   .   .   .
        Ma vie importe à la vertu.
Car l'honnête homme enfin, victime de l'outrage,
    Dans les cachots, près du cercueil,
Relève plus altier son front et son langage.

    .   .   .   .
        Sauvez-moi. Conservez un bras
Qui lance votre foudre, un amant qui vous venge.
    .   .   .   .
O ma plume! fiel, bile, horreur, Dieu de ma vie!
    Par vous seuls je respire encor:

    .   .   .   .

Nul ne resterait donc pour attendrir l'histoire
Sur tant de justes massacrés?
Pour consoler leurs fils, leurs veuves, leur mémoire,
Pour que des brigands abhorrés
Frémissent aux portraits noirs de leur ressemblance,
Pour descendre jusqu'aux enfers
Nouer le triple fouet, le fouet de la vengeance
Déjà levé sur ces pervers?
Pour cracher sur leurs noms, pour chanter leur supplice?
Allons, étouffe tes clameurs;
Souffre, ô coeur gros de haine, affamé de justice.
Toi, Vertu, pleure si je meurs.
("Iambe IX," *Oeuvres*, pp. 193–95)]

André Chénier did not write a fictional account of his sufferings nor did he sublimate them poetically. Drawn into the whirl of a mad world, he had no time to gain the necessary distance that fiction requires. And so he cast anathema at injustice, atrocity, and horror.

His militant poetry does not always possess the high art that pervades his lyric poems, but his genius was such that his cries of anger, of frustration, and of vengeance created a new poetry in France, one that inspired Victor Hugo's *Les Châtiments* and the defiant chants of the poets of the Resistance during the Second World War.

It has been said that, in its upheavals, Spain kicked its brains out. The French Revolution went it one better: it cut off the head of its greatest poet and left an indelible stain on a record that already had been far from clean.

The Great Woman and the Great Man: Mme de Staël's
Delphine *and* Corinne

History does not inform us whether Napoleon decided to exile Mme de Staël because he feared her or because he simply could not stand her. As for Mme de Staël, it was not all hate at first sight. On the contrary, she did her best to court the Great Man, but he had no use for *femmes savantes* and rewarded her efforts with cutting remarks.

At a dinner party in 1807, Mme de Staël asked him, "Who is the greatest woman, dead or alive?" He replied, "The one who has borne the most children."

Napoleon had good reason to suspect that, in her salon, he was not always praised as he felt he should be, and that she was a quarrelsome woman. Yet his decision to have her exiled from France and to have all copies of her book *De l'Allemagne* destroyed reminds us of Stendhal's prince of Parma who lived in fear of enemies under his bed.

Mme de Staël's novels *Delphine* (1803) and *Corinne* (1807) can hardly be called masterworks,[9] nor do they properly fit the definition of opposition literature. Both are overlong and at times exclamatory; yet both deal with a profound problem: the plight of a superior woman in a prejudiced society, and her difficult relations with indecisive men, who do not measure up to her and who are unable to throw off the shackles of family obligations and social etiquette.

In a way, Mme de Staël expresses strong criticism of her society, but she is dealing with age-old problems that, during the Revolution, had been intensified by hopes of greater equality for women, hopes that vanished in the face of reality. Nevertheless, both novels do contain attacks against Napoleon, but presented in the only way a writer could dare express criticism of the Great Man: obliquely.

Although the action of *Delphine* takes place between the years 1790 and 1792, the causes supported in the novel enraged Napoleon. While he was trying to lend respectability to his regime by insisting on strict morality, Mme de Staël was attacking conventional marriage and religious bigotry, pronouncing herself in favor of divorce and women's rights, and proposing England as a model state.

The one unmistakable reference to a person associated with Napoleon, however, is personal rather than political. Critics generally agree that she used Talleyrand, Napoleon's foreign minister, as the model for Madame de Vernon, a treacherous although charming woman who betrays Delphine's trust and succeeds in marrying off her own daughter to Léonce, whom Delphine loves. But Mme de Staël was attacking not so much Talleyrand's policies as the perfidy of a former lover, the only one who eventually dropped her altogether. The witty ex-abbé, when told of his changed sex role in *Delphine*, quipped, "I understand that Madame de Staël, in her novel, has disguised both herself and me as women."[10]

The heroine of *Corinne* is a far more imposing figure than the virtuous and gentle Delphine. She is idolized in Italy as a poetess, a singer, and a dancer. Not only do we find here the same social views as in *Delphine*, but, underneath the harrowing love story, a defiant Corinne realizes Mme de Staël's dream: she is crowned, she represents the female Napoleon: "A whole people at her feet, and all that without a single death, . . . the kingdom of Corinne was that of the Spirit. If Corinne was right, the Spirit, too, was a force."[11]

And her kingdom, an imaginary and ideal Italy, is joyful and appreciates its artists, contrary to the morose and stuffy atmosphere of the First Empire in France. Like most of her contemporary opposition writers during that period (and there were not many, as we have seen), Mme de Staël operated in the darkroom—by developing the negative and not the print.

Napoleon was the greatest man of his time and Mme de Staël the greatest woman. It is a pity that the two did not hit it off, but it should not surprise us: their egos were of such dimensions that there was only room for one of them in France, the more powerful one.

Who's Afraid of Napoleon? Chateaubriand's Les Martyrs de Dioclétien

Alphonse de Chateaubriand carried on a similar sort of love-hate relationship with Napoleon as did Mme de Staël. He had dedicated the second edition of his *Génie du christianisme* (1802) to the "Citoyen premier Consul," and he had accepted a diplomatic mission to Rome. But the assassination of the duc d'Enghien, vaguely accused of plotting against Napoleon, and the execution of his cousin Armand de Chateaubriand had cooled off his enthusiasm for the emperor and rekindled his inherent loyalty to the Bourbons.

Chateaubriand's epic work *Les Martyrs* (1809) contains a great number of allusions to the contemporary political scene. It was easy to recognize Napoleon in the portrayal of Diocletian, and most critics claim to see Fouché, Napoleon's chief of police, in the vicious description of Hiéroclès. The original version of this epic, which takes place in the third century A.D., was contained in an unpublished novel entitled "Les Martyrs de Dioclétien."[12] In this version, references to contemporary events and characters abound. Had it been published as written, then Chateaubriand would have been the most important (in fact, the only true) opposition writer of his time.

Judgments are contained in it about governments that have produced a succession of monsters; the one who is about to restore this sort of reign is called "the greatest enemy of mankind"; and despair is expressed in the outcry, "Will people always arm only against kindness and virtue, and will their crimes always serve to legitimize tyranny."[13]

Alas, pressured by friends close to the emperor, Chateaubriand eliminated almost all offending passages, and what little real criticism remained was so innocuous that Napoleon was highly pleased by the flattering image in which he could mirror himself.

98 SUBVERSIVE TRADITION, VOLUME I

The Big King and the Little King: Béranger's Le Roi d'Yvetot

Since vicious censorship and a concomitant lack of daring did not allow the production of strong opposition works during the First Empire, it was left to a poet, who wrote satiric songs and who was actually a great admirer of Napoleon, to create an immortal little ditty that even the Great Man could not help but hum.

In 1813, just before the battle of Leipzig, when the French were tiring of the enormous bloodletting caused by Napoleon's wars, Pierre-Jean Béranger composed a song that no one could fail to understand. He too had to employ the indirect method. Still, his *Roi d'Yvetot* (13 May 1813), by the very contrast he represents with the failing "Ruler of Europe," expressed the deep desire of the French people for peace, calm, and a normal, uncomplicated life.

> A King once lived of Yvetot,
> Though little known his name,
> Rose late, to bed did early go,
> Slept well, nor cared for fame,
> And Jenny clapped his crown instead,
> A cotton night-cap on his head,
> 'Tis said.
> Ho! ho! ho! ho! he! ha! he! ha!
> What a good little king, hurrah!
> Hurrah!
>
> He ate four meals a day inside
> His palace thatched with straw,
> And pace by pace, an ass astride,
> His kingdom travelling saw.
> Plain, jovial, thinking good, agag,
> He'd but for guard, as forth he'd jog.
> A dog.
> Ho! ho! etc.
>
> But one onerous taste had he,
> His thirst was somewhat *vif;*
> For though his people happy be,
> Of course a king must live.
> For table he directly got
> From every puncheon taxed, a pot
> By lot.
> Ho! ho! etc.

Since maidens of good birth were glad
To bow to his desire,
His folk a hundred reasons had
To call the king their sire.
He'd bring to butts his train-bands crack
Each quarter day, the bull's-eye's black
To whack.
Ho! ho! etc.

He ne'er enlarged his proper states
With all at peace abroad;
He was your model, potentates!
For pleasure was his code.
Till death his people's love he kept,
They ne'er, till in the tomb he slept
Had wept!
Ho! ho! etc.

They kept the portrait, painted fine,
Of that right-worthy prince;
It hangs a famous tavern sign
In that good land long since.
As of a fête they drink once more,
The crowd still shouts the wine-shop door
Before:
Ho! ho! etc.[14]

[Il était un roi d'Yvetot
Peu connu dans l'histoire,
Se levant tard, se couchant tôt,
Dormant fort bien sans gloire,
Et couronné par Jeanneton
D'un simple bonnet de coton,
Dit-on.
Oh! oh! oh! oh! ah! ah! ah! ah!
Quel bon petit roi c'était là!
La, la.

Il faisait ses quatre repas
Dans son palais de chaume,
Et sur un âne, pas à pas,
Parcourait son royaume.

Joyeux, simple et croyant le bien,
Pour toute garde il n'avait rien
  Qu'un chien.
Oh! oh! etc.

Il n'avait de goût onéreux
Qu'une soif un peu vive;
Mais, en rendant son peuple heureux,
Il faut bien qu'un roi vive.
Lui-même, à table et sans suppôt,
Sur chaque muid levait un pot
  D'impôt.
Oh! oh! etc.

Aux filles de bonnes maisons
Comme il avait su plaire,
Ses sujets avaient cent raisons
De le nommer leur père;
D'ailleurs, il ne levait de ban
Que pour tirer quatre fois l'an
  Au blanc.
Oh! oh! etc.

Il n'agrandit point ses états,
Fut un voisin commode,
Et, modèle des potentats,
Prit le plaisir pour code.
Ce n'est que lorsqu'il expira
Que le peuple qui l'enterra
  Pleura.
Oh! oh! etc.

On conserve encor le portrait
De ce digne et bon prince:
C'est l'enseigne d'un cabaret
Fameux dans la province.
Les jours de fête, bien souvent,
La foule s'écrie en buvant
  Devant:
Oh! oh! oh! oh! ah! ah! ah! ah!
Quel bon petit roi c'était là!
  La, la.][15]

The contrast here is great, not only between the political ambitions of the two kings, but also between the gay, carefree atmosphere in the small province in Normandy, ruled over by the "little" king, and the morose and pompous tone that rendered the court of the "big" king so unbearable.

This was the only song in which Béranger criticized Napoleon. He will become his lyric worshipper during the Restoration and the July Monarchy, but he will celebrate not so much Napoleon himself as his legend.

Chapter Six
Songs, Kings, and Social Climbers
The Restoration, 1814/15–30

They had learned nothing and forgotten nothing: that is the phrase usually applied to the Restoration in France. While it may accurately describe the mentality of most of the émigré extremists (*ultras*) and of the king's younger brother, Artois, it does not do justice to Louis XVIII.

True, he had forgotten nothing. For him the monarchy had never ceased to exist, and he referred to the time of his return to France in 1814 as the nineteenth year of his reign. But he had learned a great deal. What he offered France was a policy of national reconciliation characterized by unexpected concessions.

The Charte assured the people of forgetfulness and forgiveness. Essentially, existing laws and administrations were to continue in force, the public debt was assumed, and the proprietorship of land nationalized during the Revolution was recognized. Moreover, and even more surprising, the country was to be governed by a parliament of two chambers chosen by an electorate limited to seventy-two thousand; and religious tolerance was proclaimed. Finally, it should not be forgotten that only a Bourbon king was in a position to placate the victorious enemies of Napoleon and bring about the relatively favorable peace that France desired and needed so badly.

There is little doubt that, even if he did not adhere to every detail of the Charte, Louis XVIII believed in the spirit of this moderate policy. Alas, the king was rather weak. Very fat and able to walk only with difficulty, he possessed the intelligence but not the strength of character to maintain his principles against the enormous pressure exerted on him by his brother and the ultraconservative nobles who were hungry for revenge and compensation. Caught between this group, the Bonapartists, and the liberals, he steered an unsteady course between them, often choosing his ministers for reasons of personal preference rather than for their qualifications. Nor did he show any particular courage when Napoleon returned to France for a hundred days. He prudently took refuge in Belgium.

These events strengthened the ultraconservatives, who demanded and obtained the execution of Marshall Ney, who had rallied to the cause of Napoleon's forces. A royalist chamber, the *chambre introuvable,* was elected in 1815, but Louis XVIII dissolved it the following year. Since the election results represented a defeat for Talleyrand and Fouché, the king appointed the duc de Richelieu to head the government. During his administration the reparations imposed on France by its victorious opponents were paid off, and the occupying armies withdrew in 1818.

But the assassination in 1820 of the duc de Berry, the second son of the king's brother, gave renewed impetus to the demands of the ultras and brought down Richelieu's successor, Decazes, who had tried to govern with the support of the liberals. Richelieu was recalled to power and had to face revolutionary attempts from the left, inspired in part by Napoleon's death in 1821; the most famous attempt was undertaken by the four sergeants of La Rochelle. In 1822 Louis XVIII replaced Richelieu with Villèle, recommended to him by his favorite lady (mistress would be too strong a term), Mme du Cayla. Villèle, a hard worker, established the first workable budgetary system in France.

The Restoration might have become durable, if Louis XVIII had not died in 1824. His brother, who succeeded him as Charles X, was the head of the ultraconservative group. He had himself crowned at Reims, the way it had been the custom during the ancien régime. To please Charles X and his party, Villèle had laws passed concerning sacrilege, the press, and education. Religion had enjoyed a remarkable revival. Between 1815 and 1830, convents increased from 1,829 to 2,875. And the Congrégation, the secret political arm of the Jesuits, exerted a great influence over the government. Fear of another return by Napoleon or of a revolutionary takeover was shared by Jesuits and royalists alike, and Louis XVIII had already joined the sovereigns of Austria, Prussia, and Russia in a Holy Alliance designed to protect religion, peace, and justice. The specter of Napoleon led certain ultras to plan the possibility of calling in foreign troops for protection in case of a revolutionary uprising.[1]

The most important victory of the ultras, however, was the 1825 vote of indemnification of the émigrés for their lost property. Reaction was swift. The people were outraged at the expense of one billion francs, and Chateaubriand, who as foreign minister had supported a successful intervention in Spain in favor of Ferdinand VII, now joined the opposition.

Charles X first called on Martignac, who tried to win over the liberals but failed for lack of support from the king. When Polignac took over the government, even the Chamber addressed a note to the king which respectfully expressed the concern of the nation. In reply Charles X dissolved the Chamber. The new elections resulted in a resounding victory for the opposition. Now Polignac published four ordinances that went far beyond the powers granted the king under the Charte. They controlled the press, dissolved the new Chamber, restricted the vote even further, and ordered the electoral college to elect a new Chamber.

Riots broke out on 28 July 1830, and by 2 August Charles X abdicated. He agreed to have the duc d'Orléans installed as regent until his grandson, the duc de Bordeaux, would come of age. It was a critical moment. Those who had overthrown Charles X were, for the most part, republicans and Bonapartists, both opposed to a Bourbon or Orleanist king, but La Fayette presented the duc d'Orléans to the people at the *Hôtel de Ville* (city hall) and had him acclaimed by putting a tricolored flag in his hands and embracing him.

The duc d'Orléans had no intention of serving as regent for the Bourbon lineage and the Chamber agreed to have him installed, not as king of France (Roi de France), but as king of the French (Roi des Français), and he assumed the throne as Louis Philippe I.

Chronology

1814–1815:   Louis XVIII returns to France

1815:   Napoleon attempts to reassume power during Hundred Days; Battle of Waterloo; Napoleon abdicates and is exiled to St. Helena; Louis XVIII restored to power; publication of first collection of Béranger's songs.

1820:   Assassination of the duc de Berry.

1821:   Béranger's second collection of songs; his trial; death of Napoleon.

1822–1824:   Chateaubriand minister of foreign affairs.

1823:   Expedition to Spain.

1824: Ultra Chamber elected; death of Louis XVIII.

1825: Coronation of Charles X at Reims; indemnification of émigré nobles voted.

1828: Second trial of Béranger.

1830: Stendhal: *Le Rouge et le noir;* autocratic ordinances; (26–30 July): revolution; Charles X abdicates.

Béranger

His Influence and Trial

The two most important writers who expressed opposition to the Restoration experienced opposite fates: the one best known and most effective has faded away in the wear and tear of literary history, while the one who died almost unknown has risen to become one of the giants of French literature.

Pierre-Jean Béranger, who had directed his popular song "Le Roi d'Yvetot" against Napoleon, remained nonetheless a fervent admirer of the emperor and felt despair at the return of the Bourbon kings after Napoleon's defeat. Eking out a living from a clerkship at the University of Paris, a government job, Béranger associated with the liberal opposition and first drew attention to himself with the publication of a collection of his songs in 1815.

His next volume, published in 1821, immediately got him into trouble. Not only was he dismissed from his humble job, but the government ordered the seizure of all copies, which had miraculously disappeared, leaving only four to be confiscated. Worse still, Béranger was put on trial for sixteen of his songs, against which four charges were leveled. A number of them were condemned for offending decency; others (including *Le Bon Dieu*) for offending public and religious morality; a third group (among them *Le Prince de Navarre* and *La Cocarde blanche*) for offending the person of the king; and a last group (e.g., *Le Vieux Drapeau*) for public display of seditious adherence.

His trial on 8 December 1821, was a sensational event attended by a huge crowd. The accused, who needed forty-five minutes to get to his seat, pronounced the memorable phrase, "Gentlemen, they can't begin without me." Maître Dupin, Béranger's lawyer, pointed out that even the ancien régime had been called "an absolute monarchy tempered by songs," and he reminded his listeners of the proverbial expression that in France everything ends with a song. All to no avail. The jury found the accused guilty of the first three charges and sentenced him to three months in prison and a fine of five hundred francs.

Just what sort of songs were these to make a government try and jail a poet? Reading them today, they seem rather good-humored, but within the historical context of a Restoration monarchy fearful of anything connected with Napoleon and aware of its unpopularity, these songs took on an air of rebellion.

Béranger's political views are uncomplicated, but this very simplicity befitted not only the lyrics written on popular airs but also appealed to a large number of his contemporaries. He is a resolute partisan of the Revolution and of Napoleon. Even though the Restoration had established a constitutional regime and had granted privileges in the Charte, every effort was made by extreme royalists to take them back. Censorship was increased and the right to vote restricted to several thousand big landowners, while those officers and veterans who had not disowned Napoleon were increasingly mistreated.[2] Béranger attributed much responsibility for these repressive measures to the Congrégation, a secret religious society that spied on suspected individuals, and exerted great influence in the government.

Against these forces of reaction Béranger set the popular support of liberties resulting from the Revolution (symbolized by the tricolored flag) and the example of former popular rulers, such as Henri IV, but especially Napoleon, no longer seen as a despot but as the author of the legal code, as the creator of the Legion of Honor, and as the great national hero who always remained close to his soldiers.[3]

Songs against Louis XVIII

The poet began his attacks gently and indirectly by suggesting that the king take the kindly advice he gave Mathurin Bruneau, the son of a maker of wooden shoes, who pretended he was the prince de Navarre: to go back to making shoes (*Le Prince de Navarre; ou, Mathurin Bruneau*). Louis XVIII, who was far more tolerant than his brother and the ultras, laughed at these verses, but he can hardly have been amused by those Béranger wrote about the royal flag, *The White Cockade*. The occasion for these verses was a dinner on 30 March 1816, at which the ultraroyalists celebrated the anniversary of the day when Austrian, Russian, and Prussian soldiers first entered Paris after the defeat of Napoleon.

The White Cockade

O Day of peace and freedom! joyous then
    Were the vanquished made.
Glad day, when France her honor found again
    And the white cockade!

Let's sing that day, our fair one's pride
    When monarchs, not a few,
Scourged—by success—the rebel French;
    Saved all the good and true.
O Day of peace and freedom! etc.

The aliens and their cohorts came,
    Invoked by us; with ease
They forced an entry through our gates—
    When we gave up the keys.
O Day of peace and freedom! etc.
.   .   .   .
At this our patriotic feast,
    Props of the old noblesse—
After such dangers—come, let's toast
    The foreigner's success!
O Day of peace and freedom! etc.

Lastly, the flower of Henry's race,
    For such rare lenience shown,
Let's pledge the king who could, himself,
    Take Paris—and his throne!
O Day of peace and freedom! joyous then
    Were the vanquished made.
Glad day, when France her honor found again,
    And the white cockade![4]

[La Cocarde blanche
30 mars 1816
Air des Trois Cousines

Jour de paix, jour de délivrance,
Qui des vaincus fit le bonheur;
Beau jour, qui vint rendre à la France
La cocarde blanche et l'honneur!

Chantons ce jour cher à nos belles,
Où tant de rois par leurs succès
Ont puni les Français rebelles,
Et sauvé tous les bons Français.
Jour de paix, jour de délivrance, etc.

Les étrangers et leurs cohortes
Par nos voeux étaient appelés.
Qu'aisément ils ouvraient les portes
Dont nous avions livré les clés!
Jour de paix, jour de déliverance, etc

. . . .
Appuis de la noblesse antique,
Buvons, après tant de dangers,
Dans ce repas patriotique,
Au triomphe des étrangers.
Jour de paix, jour de délivrance, etc.

Enfin, pour sa clémence extrême,
Buvons au plus grand des Henris,
A ce roi qui sut par lui-même
Conquérir son trône et Paris.
Jour de paix, jour de délivrance, etc.
(Oeuvres, pp. 173–74)]

In his song *Le Bon Dieu*, Béranger lashes out at his two favorite targets, the Restoration king and the conservative clergy. To the severe God of the clergy, always ready to punish, he opposes a kindly, understanding, merciful God, benignly indifferent to those he created long ago, and shocked and amazed at what is being done in his name on the planet Earth.

Jupiter

Jove, waking up from a nap t'other day,
Gave us thought, in a kind enough way.
"May be their planet hath perished," he cries,
As from his window he peers at the skies.
But, at the word, far away he still found
Snug in a corner earth spinning around.
"If in what they're about head or tail I can see,
May the devil," quoth Jove, "may the devil take me!"

. . . .

"What are those dwarfs doing, gaily tricked out,
Seated on thrones with gilt nails stuck about?
Brows are anointed, and pride has full sway,
Whilst—but the chiefs of your ant-hillock—they
Tell you I've blessed all the rights of their race,
Bid you believe that they're kings by my grace.
If to reign in their fashion could be my decree,
May the devil, my children, the devil take me!

"Others live on me, in black all arrayed—
Dwarfs, of whose censers my nose is afraid.
Life to a Lent they're essaying to tame,
Launching anathemas couched in my name
In sermons sublime and severe as can be,
But which, to be frank, are Greek to me.
If I credit a word that is found in their plea,
May the devil, my children, the devil take me!

"Children, no longer ill-will to me bear;
Good honest hearts my elect I declare.
Love when ye can, and all pleasures secure;
'Tis not for this that I'll drown you, be sure.
Nabobs and hypocrites learn to defy! . . .
But, fare ye well; I'm afraid of yon spy!
Ah, if e'er to those fellows my gates I set free,
May the devil, my children, the devil take me!"[5]

[Le Bon Dieu

Air: Tout le long de la rivière
Un jour, le bon Dieu s'éveillant
Fut pour nous assez bienveillant;
Il met le nez à la fenêtre.
"Leur planète a péri peut-être."
Dieu dit, et l'aperçoit bien loin
Qui tourne dans un petit coin.
"Si je conçois comment on s'y comporte,
Je veux bien," dit-il, "Que le diable m'emporte,
Je veux bien que le diable m'emporte."

·   ·   ·   ·   ·   ·   ·   ·   ·   ·   ·   ·

"Que font ces nains si bien parés
Sur des trônes à clous dorés?
Le front huilé, l'humeur altière,
Ces chefs de votre fourmilière

Disent que j'ai béni leurs droits,
Et que par ma grâce ils sont rois.
Si c'est par moi qu'ils règnent de la sorte,
Je veux, mes enfants, que le diable m'emporte,
Je veux bien que le diable m'emporte.

"Je nourris d'autres nains tout noirs
Dont mon nez craint les encensoirs.
Ils font de la vie un carême,
En mon nom lancent l'anathème
Dans des sermons fort beaux ma foi,
Mais qui sont de l'hébreu pour moi.
Si je crois rien de ce qu'on y rapporte,
Je veux, mes enfants, que le diable m'emporte,
Je veux bien que le diable m'emporte.

"Enfants, ne m'en veuillez donc plus;
Les bons coeurs seront mes élus.
Sans que pour cela je vous noie,
Faites l'amour, vivez en joie;
Narguez vos grands et vos cafards.
Adieu, car je crains les mouchards.
A ces gens-là si j'ouvre un jour ma porte,
Je veux, mes enfants, que le diable m'emporte,
Je veux bien que le diable m'emporte."

(Oeuvres, pp. 270–71)]

Songs against Charles X

If Béranger had attacked the relatively tolerant Louis XVIII, imagine his detestation of the fanatically reactionary Charles X, who assumed the throne after his brother's death. He promptly wrote *Le Sacre de Charles le Simple* and *Les Infiniment Petits; ou, La Gérontocratie,* which led to his second trial on 5 December 1828. As it had seven years earlier, the event drew an immense crowd, and again he was found guilty of having insulted the king and his family and of outraging public morality. This time he was sentenced to nine months in prison and fined ten thousand francs, an enormous amount of money, which was raised by his friends, but not without difficulty.

In *Le Sacre de Charles le Simple,* Béranger presents his version of the coronation of Charles X. By choosing Charles III, called the Simple, he implies that the position of kings is not secure (a less daring statement in 1824 than at the time Voltaire suggested this in *Candide*), since

Charles the Simple was first denied the throne by Eudes, count of Paris (crowned in 898), and later dethroned and imprisoned. At the coronation of Charles X everything was done to restore the pomp of the old traditional ceremonies. The holy phial, publicly broken at Reims in 1793, was to have been miraculously found again, and the ancient custom of setting birds to flights of liberty was renewed. But Béranger turns this symbol of joy into one of sorrow over the liberty the French people have lost.

Coronation of Charles the Simple

Frenchmen, to Rheims who thronging crowd,
"Montjoie!" "Saint Denis!" shout aloud!
The holy cruise with oil once more
Is filled; and, as in days of yore,
Sparrows by hundreds tossed on high
Through the cathedral joyous fly—
    Vain symbol of a broken yoke,
    That from the king a smile provoke.
"Be wiser than ourselves!" the people cry;
"Hold fast, O birds, hold fast your liberty!"

. . . .
    In tawdry lace bedizened bravely,
    This king, who gulped down taxes gravely,
    Walks 'mid his faithful subjects; they
    Had, in a less auspicious day,
    To rebel standard all adhered,
    By generous usurper reared.
    Their tongues some hundred millions buy—
    A price for fealty none too high.
"We're paying for our chains!" the people cry;
"Hold fast, O birds, hold fast your liberty!"

. . . .
    In belt of Charlemagne arrayed,
    As though just such a roystering blade,
    Charles in the dust now prostrate lies;
    "Rise up, Sir King!" a soldier cries.
    "No," quoth the bishop, "and by Saint Peter,
    The Church crowns you; with bounty treat her!
    Heaven sends, but 'tis the priests who give;
    Long may legitimacy live!"
"Our ruler's ruled himself!" the people cry;
"Hold fast, O birds, hold fast your liberty!"

This king, O birds, in miracles dealing,
Will all the scrofulous be healing;
But ye, the sole redeeming sight
For yawning escort, take to flight,
Lest sacrilege you be committing,
As o'er altars you are flitting!
Religion here plants guards; and hers
Just now are executioners.
"Your wings we envy you!" the people cry;
"Hold fast, O birds, hold fast your liberty."

[Le Sacre de Charles-le-Simple

Air: Du beau Tristan (de Beauplan)
Français, que Reims a réunis,
Criez: "Montjoie et Saint Denis!"
On a refait la sainte-ampoule,
Et, comme au temps de nos aïeux,
Des passereaux lâchés en foule
Dans l'église volent joyeux.
D'un joug brisé ces vains présages
Font sourire sa majesté.
Le peuple s'écrie: "Oiseaux, plus que nous soyez sages;
Gardez bien, gardez bien votre liberté." (bis.)
.   .   .   .
Chamarré de vieux oripeaux,
Ce roi, grand avaleur d'impôts,
Marche entouré de ses fidèles,
Qui tous en des temps moins heureux,
Ont suivi les drapeaux rebelles
D'un usurpateur généreux.
Un milliard les met en haleine:
C'est peu pour la fidélité.
Le peuple s'écrie: "Oiseaux, nous payons notre chaîne;
Gardez bien, gardez bien votre liberté."
.   .   .   .
De Charlemagne, en vrai luron,
Dès qu'il a mis le ceinturon,
Charles s'étend sur la poussière.
"Roi!" crie un soldat, "levez-vous!"
"Non," dit l'évêque; "et par saint Pierre,
"Je te couronne: enrichis-nous.
Ce qui vient de Dieu vient des prêtres.
Vive la légitimité!"

Le peuple s'écrie: "Oiseaux, notre maître a des maîtres;
Gardez bien, gardez bien votre liberté."

Oiseaux, ce roi miraculeux
Va guérir tous les scrofuleux.
Fuyez, vous qui, de son cortège,
Dissipez seuls l'ennui mortel:
Vous pourriez faire un sacrilège
En voltigeant sur cet autel.
Des bourreaux sont les sentinelles
Que pose ici la piété.
Le peuple s'écrie: "Oiseaux, nous envions vos ailes;
Gardez bien, gardez bien votre liberté."

(*Oeuvres*, pp. 403–5)]

In *Les Infiniment Petits; ou, La Gérontocratie*, Béranger no longer proceeds by indirection. Taking advantage of the similarity in sound of *barbon* (graybeard) and Bourbon, he lashes out at the old Restoration kings (Louis XVIII, born in 1755; Charles X, born in 1757) whom he accuses of having taken over a great nation, which, with the help of the clergy, they are reducing to a miniature state. The word *petit* pervades the song with obsessive frequency, comparing, as Victor Hugo will do during the Second Empire, the little kings to the grandeur of the Napoleonic era.

The Infinitely Little;
Or, The Rule of the Grey-Beards

I've faith in magic; t'other night
A great magician brought to light
Our country's destiny; the sight
Was in the mirror plain.
How threatening was the picture! there
Paris and all its fauxbourgs were.
'Tis 1930, I declare—
But still the grey-beards reign.

A set of dwarfs have got our place;
Our grandsons are so squat a race,
That if beneath their roofs I trace
Such pigmies, 'tis with pain.
France, but the shadow of a shade
Of France that I in youth surveyed,

Is now a petty kingdom made—
But still the grey-beards reign.

How many a tiny little mite!
What little Jesuits full of spite!
Other small priests in shoals unite
Small Hosts to bear in train.
Beneath their blessing all decays;
Through them, the oldest court betrays
The little school in all its ways—
But still the grey-beards reign.

All's little—workshop, lordlings' hall;
Trade, Science, the Fine Arts, are small;
On tiny fortress vain the call
Small famines to sustain.
Along their badly closed frontier
Poor little armies, when they hear
Their little drums, on march appear—
But still the grey-beards reign.

At length in this prophetic glass,
Crowning our woes, is seen to pass
A giant—earth can scarce, alas!
The heretic contain.
This pigmy people quick he reaches,
And, braving all their little speeches,
Pockets the kingdom in his breeches—
But still the grey-beards reign.

[Les Infiniment Petits; Ou, La Gérontocratie
      Air: Ainsi jadis un grand prophète

      J'ai foi dans la sorcellerie.
      Or un grand sorcier l'autre soir
      M'a fait voir de notre patrie
      Tout l'avenir dans un miroir.
      Quelle image désespérante!
      Je vois Paris et ses faubourgs:
      Nous sommes en dix-neuf cent trente,
      Et les barbons règnent toujours.

      Un peuple de nains nous remplace
      Nos petits-fils sont si petits,

Qu'avec peine dans cette glace,
Sous leurs toits je les vois blottis.
La France est l'ombre du fantôme
De la France de mes beaux jours.
Ce n'est qu'un tout petit royaume;
Mais les barbons règnent toujours.

Combien d'imperceptibles êtres!
De petits jésuites bilieux!
De milliers d'autres petits prêtres
Qui portent de petits bons dieux!
Béni par eux, tout dégénère;
Par eux la plus vieille des cours
N'est plus qu'un petit séminaire;
Mais les barbons règnent toujours.

Tout est petit, palais, usines,
Sciences, commerce, beaux-arts.
De bonnes petites famines
Désolent de petits remparts.
Sur la frontière mal fermée,
Marche, au bruit de petits tambours,
Une pauvre petite armée;
Mais les barbons règnent toujours.

Enfin le miroir prophétique,
Complétant ce triste avenir,
Me montre un géant hérétique
Qu'un monde a peine à contenir.
Du peuple pygmée il s'approche,
Et, bravant de petits discours,
Met le royaume dans sa poche;
Mais les barbons règnent toujours.
                    (*Oeuvres*, pp. 407–9)]

Imprisoned again after his condemnation in 1828, Béranger felt resentment, but his bitterness was somewhat sweetened by visits of distinguished guests. Victor Hugo, Alexandre Dumas, Alfred de Vigny, Sainte-Beuve, Chateaubriand, Mérimée, Mignet, Michelet, and Thiers were among those who came to console him. But he had to ask for money to pay his fine and this humiliation he could not forgive. And so the little ex–government clerk cast defiance at the Bourbon king in one of the boldest songs ever written by a poet.

My Mardi Gras, 1829

My goodly king, may God grant you much joy.
Cause of your anger you avenged so well,
I spend again, thanks to Bridoie, your boy,
A carnival in a dark prison cell.
I could think of far better ways
To celebrate these sacred holidays.
Ranc'rous as a prince, I'm itching for a spat:
My goodly king, you'll pay for that.

In your message from the throne,
How wicked, you pronounced my humble name.
That means I'll be worn down to the bone,
And I'm resigned to lose that game.
But sad and lonely, hearing sounds
Of joy in Paris without bounds,
Satire in me revives its bitter ring:
You'll pay for that, my goodly king.

Just look! All my good friends, toasting,
Eating, madly masked and boasting,
Forget that I exist; yet all day long
They sing—hark! It's a Béranger song.
With them, it would have been my tendency
To raise my glass in praise of clemency.
My verses might have lost their sting:
You'll pay for that, my goodly king.

You know my mistress, Lise, quite mad,
Who o'er my troubles tears has shed.
Tonight a ball consoles her sorrow:
"Too bad," she says. "For him there's no tomorrow."
To please her, a poem I had planned
Depicting us as happy in your royal land.
Not so! My Lise unfaithful, a depressing thing:
You'll pay for that, my goodly king.

In my old quiver full of gaping holes
Made by your judges (th'Devil take their souls),
One arrow still is subject to my pen.
I write on it: For old King Charles Number Ten.

Despite these walls that make me sad,
Despite these bars 'gainst which I press my head,
The bow is taut, my arrow I shall fling:
You'll pay for that, my goodly king.[6]

[Mes Jours Gras de 1829

Air: Dis-moi donc, mon p'tit Hippolyte

Mon bon Roi, Dieu vous tienne en joie!
Bien qu'en butte à votre courroux,
Je passe encor, grâce à Bridoie,
Un carnaval sous les verroux.
Ici fallait-il que je vinsse
Perdre des jours vraiment sacrés!
J'ai de la rancune de prince:
Mon bon Roi, vous me le paierez.

Dans votre beau discours du trône,
Méchant, vous m'avez désigné.
C'est me recommander au prône;
Aussi me suis-je résigné.
Mais triste et seul, quand j'entends rire
Tout Paris en joyeux émoi,
Je reprends goût à la satire:
Vous me le paierez, mon bon Roi.

Voyez, verre en main, bouche pleine,
Fous déguisés de vingt façons,
Mes amis m'oublier sans peine,
Tout en répétant mes chansons.
Avec eux, ma verve en démence
Eût perdu ses traits acérés.
J'aurais pu boir à la clémence:
Mon bon Roi, vous me le paierez.

Vous connaissez Lise la folle,
Qui sur mes fers pleure d'ennui;
Ce soir même un bal la console:
"Bah!" dit-elle; "tant pis pour lui!"
J'allais, pour complaire à la belle,
Nous peindre heureux sous votre loi;
Serviteur! Lise est infidèle:
Vous me le paierez, mon bon Roi.

> Dans mon vieux carquois où font brèche
> Les coups de vos juges maudits,
> Il me reste encore une flèche;
> J'écris dessus: Pour Charles dix.
> Malgré ce mur qui me désole,
> Malgré ces barreaux si serrés,
> L'arc est tendu, la flèche vole:
> Mon bon Roi, vous me le paierez.
>
> (*Oeuvres*, pp. 476–77)]

Béranger made good on his threat: the king did pay him back—with interest! Once released, the poet used his great popularity and influence to get liberal party candidates elected and helped prepare the way for the 1830 revolution. He lent his support to an idea that until then had not been widespread: to entrust the new government to the duc d'Orléans, the future Louis Philippe, not because he believed in monarchy, but because he felt that the July Monarchy was the best solution under the circumstances. For all practical purposes this position put an end to strong political opposition in his songs.

Béranger has not enjoyed the kind of favor bestowed by posterity on André Chénier or Victor Hugo, and in absolute terms, he was obviously not as great a poet as these two men. But if effectiveness is to be used as a yardstick, then Béranger may well be the greatest political poet France has produced. His satiric vein, the light mocking tone, the irreverent references to authority and religion, and his emphasis on enjoyment and liberty as opposed to severity of manners are in the best Gallic tradition of Rabelais, Molière, La Fontaine, and Voltaire, all of whom would have recognized a kindred soul in him.

It is true that Béranger can be fully appreciated only with an understanding of the historical context in which he wrote and that the popular airs on which he composed his verses added to their attractiveness. Let us hope that, one day, a singer will come along who will revive Béranger's popularity by recording his songs.

Stendhal

The Ideal Political Novelist

Just as Voltaire is the master of satire and Guy de Maupassant the master of the French short story, so Stendhal is the master of the political novel. It is a marvelous experience to observe what happens when the right writer encounters the right genre at the right time. With no apparent effort, masterworks pour forth.

Le moment—as Taine so aptly defined it, a given moment in time carrying the momentum of what has gone before—was propitious. Young ambitious commoners were thwarted by an established aristocracy, as had been the case in Voltaire's time, with this difference: their expectations had been raised immensely by the Revolution and by the meritorious promotions in Napoleon's army. But the return of the Bourbon kings had smashed all their legitimate hopes by reestablishing a rigid caste system. No wonder Napoleon rose from ignominious defeat to become a symbol of unlimited possibilities for the most capable.

Showing an early talent for mathematics, and apparently destined for the Ecole polytechnique in Paris, Stendhal ended up in the army and rose so high in Napoleon's service that he could have aspired to a post as prefect—if Napoleon had not been defeated. As it turned out, with the return of the Bourbon kings all the important doors were closed to men like Stendhal, who eventually was appointed by the July Monarchy as consul at the Vatican city of Civitta Vecchia, a dull place perfect for a bureaucrat but hardly for Stendhal.

Unfortunate as all this may seem, it was perhaps a blessing in disguise for literary posterity, because it left Stendhal with the necessary time (and enforced leisure) to meditate and write three masterful novels: *Le Rouge et le noir* (1830), the unfinished *Lucien Leuwen* (1834), and *La Chartreuse de Parme* (1839). Although different in period and setting, they have a number of features in common: a young and handsome hero, liberal ideas (for the time and place), one or more love stories, adventures, and a political atmosphere ever present and so naturally part of the novel that the reader rarely is disturbed by its intrusion.

What makes Stendhal stand out among opposition writers is that he is first and foremost an artist. He does not write in order to advocate a political point of view for which his hero serves as model or spokesman or convert. He primarily tells the story of his hero, and his characters achieve such independence, such life of their own, that we can never quite predict what their attitudes are going to be in a particular situation.

Stendhal's basic method is very simple. He supplies his hero with the necessary background: family, environment, class status, economic status. But to this he adds intellectual baggage, and as a follower of the

French ideologues Cabanis and Destutt de Tracy, he adheres to the rule
that our knowledge is not inborn but induced by sensations and experience, which leave their impressions on the basic constitution of the
individual. Once this constitution is determined, the author sends out
his heroes on their daily *chasse au bonheur*. It is happiness they want to
find in the final analysis, happiness for themselves in the company of
"the happy few."[7]

The Dangers of Social Climbing: Le Rouge et le noir

Julien Sorel, the hero of *Le Rouge et le noir*, is an excellent example of
Stendhal's method. The youngest son of a tyrannical sawmill owner,
weaker than his brothers and given to reading and dreaming, he is
mistreated by his family and desperately wants to leave home. But he
has no formal education. He has studied with a kindly priest and can
recite the New Testament by heart, and in Latin at that. He has also
read *Du pape* by Joseph de Maistre and Rousseau's *Confessions,* and
through the influence of a former Napoleonic veteran, he has developed
a great enthusiasm for the emperor, devouring the *Mémorial de St.
Hélène* and the bulletins of the Grand Army. Thus three books, a
prodigious memory, and pride and ambition constitute Julien's intellectual and emotional makeup, and he looks at the world through this
limited vision.

He wants to succeed by going to the top like his model, Napoleon.
He dreams of being the lover of elegant and noble women, the same
dream Rousseau had. But times have changed. A young commoner can
no longer aspire to a military career during the Restoration. And
although very handsome, Julien, unlike Rousseau, will find no philosophes to ease his way into noble society. The only road to success for
someone in his situation is through the clergy. Believing neither in
religious dogma nor in the Church, and forced to hide his adoration of
Napoleon, Julien will have to learn to dominate his feelings and to be a
hypocrite.

His opportunity arrives when M. de Rênal, the mayor of Verrières,
decides that his children should have a tutor. While his recitations in
Latin impress M. de Rênal and other dignitaries, his great beauty and
sensitivity strike the mayor's wife. But Julien spoils potential happiness
by his imaginary, bookish view of the world. To him all nobles are
enemies who stand between him and success. His inability to distin-
guish between individual nobles puts him in a false position and pre-

vents him from appreciating Mme de Rênal for a long time. Were it not for the enormous tension of Julien's having to constantly watch what he says and does (owing both to the political circumstances and his ignorance of social facts and behavior), *Le Rouge et le noir* could be read as a comic novel about a young man who misjudges the world around him and commits one blunder after another, while believing all the while that he is very clever; one who, in fact, succeeds mostly, not when he follows carefully prepared plans, but when he gives way to his natural feelings and charming spontaneity, the type of behavior that Stendhal calls *espagnolisme*. He quickly learns, however, from experience and has an affair with Mme de Rênal, succeeding with her less because of his almost militarily planned seduction than because of his tears, which are sincere and move his somewhat older mistress. Yet he does not find happiness; he looks on his affair as a conquest, as part of his duty to live up to the model he has set for himself. Unable to give himself over to his natural emotions and experience the joy of being loved by a natural and generous woman, he considers his seduction of Mme de Rênal a victory over the nobility.

When M. de Rênal becomes suspicious, Julien has to leave Verrières, and he enters a seminary to prepare for the priesthood. There too his ignorance makes him choose the wrong confessor, a Jansenist, at a time when the Jesuits are the dominant religious group. Eventually he receives a low grade in his examination, because he falls into the trap of quoting Horace, whom he had meanwhile read. But he makes an excellent impression on a humanistic bishop, and his confessor takes him along to Paris where M. de La Mole needs the Jansenist for a lawsuit. Julien, whose spelling is somewhat shaky, is chosen as M. de La Mole's personal secretary and rapidly becomes indispensable to this important nobleman.

In high Paris society now, Julien is again totally ignorant of social customs and has to learn all over again. The results are often very comic. He challenges a man who insulted him to a duel—but his opponent turns out to be a coachman. He falls constantly off his horse when M. de La Mole's son takes him out riding, but the most comic scene in the book is Julien's "seduction" of Mathilde de La Mole, the daughter of the house.

Haughty, strong willed, and bored with those around her, Mathilde has ordered him to come to her room late at night. He arrives there via a ladder, convinced that he is going into a trap set for him. Fully armed and looking for his "assassins," Julien has no mind to speak of love, and since Mathilde is inexperienced, the two do not know what to do or say. After looking in the closet for his imaginary assailants and finding none, Julien finally makes the obligatory gestures and gets rewarded for his bravery. What develops is a tug of war between two lovers, in which Mathilde now rejects him out of pride and now bows to him again. Desperate at being rejected, Julien makes the mistake of confessing that he loves her and faces the prospect of losing her altogether. But a scheme he learns from a Russian nobleman (writing letters to another woman to make Mathilde jealous) brings her back to him.

Both Julien and Mathilde carry within themselves an ideal and a model. Julien, the capable and energetic lower-class individual who wants to (and should) rise in society has made Napoleon his model. Mathilde, the true aristocrat, who wants her class to be courageous and proud rather than fearful (of the Revolution, of Napoleon) and ashamed (of not deserving their rank and privileges), has chosen as her model her ancestor Boniface de La Mole, who had been decapitated after an unsuccessful attempt in 1574 to free his friends held prisoner by Catherine de Médicis.

Once Mathilde is pregnant, even M. de La Mole has to accept Julien, who feels guilty for having abused the kindness of his benefactor. Now he is about to realize all his ambitions: he has been given a title, land, and a commission in the cavalry. Besides, he is about to marry a beautiful and important noblewoman.

But just then a letter from Mme de Rênal is received by M. de La Mole, accusing Julien of having seduced her and of being an unscrupulous man who uses women to advance himself. When Julien is shown this letter, he enters into an alternate state of consciousness.[8] Almost hypnotically, he leaves Mathilde and returns to Verrières, where, in the church, he shoots Mme de Rênal. Fortunately, his former mistress is not seriously wounded, but Julien is arrested.

Mathilde now takes charge and makes arrangements for Julien's acquittal (or, at the worst, a light sentence) by buying off the important jurors, chief among whom is M. Valenod, a dishonest commoner who has risen to the rank of baron by serving the Jesuit Congrégation. In prison Julien has his first real opportunity to be at peace, away from the tensions of his ambitious and nerve-racking life. He receives visits from Mme de Rênal, learns that she had written the letter under pressure from her confessor, and realizes that it was she he had loved all along—and not capricious and demanding Mathilde. Tired of ambition and heroism, Julien decides that he does not want to live with

Mathilde. And since he cannot enjoy happiness with Mme de Rênal, he practically condemns himself by making an inflammatory speech against the jurors. Stating that his crime was premeditated (which it was obviously not), Julien continues:

> But even if I were less guilty, I see before me men who, without being moved by the pity my youth might inspire, want to punish in me, and discourage forever, that class of young people who, born in an inferior class and in some way oppressed by poverty, have had the good fortune to obtain a decent education and have had the audacity to mix into what the pride of rich people calls society.

> [Mais quand je serais moins coupable, je vois des hommes qui, sans s'arrêter à ce que ma jeunesse peut mériter de pitié, voudront punir en moi et décourager à jamais cette classe de jeunes gens qui, nés dans une classe inférieure et en quelque sorte opprimés par la pauvreté, ont le bonheur de se procurer une bonne éducation, et l'audace de se mêler à ce que l'orgueil des gens riches appelle la société. (*Le Rouge et le noir,* p. 675)][9]

Julien is executed, Mathilde melodramatically kisses his severed head, and Mme de Rênal dies shortly after of a broken heart.

This, very sketchily, is the main plot of Stendhal's *Le Rouge et le noir.* As we have seen, the work can be read in several ways: as a dramatic novel, as a psychological novel, as a comic novel, or as a political novel. Let us deal with the last mentioned first.

Julien attempts to penetrate a political world of closed doors. Like in Kafka's fable of the Law, in *The Trial,* there seems to be a redoubtable doorman in front of every door, and the hero cannot force his way in. But the doors are not definitely closed. They are left ajar (like the light visible behind Kafka's doors) for those who learn the rules of the game and who can take advantage of the loopholes in a given situation. Julien stumbles into some of the doors by accident rather than design (the way K. finds himself in a room with Bürgel, in *The Castle*),[10] and through influential women and through his natural aptitudes, he reaches heights he had not dreamed of in his wildest imagination.

His success in Paris is also due to the freshness he brings, dispelling the atmosphere of boredom pervading the Restoration period, when most interesting topics of conversation were taboo. In a manner reminiscent of Figaro, Stendhal describes the limits imposed on what could be discussed.

Provided you made no jocular remarks about God or priests, or the king, or
people in high office, or artists protected by the court, or about anything that
was part of the establishment; provided you did not speak favorably of
Béranger, of the opposition papers, of Voltaire, of Rousseau, or of anything
that dared to speak a bit frankly; provided especially you never talked about
politics, you could argue freely about anything."

[Pourvu qu'on ne plaisantât ni de Dieu, ni des prêtres, ni du roi, ni des gens en
place, ni des artistes protégés par la cour, ni de tout ce qui est établi; pourvu
qu'on ne dît du bien ni de Béranger, ni des journaux de l'opposition, ni de
Voltaire, ni de Rousseau, ni de tout ce qui se permet un peu de franc-parler;
pourvu surtout qu'on ne parlât jamais politique, on pouvait librement rai-
sonner de tout (Le Rouge et le noir, p. 457)].

It would be an exaggeration to see in Julien a revolutionary. Stendhal
quite properly calls him a plébéien irrité. He does not want to overthrow
the existing power structure—all he asks is the chance to rise in it. He
does not shout, "Down with aristocracy." His demand is, "Open the
doors to the most capable from the lower classes." He reads Danton,
but, contrary to Mathilde's romantic imagination, he will never be one.
He invokes the Revolution because it opened the way upward for
peasants and bourgeois, and he makes Napoleon his model because the
humble Corsican rose to be emperor. To ascribe any deeper political
philosophy to Julien would be contrary to Stendhal's epistemological
system.

Of course, Julien has to learn how to behave in Restoration society,
and he feels a greater kinship with liberals and revolutionaries than
with conservative monarchists. But at the same time he remains totally
loyal to M. de La Mole, who holds a high position among reactionary
monarchists. This unexpected affection can be understood only in terms
of Julien's aesthetic and emotional reactions. M. de La Mole is elegant,
gracious, and intelligent; besides, Julien sees in him his benefactor, the
sort of ideal father he never had.

Yet M. de La Mole participates in terrible projects; in fact, he is
engaged in outright treason. Chapter 21 of part 2, entitled "The Secret
Note," recounts a plot by the ultraroyalists, joined by high-ranking
clergy, to call for the aid of foreign troops to crush what they fear are
Jacobin efforts to overthrow the royal government. Stendhal was well
aware of the distraction represented by political intrusions in a novel,
yet he considered this matter so important that he was willing to take
the risk of irritating his readers for several chapters of veiled references.

These meetings expose, through concrete example, the collaboration of the ultraconservatives and the Jesuit Congrégation in an effort not only to prevent a reoccurrence of revolutionary activities or a return of Napoleon but also to repress liberal ideas of any sort by any means, including treason. One would expect Julien, the liberal at heart, to use the information he obtains as an observer at the clandestine meeting to thwart the malicious scheme of the conspirators. Yet he does nothing of the sort. On the contrary, he faithfully relays the secret note (so secret that it is not committed to paper but only to his prodigious memory) to an important personage in Strasbourg. It matters little here that the plot does not come off. The fact remains that Julien, slave to his loyalty and his aesthetic instinct, becomes an active and knowing collaborator in an action he considers nefarious to his country, to his class, and even to his own long-range ambitions.

The Character of Julien Sorel

This and other actions of Julien seem inconsistent, but they must be understood as those of a man in a false situation. Julien is a man divided between his rational self, on the one hand, and his emotional and aesthetic self, on the other. His mind tells him that the plotters are evil, his heart beats to a liberal tune, but his aesthetic (and contradictory emotional) reactions make him obey the orders of the Marquis de La Mole. We must never forget, either, that Julien can act only within the limited knowledge he has acquired and that he has a peasant background, which makes him think in immediate and practical terms.

It is likewise aesthetic judgment that contributes to his intense dislike of M. Valenod, who is, in a way, the villain of the story. Of course, Valenod has climbed the social ladder by questionable means and has gained the support of the hated Congrégation. But then Julien's means of rising socially are not beyond reproach, either. What he absolutely cannot stand in Valenod are the bad manners of a nouveau riche. "M. Valenod was what, a hundred leagues from Paris, people call a *faraud;* that is a sort of natural manner of being impudent and coarse." [M. Valenod était ce qu'on appelle, à cent lieues de Paris, un *faraud;* c'est une espèce d'un naturel effronté et grossier (*Le Rouge et le noir*, p. 354).] Julien will forgive M. de La Mole for engaging elegantly in treason, even with the Congrégation, but he cannot forgive Valenod's bad manners in matters of far less serious consequences.[11]

He realizes that a class revolution, for him at least, is a mere "pie in the sky," the rewards of which he may perhaps never taste, since there are no new Dantons on the horizon. [12] His fortune and advancement are tied to M. de La Mole, and the marquis can succeed only if the Restoration government remains in power. He also realizes that if M. de La Mole fails, it will be the turn of the Valenods, the clever "operators" who always survive, because they change loyalties the way they change their shirts. That is why Stendhal's condemnation of the Restoration is not complete. It concentrates on the unholy alliance of blind reactionary nobles and the ultramontane clergy. But if he had to choose between government by the marquis de La Mole or government by Valenod, Julien would unhesitatingly prefer the aristocrat.

Julien is neither good nor evil. He behaves the way a young man is bound to behave who has his particular intellectual and emotional formation, who comes from peasant stock, who is ambitious and handsome, and who has will power. It is unreasonable to expect more or different things from one who lives under daily pressures: inferior in class, inferior in knowledge, ignorant of social customs, he is superior only in that he has forged for himself a character based on the model of Napoleon.

But this very creation of will places him under an even greater, almost unbearable, strain, because the model he has willed himself to emulate is contrary to his true self and makes him live a false life in a false situation. It forces him to concentrate on material matters, to think in terms of career, of money, of rank, when in reality he is a meditative person who experiences peace and fulfillment only in calm self-communion in nature, in prison, or in the intimate company of those he loves.

While at the seminary, instead of thinking how to reduce the cost of decorating a cathedral for a religious ceremony, Julien is exalted by the sound of bells striking the hour. "He will never become a good priest nor a great administrator," Stendhal comments. "People whose souls are moved like that can at best turn into artists." [Au lieu de ces sages réflexions, l'âme de Julien, exaltée par ces sons si mâles et si pleins, errait dans les espaces imaginaires. Jamais il ne fera ni un bon prêtre, ni un grand administrateur. Les âmes qu s'émeuvent ainsi sont bonnes tout au plus à produire un artiste (*Le Rouge et le noir*, p. 399).]

Although the author went out of his way to expose this key element in Julien's character, few critics have paid proper attention to it. [13] The simple fact is that Julien has followed a wrong path ("il a fait fausse route," as the French put it so aptly), one that is contrary to his profound nature.

He failed to judge his situation and his feelings correctly most of the time. He was happy without knowing it during his liaison with Mme de Rênal: his dance before the Napoleonic mirror prevented him from enjoying happiness. He whipped himself into passionate feelings for Mathilde, believing his emotions to be love when his heart beat only in the excitement of a tug of domination. He thought his deepest wish was to hold an exalted position in the tumult of the social and political whirl, when his innermost desires craved for calm affection and intimacy. And when he finally realized what he was really like, it was too late. He was in prison, Mme de Rênal was beyond reach, and his choice was limited to life with Mathilde or death.

And from the eventual realization of his error follows a final value judgment: namely, that personal, intimate happiness cannot be attained "in the storm of the world" (to use Goethe's expression), and that next to this supreme goal, politics, success, titles, and social advancement pale in comparison.

This may strike us as a strange conclusion for a political novel, but for the artist it represents a magic formula. He can have his cake and eat it, artistically speaking, exposing the political situation in question and expressing his judgment of it while at the same time writing a novel in which the interest of the reader is held by the fate of the hero and not by the success or failure of one political system or another. At the same time, the author can criticize the government without taking personal responsibility—by having his young and inexperienced hero express ideas that are in keeping with his character but that the author can disclaim as fictional or farfetched.

Stendhal had reason to take precautions. Between the writing and publication of *Le Rouge et le noir,* the revolution of July 1830 had put an end to the Restoration, but the author could not have bet on that eventuality at the time he wrote his work. And since he had no desire to become an imprisoned martyr, he used his hero as a spokesman for his own criticisms of the regime in power.

Still, once in a while, he slipped in a casual remark that he hoped might escape the vigilance of a busy censor. In describing the pitiful comte de Thaler, who has inherited a fortune from his rich Jewish father, a banker,[14] Stendhal dared to write: "What this poor comte de Thaler lacked perhaps most was willpower. In this aspect of his character he would have been worthy of being king. Taking constantly advice from everybody, he did not have the courage to follow through with any of the advice to the end." [Ce qui manquait peut-être le plus à ce pauvre comte de Thaler, c'était la faculté de vouloir. Par ce côté de son caractère il eût été digne d'être roi. Prenant sans cesse conseil de tout le monde, il n'avait le courage de suivre aucun avis jusqu'au bout (*Le Rouge et le noir,* p. 466).]

In his next novel, Stendhal was to be far more outspoken—but then he did not publish it.

Chapter Seven

Much Ado about Kings, Umbrellas, and Petty Tyrants

The July Monarchy, 1830–48

Louis Philippe was what the French needed in 1830, but he was not what the French wanted. He represented an almost perfect compromise between a Bourbon restoration and a republican government. It is true that 1830 (like 1848) was a pivotal moment in French and European history, and historians are tempted to suggest that at those moments a republican government could have been set up in France, but they forget to mention the rest of Europe. The ruling monarchies would not have stood idly by in the face of a real or imagined threat from France to their territories and even to their thrones; the example of a republican government in France would no doubt have been contagious, leading to similar attempts in their own countries.

It must not be forgotten, either, that the number of republicans was a mere fraction of the group that had overthrown Charles X and Bourbon rule. It had included Bonapartists, financiers, and property owners, none of whom felt any desire to exchange a disliked monarchy for a republic that would have jeopardized everything they had acquired. The real losers in the changeover were the ultras among the émigré nobles, who could no longer count on support from the throne for their never-ending claims of compensation. Already of little use during the Restoration, these aristocrats now went full circle: Starting as "kept" nobles under Louis XIV, they became, in effect, an "interior emigration," refusing to have anything to do with the July Monarchy. Stendhal describes the ridiculous extremes to which these ultras went in *Lucien Leuwen.*

The disparate nature of the July revolution was reflected in its first government: La Fayette represented the Revolution, Sébastiani the Napoleonic era, Guizot the Restoration, the banker Lafitte and Thiers the Orleanist movement, and Casimir-Périer and the duc de Broglie the uncommitted center.

If a republic appeared unlikely, a constitutional monarchy on the British model could have been instituted. Although the July Monarchy moved much more in that direction than the Restoration had, the personality of Louis Philippe got in the way here. He intended to be an activist king and was therefore reluctant to tolerate a strong premier or foreign minister. Although the king possessed considerable political skill, he left just about everyone dissatisfied: the ultras sulked in their domains; the Bonapartists dreamed of a revived Napoleon, even though attempts by Louis-Napoleon to arouse French enthusiasm for him had found little echo; and the republicans were stuck with another monarchy.

The real cause of the generalized disaffection for Louis Philippe should, however, be sought elsewhere: deep down, most French men and women simply wanted no more kings. What had been the use of the 1789 and the 1830 revolutions, with all the sacrifices and the bloodshed, if the result was just another king? And what a king! He had none of the ceremonious splendor of the divine-right Bourbons and none of the panache of Napoleon. The French might have accepted hating the former and loving and sacrificing for the glorious conquests of the latter. But a king who carried an umbrella, a bourgeois king without splendor or panache simply would not do! This may explain the numerous attempts on his life, the most serious of which occurred in 1835 and led to the reestablishment of censorship.

Ruling by ruse rather than by force, Louis Philippe thoroughly overhauled the governmental administration, and used his prefects to maneuver elections in favor of his party, known as *le juste-milieu,* and made up of financiers, merchants, and property owners. Moderation was the key to Louis Philippe's policy. In order to keep peace with Great Britain, he refused an offer to make his son, the duc de Nemours, king of a newly independent Belgium; he managed to save the last ministers of Charles X from severe punishment, and he did not even wreak serious revenge on those who had used violence against him.

At the same time he had to defend himself on all sides. Anticlericalism burst out, resulting in the destruction of the archbishop's palace, next to Notre-Dame, and the burning of the books in his library. The legitimists pinned their hopes on an attempt by the duchesse de Berry, the mother of the legitimist heir, the comte de Chambord, to arouse the population, but she turned out to be pregnant and the French felt that one miraculous child (the comte de Chambord was born after his father's assassination) was enough. The republicans, joined by the legitimists and Bonapartists, attempted to overthrow the government in 1832 at the occasion of the funeral of General Lamarck, who had served Napoleon and had been a liberal member of the Chamber of Deputies, but the army and the National Guard crushed the uprising. The most serious threat to the July Monarchy, however, came from the Lyons silk weavers, who had already demonstrated against lower prices paid to them in 1831 and who struck again for the same reason in 1834. An attempt at insurrection was put down, but the news reached Paris, where serious trouble for the government arose as barriers were set up in the Marais quarter. The uprising was soon quelled, but members of the National Guard sought out an apartment in the rue Transnonain for special attention and massacred its inhabitants. This atrocity, which Daumier depicted in one of his cartoons, was to be constantly held against the regime by its opponents.

After nearly ten years of struggle and changes of ministries, the July Monarchy seemed to be firmly established at last, so much so, in fact, that it could return the remains of Napoleon to France and exploit his legend. In Guizot, the king had found a minister to his liking, and economic conditions had improved considerably. Almost against the government's wishes, a colonial empire was established with the conquest of Algeria; and Guizot arranged an entente with Great Britain. All seemed to go well for the government, as evidenced by a large victory in the elections of 1846.

But governments do not live by laws and elections alone; they also depend on the mood of the country. And the mood of France was romantic. Starting out as royalists enamored of the Middle Ages, writers like Victor Hugo and Lamartine soon identified romanticism with liberalism. Although Hugo, charmed by the king's daughter-in-law, Hélène de Mecklenbourg, became a member of the upper house and remained faithful to the regime, Lamartine joined the liberal opposition.

To the young romantics who dreamt of ideal states, of ideal lives and loves, to the adorers of the Napoleonic legend, this practical and pedestrian government had no appeal. "La France s'ennuie," they complained. Accusations of corruption, a bad harvest in 1846, and an economic recession in 1847 that led to unemployment gave new impetus to the opposition, which was joined by Thiers, who wanted to unseat his rival Guizot. Political banquets were organized at which governmental corruption was denounced and parliamentary reforms demanded.

In a counterdemonstration, Louis Philippe reviewed the National Guard but was greeted with shouts demanding reforms and the resignation of Guizot. Reluctantly the king agreed to part with his favorite minister. This seemed to relieve the tension, but on 23 February 1848, a seemingly harmless crowd was stopped as it surged toward the Foreign Ministry. Shots rang out and panic followed. In no time barricades were erected all over Paris, and the next day Louis Philippe abdicated in favor of his grandson, the comte de Paris.

The July Monarchy had lasted for eighteen years, longer than any of its predecessors since the Revolution. Was this finally going to be the end of kings and emperors for France? Would the Revolution at last give birth to a lasting republic? France had reached another turning point in its history.

Chronology

1830:   Louis Philippe becomes king of the French.

1831:   French expel Dutch from Belgium.

1832:   Death of duc de Reichstadt, Napoleon's son.

1834:   Lyons weavers strike; massacre in rue Transnonain. Stendhal: *Lucien Leuwen*.

1836:   Louis-Napoleon's abortive attempt at Strasbourg.

1839:   Stendhal: *La Chartreuse de Parme*.

1840:   Napoleon's remains transferred for burial at the Invalides; Louis-Napoleon's attempt at Boulogne; he is imprisoned.
        Ministry of Guizot.

1846:   Louis-Napoleon escapes from prison.

1847:   Conquest of Algeria; economic crisis.

1848:   Political banquets; resignation of Guizot; revolution in Paris; abdication of Louis Philippe.

Stendhal

A Halt in the Mud: Lucien Leuwen

It is regrettable that Stendhal's political novel par excellence is beset by all sorts of problems. To begin with, *Lucien Leuwen* is unfinished;

next, Stendhal could not decide on a definitive title;[1] and finally, it was not published during the author's lifetime; in fact, the complete version of the novel appeared only in 1926–27.

Fortunately, none of these handicaps is fatal. The finished portion of the novel thoroughly describes the political situation during the July Monarchy, and the projected final part was to transport the hero to Italy. The editors definitely opted for *Lucien Leuwen* as the title. And it was unthinkable that Stendhal, employed by the government, should publish a novel exposing its corruption.

For lovers of Stendhal, *Lucien Leuwen* makes delightful reading. The atmosphere is more relaxed than in the always tense *Rouge et noir;* the tone is lighter, often mocking and ironic, in the eighteenth-century manner of Voltaire and Crébillon fils. As in *Le Rouge et le noir,* the tone fits the subject. There Stendhal attacked a regime he hated and created a young hero who was under constant pressure; hence the tense and serious tone when political or social matters are related, a tone that changes to irony only when the author intervenes to make affectionate fun of his inexperienced hero or when comic scenes are depicted.

Lucien Leuwen is a brilliant variation on *Le Rouge et le noir.* Again the hero is young, handsome, inexperienced, and idealistically liberal. But Lucien is neither poor nor a peasant nor the intellectual and emotional product of having read only three books. He has almost all the advantages Julien lacks. Lucien's father is not only a rich and influential banker but also a witty and cultured gentleman, probably the sort of ideal image Stendhal had of an intellectual father. The only shortcoming one can find in M. Leuwen is that he shies away from close and sentimental relationships. Obviously, Lucien has received an excellent education. He studied at the Ecole polytechnique but was expelled for having taken part in the funeral procession of General Lamarck, a gesture considered hostile to the July Monarchy. Finally, Lucien possesses social know-how, having been brought up in one of the most fashionable salons in Paris.

What will Stendhal, the follower of the ideologues, make of a young man so fortunately endowed? A seducer? An ambitious politician? An artist? He will do nothing of the sort, because with his remarkable insight he realized two things: (1) that sons who have successful and overpowering fathers tend to live in their shadow and find it difficult to choose a profession; (2) that sons of well-to-do parents tend to rebel and adopt liberal or even radical political and social views.

Both of these factors apply in the case of Lucien, whose liberal inclinations do not prevent him from admiring his father. After working for a while (one day a week) in his father's bank, the latter obtains for him a lieutenant's commission in a cavalry regiment. Stationed near Nancy, Lucien must get accustomed to the military tone, so different from what he was used to at home in Paris. As the regiment enters Nancy, Lucien is charmed by the view of a blond woman, watching from behind blinds. He spurs his horse and is thrown off exactly in front of that house.

In Nancy, Lucien faces the same dilemma that Julien Sorel must deal with. The government party is centrist (*le juste-milieu*) and stands for the status quo. His political preferences lead him to Gauthier, the editor of the republican newspaper *L'Aurore,* but he cannot stand the dogmatic and boring sermonizing of this honest and poor land surveyor. His aesthetic sense leads him to the aristocrats of the town, all the more so since Mme de Chasteller, the woman behind the blinds, is part of this society. But he must call on all of his patience to put up with the ridiculous politics of these legitimists, who, sulking in their provincial estates, recognize only Bourbon kings and celebrate the birthdays of exiled pretenders to the throne. At least they have some semblance of elegant manners, however provincial, and their leader, the ridiculous and grotesque Dr. Du Poirier, amuses him greatly.

Lucien accepts the drudgery of pretending to be sympathetic to the views of the aristocrats in order to be able to see Mme de Chasteller, a young widow with whom he engages in a long, drawn out, and delicate love affair. But a plot by Dr. Du Poirier makes Lucien believe that the woman he loves is pregnant by another man, and he leaves both Nancy and the cavalry and returns to Paris.

Not only does his father smooth over the mess Lucien has made by his impetuous departure but he also obtains a position for Lucien as assistant to M. de Vaize, the minister of the interior. Although the minister is reputed to be a great administrator, Lucien soon discovers that he is just a vulgar politician who plays the stock market by taking advantage of the inside information at his disposal—and apparently the king does likewise.

Worse still, Lucien has to do the dirty work his job demands. He is told to prevent a severely wounded secret government agent from talking. And he is sent out into the provinces to fix elections in favor of the government.

Miserable as he feels about these assignments, Lucien is fortunate in having the support of his father and of Coffe, a former fellow student, poor but honest, who serves the same function as Martin does in Voltaire's *Candide*. While Lucien, ever idealistic, is shocked by what he sees and learns, Coffe the realist considers all this to be quite natural, just as Martin judged wicked human behavior. Coffe is amused by Lucien, who thinks he can do the government's dirty business while maintaining intact his personal sense of honor.

Stendhal can satirize and castigate the low politics of the July Monarchy without compromising his young hero, because Lucien is able to maintain a position of independence, owing to his father's influence. Treated impolitely by the minister of foreign affairs, Lucien can challenge him to a duel and threaten to resign at any time. Angered by the foreign minister's efforts to harm Lucien, M. Leuwen decides to enter politics himself. Once elected, he gathers around himself the most insignificant and neglected deputies he can find and organizes them into a voting block, which he calls *La Légion du midi,* since most of them hail from southern France.

In the Chamber, M. Leuwen wakes up the bored assembly with witty speeches in which he pokes fun at the ministers and threatens to overthrow the administration. The king himself finally has to intervene and ask M. Leuwen to moderate his attacks and to vote in favor of governmental proposals. M. Leuwen promises the votes of his group but refuses to give up his pleasure of heaping ridicule on the ministers.

He has not forgotten the interests of Lucien, either. Since the hostile minister has had rumors spread that Lucien is a liberal Saint-Simonian, M. Leuwen decides that his son has to take a conservative mistress to give the lie to these reports. Lucien, still sighing for Mme de Chasteller, reluctantly agrees to court Mme Grandet, who soon falls in love with him.

Then suddenly M. Leuwen dies and Lucien finds himself nearly destitute, all the more so since he insists on paying off all his father's debts and on providing for his mother.

The novel breaks off just as Lucien receives an appointment as second secretary at the French embassy in Rome. Stendhal had planned to write a third part in which Lucien would have become involved with the duchesse de Saint-Mégrin and would have been forced to resign his position. Retired at Fontainebleau, he would have met Mme de Chasteller again, discovered her innocence, and married her.

For all practical purposes, *Lucien Leuwen,* which is longer than *Le Rouge et le noir,* is no more of an unfinished work than *La Chartreuse de Parme*. Both were to have a third part, which was never written. The

difference is that in the latter Stendhal summarized the projected part
and tacked it on to what he had written. He could have done likewise
for *Lucien Leuwen* by dropping the hero's projected soujourn in Rome;
instead, Lucien could have returned to Nancy and been reunited with
Mme de Chasteller on learning of her innocence.

Given the way he exposed dishonesty in the July Monarchy government, Stendhal could never have seriously envisioned publishing the
novel during his lifetime. As it is, he pulled no punches, referring
contemptuously to Louis Philippe as a "procurator of Lower Normandy
who occupies the throne" (p. 1305),[2] indicating a cunning and crafty
person; and openly revealing the corruption, haughtiness, and dubious
behavior of those who ran the government, which General Lamarck had
characterized as a "halt in the mud," a static and corrupt regime.

Stendhal described these machinations in great detail, especially the
efforts to fix the elections, and he might have tried the reader's patience, were it not for his light and ironic tone. Distancing himself
from the events he describes, not only as the author but doubly so by
means of the detached Coffe, he places us in the role of the amused
observer. And what comes through the minute descriptions of specific
political situations is a series of general judgments concerning the "art
of politics."

The first is that politics is based on a pretentious facade, created by
pomp, titles, and a hypocritical language; and that, if we penetrate
behind the smoke screen so created, we discover that the emperor (in
this case, the king) wears no clothes.

Thus, Lucien is prepared to admire M. de Vaize, the great administrator. But he quickly discovers the disparity between outward appearance and inward intellectual qualities.

His nice, graying hair, his very regular features, his head held high, created a
favorable impression. But it did not last. A second look revealed a low fore-
head, covered with wrinkles and excluding any possibility of ideas. Lucien was
terribly astonished and disappointed to discover that this great administrator
had very common manners, the manners of a valet. He had long arms and did
not know what to do with them; worse still, Lucien thought he perceived that
His Excellency tried to assume imposingly graceful airs. He spoke too loudly
and listened to himself talk.

[De beaux cheveux grisonnants, des traits fort réguliers, une tête portée haute
prévenaient en sa faveur. Mais cette impression ne durait pas. Au second
regard, on remarquait un front bas, couvert de rides, excluant toute idée de

pensée. Lucien fut tout étonné et fâché de trouver à ce grand administrateur l'air plus que commun, l'air d'un valet de chambre. Il avait de grands bras dont il ne savait que faire; et, ce qui est pis, Lucien crut entrevoir que Son Excellence cherchait à se donner des grâces imposantes. Il parlait trop haut et s'écoutait parler. (*Lucien Leuwen,* p. 1099)]

The second judgment is that governments insist on bureaucracy and bureaucratic language and are suspicious of anyone who has character and ideas of his own. Coffe compliments Lucien for having done what his minister would consider a good job in dealing with a prefect. "And you have been an infinitely better statesman, that is to say: insignificant and using elegant and empty commonplaces." [Et vous avez été infiniment plus homme d'Etat, c'est-à-dire insignifiant et donnant dans le lieu commun élégant et vide. (*Lucien Leuwen,* p. 1223).] That sort of style is indispensable in a bureaucracy. When Julien remarks that Coffe's reports are badly written, his assistant explains, "Blown up and insipid, and, above all, never simple; that's what the government agencies want." [Emphatique et plat, et surtout jamais simple, c'est ce qu'il faut pour les bureaux (*Lucien Leuwen,* p. 1255).]

The third judgment is that a parliamentary system of government encourages the game of party politics, of manipulating undistinguished legislators, and of block voting. M. Leuwen's *Légion du midi* is more than a satire on parliamentary maneuvering. It is a recipe for the way in which even a small minority can acquire the power to unseat an administration.

Finally, and the most important of the lessons Lucien receives, Stendhal submits that politics requires one to be a crook and a hypocrite at all times. When M. Leuwen suggests that his son take a political office, he exposes the change that has taken place in France since the Revolution and the First Empire: it is no longer a question of shedding blood but of amassing money and of being a scoundrel. And he points out to his shocked son that all political leaders, from Sully to Colbert, have played that game; in fact, lying is an integral part of politics.

The principle is this: all governments, even that of the United States, lie always and about everything; when they cannot lie about substance, they lie about details. Next, there are good and bad lies; the *good ones* are those which little people with pensions of fifty louis to twelve or fifteen thousand francs believe, the *excellent ones* are those that fool even some people who own a carriage; the *detestable ones* are those which nobody believes and which are proffered only by shameless people in the governmental ministries.[3]

[Voici le principe: tout gouvernement, même celui des Etats-Unis, ment toujours et en tout; quand il ne peut pas mentir au fond, il ment sur les détails. Ensuite, il y a les bons mensonges et les mauvais; les *bons* sont ceux que croit le petit public de cinquante louis de rente à douze ou quinze mille francs, les *excellents* attrapent quelques gens à voiture, les *exécrables* sont ceux que personne ne croit et qui ne sont répétés que par les ministériels éhontés. (*Lucien Leuwen*, p. 1080)]

Concerning the July Monarchy specifically, M. Leuwen reveals where the real power lies. "M. Grandet is, like myself, a bank director, and since July, the bank runs the state. The bourgeoisie has replaced [the nobles] of the faubourg Saint-Germain, and the bank is the nobility of the middle class." [M. Grandet est, ainsi que moi, à la tête de la banque, et depuis Juillet, la banque est à la tête de l'Etat. La bourgeoisie a remplacé le faubourg Saint-Germain, et la banque est la noblesse de la classe bourgeoise (*Lucien Leuwen*, p. 1333).]

In the final analysis, Stendhal points out the inherent contradiction of a constitutional monarchy in which the king is not content to be a symbolic figurehead but wants to be the head of the government. He has to play the parliamentary game and thereby loses all pretense of royal stature. Louis Philippe has to humiliate himself by begging M. Leuwen not to overthrow his cabinet. This, much more than his umbrella, produced a ruler who could be neither king nor president of a republic.

Since Stendhal could not publish a novel that dealt too directly with contemporary events, he left it unfinished and turned to one that could pass censorship, because its action took place in Italy and contained only slight references to France.

The Pompous Prince of Petty Parma: La Chartreuse de Parme

It is fascinating to follow Stendhal's evolution as a novelist. The casual reader may feel that he always deals with the same subject: a young hero in a more or less favorable situation, affected by politics; his protectors and detractors; and one or more love affairs.

On closer acquaintance with his work, we discover that the hero changes, as do political circumstances and those around him. With each successive novel since *Le Rouge et le noir,* the hero gains advantages. Julien Sorel was a proletarian, Lucien Leuwen the well-educated son of a rich and influential banker. Fabrice del Dongo, the hero of *La Char-*

treuse de Parme, is a young Italian nobleman. Yet as their social rank increases, the importance of these young men decreases in the novel. While Julien Sorel dominates *Le Rouge et le noir,* Lucien Leuwen has to share the spotlight with his father but still remains the principal character of the novel that bears his name. By contrast, Fabrice del Dongo is somewhat like the naive young man in the Italian commedia dell'arte who gets himself in trouble and must be extricated from dire consequences by the clever servant, who actually has the principal role; the difference being that in *La Chartreuse de Parme* that function is assumed by noble persons: La Sanseverina and Count Mosca.

Although the least assertive of the three heroes, Fabrice is not lacking in energy. The son of an ultraconservative nobleman and a beautiful mother, he admires the emperor Napoleon so much that he sets out to join the Imperial Army during the battle of Waterloo. In that famous episode, which foreshadows later battle descriptions by Barbusse and Aragon, he sees Napoleon ride past but does not recognize him, finally wondering whether it was really the battle of Waterloo he has witnessed. Slightly wounded, he eventually returns home to find that the Austrian troops have again taken over and that he now has the bad reputation of a liberal, to the horror of his hated father and brother.

He has been studying with a priest, but his career will be determined by his beautiful aunt, La Sanseverina. Having lost her beloved husband, she is being courted by Count Mosca, the foreign minister at the court of Parma, where she will later join him and call her nephew to her side.

The prince of Parma, Ranuce-Ernest IV, is a petty tyrant, who thinks of himself as a modern-day Louis XIV, but who possesses only the Sun King's petty traits without any of his grandeur. Mosca, a former liberal, has to maneuver among the many intrigues that go on in the absolute miniprincedom.

The couple decides that Fabrice is to study theology in preparation for being named archbishop of Parma, but the young madcap gets involved with an actress and kills her jealous companion when threatened by him. Although Fabrice has the advantages of a nobleman and has killed in self-defense, a plot is worked out at the court by the minister of justice to arrest him; and, although his aunt strictly forbids him to set foot in Parma, he returns and promptly gets arrested and imprisoned in the Citadel.

Now begins a long and somewhat tedious sequence of attempts by the couple to get Fabrice released. But he has seen Clélia Conti, the daughter of the governor of the Citadel, from his prison tower and has fallen in love with her. They communicate with signals, and, even when La Sanseverina arranges for his escape, he soon voluntarily returns to prison in order to be near the woman he loves.

Angered by the prince's failure to keep his promise to have all charges against Fabrice dismissed, La Sanseverina arranges for the prince to be poisoned by a mad poet, but Mosca protects the princedom against a popular revolt, and the prince's son assumes the reins of government. Quite inexperienced and limited in intelligence, young Ranuce-Ernest V stubbornly insists that La Sanseverina will have to give herself to him before he will free Fabrice. In despair she sacrifices herself for her favorite nephew and then leaves Parma. She marries Mosca but establishes her residence just outside the princedom, where Mosca returns as minister.

Fabrice assumes his ecclesiastic functions and manages to see Clélia again, who has had to marry a man chosen by her father, and who herself dies soon after her son has been carried off by illness. Fabrice retires to the Charterhouse of Parma, where he dies after a year; La Sanseverina follows him to the grave soon thereafter.

This, very briefly, is the involved plot of *La Chartreuse de Parme*. The novel does not have the unity of structure and tone of its two predecessors. It moves from commedia dell'arte (Fabrice's follies and efforts to get him out of trouble) to melodrama (the poet-bandit Ferrante Palla and the poisoning of the prince) to intense realism (the battle of Waterloo, court intrigues) to high romance (Fabrice falls in love while in prison and Clélia vows not to see him again, but she meets him in the dark). Finally, the ending, which summarizes the projected third part (the only place where the Charterhouse of Parma is mentioned), is as hastily patched together as the denouement of a Molière farce.

The character who holds all these disparate elements together is La Sanseverina, who stands clearly above all the other characters in the novel. Thus *La Chartreuse de Parme* is no longer the story of a young man, but equally (even more so) of a mature woman. Her only weakness is her considerably more than auntly love for Fabrice, and it is not entirely clear why she keeps her forced promise to the young prince instead of having him disposed of like his father. Her strength lies in her beauty and her independence of character. She is prepared to leave Parma (and, if need be, Mosca too) at any time, and this detachment gives her the freedom of action that no one else in the princedom enjoys.

While the political arena of the two previous novels was France during a defined regime, the court of Parma is fictional. Being small and relatively unimportant, it offers a laboratory setting for the study of an absolute regime, where political intrigues have to be minutely worked out, where enormous energy is expended to gain advantages exactly because there is so little at stake (just how much respect would a minister of Parma inspire in Milan, to say nothing of Paris?), and where decisions are made not on the basis of reason or experience but on the basis of personality and caprice.

From a political point of view, the setting no doubt appealed to Stendhal, because it enabled him to depict the caricature of a monarch with no repercussions. The result is not so much a slap at Louis Philippe, who was both courageous and far less pompous than Ranuce-Ernest IV, as a slap at all royal and absolute governments, which, to a liberal thinker like Stendhal, represented an anachronism in postrevolutionary Europe.

You would expect the ruler of such a tiny territory to be a "prince d'Yvetot," for that is what Parma amounts to, and the goings-on at this minicourt to supply an ideal subject for satire. But neither of these expectations is met in the novel.

Ranuce-Ernest IV's sense of self-importance is matched only by the insignificance of his princedom. This unimaginative, pompous imitator of Louis XIV anticipates Chaplin's film *The Great Dictator*. Stendhal bases his character partly on Saint-Simon's caricature of Louis XIV, and partly on Montesquieu's barbs at the "Roi Soleil."[4] Yet this ridiculous ruler exerts absolute power over his subjects, who fight among themselves over equally ridiculous titles and honors.

What a splendid subject for satire! It is indeed in that vein that *La Chartreuse de Parme* opens, as Napoleon's troops bring liberty and gaiety to the sad and depressing Austrian occupation of Milan. But this detached irony prevails only until Fabrice's life is threatened by poisoning in prison or condemnation by corrupt judges. From that point on, the tone changes and Stendhal seems to share the apprehension and even panic of La Sanseverina. He gets so intensely involved in the petty court intrigues that the prince's slightest gesture inspires the kind of terror that Balzac's Père Grandet's raised voice caused in Eugénie Grandet and her mother. On the other hand, the increasingly grave mood of the novel reflects Fabrice's growing maturity and the intensity of his inner life as his hopeless love for Clélia leads him into quiet despair.

The Evolution of Stendhal's Young Heroes

In light of the interpretation that has emerged from this analysis of Stendhal's major novels, a reexamination of his young heroes may produce interesting results.

It is a commonplace for critics to speak of Stendhal's cult of energy, which he contrasted with the prevailing sad and dull atmosphere of the Restoration and the July Monarchy; and his young heroes present a contrast to the romantic heroes who act but with the defeatist foreknowledge that it is all in vain. Characters like Victor Hugo's Ruy Blas, Dumas père's Antony, or Alfred de Vigny's Chatterton are inevitable losers.

Compared to them, Stendhal's principal characters are impressive in their vitality, standing out against the background of a reactionary aristocracy in a state of rigor mortis and a money-hungry but rule-obeying bourgeoisie.

Since Stendhal's novels deal mostly with the youthful adventures and struggles of his heroes, their subsequent evolution is usually relegated to the final pages of the work. Yet this evolution is unmistakable. His young heroes arrive at the same state of awareness, realizing that a life of unceasing activity, ambition, and excitement is a mere stage, definitely inferior, at least anterior, to a simpler life of emotional and intellectual fulfillment in intimate relationships. For Stendhal's novels are not only *addressed* to "the Happy Few"—they are also *about* "the Happy Few," those exquisite beings in whose company we would like to spend the rest of our life, away from pettiness and intrigue.[5]

The fact that, in terms of the novels' chronology, Julien Sorel and Fabrice del Dongo attain this level of awareness at a very young age should not detract from the significance of the discovery, because Stendhal crams into their "active" years a lifetime of events and experiences.

Setting out on his path of adventure, each believes he has a clearly defined goal (social success for Julien, career success for Lucien and Fabrice). But each gradually realizes that it is not material success of one sort or another that matters, but *the one person* who will fill his heart. A latent inclination toward private and intimate relations crystallizes once each encounters the ideal partner (Mme de Chasteller, Clélia Conti) or becomes conscious of who that partner is (Mme de Rênal). At that moment adolescence and youth cease and maturity begins. Julien's suicidal declaration to the jury at his trial can be attributed not only to a contempt for the nouveaux (and uncouth) riches but equally to a realization that only life with Mme de Rênal is worth living. The existence he would have to face if he were acquitted or if he received a light sentence, an existence with a Mathilde de La Mole, forever prisoner of her adolescent dreams of a heroic life in which her lover or husband continually must live up to an idealized image of one of her decapitated ancestors—such an existence has simply become intolerable to the new Julien, who deliberately chooses death. For Fabrice, his encounter with Clélia spells the end of adolescent indecision. Until then, torn between his search for the love-at-first-sight woman and his unavowed, probably unconscious, and, at any rate, impossible desire for his aunt Sanseverina, Fabrice puzzles the reader by his inability to become passionately involved with highly attractive and desirable women. But as soon as he sees Clélia, all these hesitations disappear: he "sees clearly in his heart," the way Marivaux's young lovers do at the moment of consciousness, and all previous goals (Napoleonic worship, clerical ambitions) give way to his definitive goal, the quest of which will lead him to an ever-deeper inner life of meditation away from the tumult of the world.

Like most young people, Stendhal's heroes have to go through the painful process of trial and error before attaining self-knowledge. They have set out (or have been sent out) on the wrong path.[6] They are sensitive, natural, and spontaneous men, who are forced (or who erroneously force themselves) to exhaust their energy seeking goals that will not make them happy. And this is perhaps the most profound criticism Stendhal makes of Restoration and July Monarchy society: that it misleads and represses the natural talents and inclinations of its best young people.

Stendhal presents us with an interesting sampling of young heroes from different social backgrounds, and his depiction of their views and behavior strikes us as extremely modern.

Julien Sorel, the son of a sawmill owner, feels very conscious of his class, but that does not make him a champion of its interests. A fine champion, indeed, whose goal is to abandon his social status! Socially, his first and foremost concern is himself. He insists on acknowledgment of his social origins only when he feels it is to his advantage (with Mathilde de La Mole, for example) or when his pride is hurt—the rest of the time he is ashamed of them. His final speech should not mislead us into thinking that he is defending his class. He cares very little about improving the conditions of the peasants or the workers. What he wants is a merit system that will allow talented young people, like himself, to rise regardless of birth. For those who work without hope or ambition, such as his father and his brothers, he feels only contempt. Thus, like most proletarians, Julien dreams only of a better life through social and economic improvement without particular concern for the betterment of his social class as a whole.

Lucien Leuwen, the son of a wealthy banker, has never known any privations and, like the sons of today's well-to-do middle-class families, he is a liberal. And, like most of his twentieth-century brethren, he has never rubbed elbows with people of the lower classes. When he finally gets to know the socialist Gauthier (the most intelligent of them), the best he can muster is a sort of bored sympathy, but he cannot stand their constant company, because they do not smell good, are humorless, and, above all, lack wit, elegance, and good manners.

In a more intensive way than Julien (because he has more leisure time), Lucien's largely self-imposed tests represent, on another level, the adolescent rite of proving one's manhood. That he has not entirely passed the test is illustrated by his fall from the horse under the window of Mme de Chasteller, when his unit enters the town of Nancy. Had it not been for the mistaken notion that Mme de Chasteller was pregnant by another man, and if Stendhal had finished the novel, Lucien would probably have experienced the same evolution toward intimate relations and a deepened inner life as Julien and Fabrice.

Fabrice represents a quite different type. Whereas Julien and Lucien are worriers who want to improve themselves or society, Fabrice is quite happy with his social status. Of noble birth, his youthful escapade to Waterloo does not signify an adherence to revolutionary ideals but an admiration of the emperor Napoleon, and his subsequent behavior reveals his unquestioning acceptance of the privileges of his class. He feels no remorse for having killed a low-class actor and he is unconcerned about the misery of the poor. His ambition for himself is very limited: he strives for a clerical career more to please his aunt and Count Mosca than for his own sake. Even his sermons, which attract primarily the noble and the wealthy, are primarily directed at Clélia and finally help him succeed in renewing contact with her.

In Search of the Ideal State and Statesman

Just as his young heroes are looking for the right woman, so Stendhal is seeking the right statesman and the ideal political system.

In each of his three major novels, one statesmen is depicted. M. de

La Mole represents a political leader of whom Stendhal approves aesthetically but not politically. The marquis is elegant, intelligent, witty, and dignified. We have seen that Julien so admires this noble statesman and feels such loyalty toward him that he will carry out missions for him that are completely opposed to his own personal and political interests. As a member of the aristocracy, M. de La Mole pursues a policy of self-interest in supporting the goals of the Restoration government while trying to assert a moderating influence on its ultraconservative elements.

In *Lucien Leuwen* we encounter the professional politician M. de Vaize, the great administrator whose principal aim is to remain in office. Competent, unimaginative, lacking the final touch of elegance, humorless, unscrupulous but pusillanimous, somewhat corrupt, the minister of the interior turns out to be half caricature, half realistic portrayal. Although such people are needed in government, Stendhal considers him no better than an ambitious bureaucrat.

M. Leuwen is quite a different type. He carries out a policy of personal politics that may or may not benefit the great majority of the people. He is protecting the interests of his son and giving a lesson in the political game to those who think they can ignore him. Always keeping his independence and tied to no political party or position, M. Leuwen exerts his influence by means of cleverness, connections, personal charm, and wit. And the ministers and the king himself tremble when this elegant banker steps up to the speaker's podium.

In *La Chartreuse de Parme* we likewise find two characters who can influence the actions of the prince. Count Mosca has received unreserved praise as a statesman from the majority of critics. He has been compared to Machiavelli by Balzac, but as I have elsewhere shown, Mosca's reputation is greatly exaggerated.[7] It is he who causes all the complications arising from Fabrice's arrest, because, when copying the agreement, his awe of the prince's authority makes him omit the sentences extracted from Ranuce-Ernest IV by La Sanseverina, which would have put an end to the entire matter. Mosca not only prevents a popular revolt after the prince's death, but he secures the succession of Ranuce-Ernest V, who will make a cuckold of him. And after all that, he returns to Parma to reassume his post as minister! A statesman has to be judged on results, and if Machiavelli could not have done better for his prince than Mosca for the woman he loved, he would have been fired and his book relegated to oblivion. Despite his air of making light of his functions in Parma, Mosca is, at heart, another M. de Vaize, although more elegant, more charming, and with a greater sense of conscience. But the two share the basic weakness of mediocre statesmen, which La Sanseverina castigates in her anger at Mosca's blunders. "He always thinks that offering his resignation is the greatest sacrifice a prime minister can make." And she tells him contemptuously, "You have all the talents to be a minister, but you also have the instincts of that profession." [Il s'imagine toujours que donner sa démission est le plus grand sacrifice que puisse faire un premier ministre. . . . "Vous avez de grands talents pour être ministre, mais vous avez aussi l'instinct de ce métier" (*La Chartreuse de Parme*, pp. 286, 292).][8]

By contrast, La Sanseverina, to the extent she has to enter the political arena, acts much in the manner of M. Leuwen. She uses her beauty, charm, independence, and sense of improvisation to impose her terms on the prince by threatening to leave the court; she forces the reluctant ruler to sign a statement (catastrophically modified by the fawning Count Mosca) putting an end to all further procedures against Fabrice. And, being an Italian woman with a Renaissance character, she does not hesitate to have the petty tyrant poisoned as a matter of personal revenge.

From these examples we can attempt to piece together Stendhal's idea of the ideal statesman. His obvious preference goes to M. Leuwen and La Sanseverina, but neither has a political philosophy or enough devotion to politics to carry through a consistent policy. It would take a liberal-minded Marquis de La Mole or someone with Mosca's experience and aptitudes but possessing a spirit of daring, imagination, and independence to be the kind of leader who, combining the qualities of character and liberal politics, would resemble Stendhal's ideal.[9]

If it is difficult for Stendhal to find the ideal statesman, it is impossible to find a system of government that would satisfy his needs and wishes. In his three major novels Stendhal surveys the principal governments France had experienced: absolute monarchy and the First Empire (*La Chartreuse de Parme*); reactionary monarchy during the Restoration (*Le Rouge et le noir*); and constitutional monarchy during the reign of Louis Philippe (*Lucien Leuwen*). None of these comes even close to meeting with Stendhal's approval.

Absolute monarchy necessarily leads to tyranny; rigid standards of behavior are imposed on the subjects of the monarch or emperor, who inevitably ends up ruling by caprice. If that ruler is Louis XIV or Napoleon, the reign has an appearance of grandeur, both through military power and outward pomp; if that ruler is a Ranuce-Ernest IV or V, the result is a cruel farce. In neither of these two systems is there any liberty; and advancement, even by the nobles, is possible only by appealing to the vanity of the ruler. Reactionary monarchy is even worse than absolute monarchy, because it is forced to make concessions, which it then undermines (la Charte), and because it looks backward instead of forward (closing off even those few upward routes for meritorious young people that had existed under Napoleon). Its only redeeming quality is a sense of elegance. A constitutional monarchy presents a bad mixture, because it has neither royal dignity nor republican virtues. Thus it combines the worst features of those two systems. The king has to abase himself to play the parliamentary game, and the politicians play their party-politics game with the resulting dishonesty and corruption. Yet, despite the criticism and abuse Stendhal heaps on the July Monarchy, he judged it the least objectionable of the three, because it left room for a man like M. Leuwen to rise and assert his influence, and it did appoint him consul—even though only at Civitta Vecchia.

During all that time Stendhal kept glancing at, and flirting with, a system of government that appealed to his political heart but not to his aesthetic sense. Lucien Leuwen's reflections are typical of Stendhal's ambivalent attitude toward the United States.

When he had met M. de Lafayette on Sundays at M. de Tracy's, he imagined that, along with his good sense, his integrity, his elevated philosophy, the American people would also share his elegant manners. He had been rudely mistaken: there rules the majority, which is largely made up of the rabble. "In New York, the chariot of the state has fallen into the rut opposite of ours. Universal suffrage reigns tyrannically and with dirty hands. If my shoemaker dislikes me, he spreads bad rumors about me, which make me angry, but I have to cater to my shoemaker. People are not weighed but counted, and the vote of the most vulgar workman counts as much as Jefferson's, and often meets with more approval. The clergymen render them even more stupid than here. . . . This universal and somber vulgarity would stifle me."

[Quand il rencontrait tous les dimanches M. de Lafayette chez M. de Tracy, il se figurait qu'avec son bon sens, sa probité, sa haute philosophie, les gens d'Amérique auraient aussi l'élégance de ses manières. Il avait été rudement détrompé: là règne la majorité, laquelle est formée en grande partie par la canaille. "A New-York, la charrette gouvernative est tombée dans l'ornière opposée à la nôtre. Le suffrage universel règne en tyran, et en tyran aux mains sales. Si je ne plais pas à mon cordonnier, il répand sur mon compte une calomnie qui me fâche, et il faut que je flatte mon cordonnier. Les hommes ne sont pas pesés, mais comptés, et le vote du plus grossier des artisans compte autant que celui de Jefferson, et souvent rencontre plus de sympathie. Le clergé les hébète encore plus que nous. . . . Cette grossièreté universelle et sombre m'étoufferait." (*Lucien Leuwen*, pp. 1357–58)][10]

The trouble is that the happy few are surrounded by the unhappy many, who either adapt to the conditions imposed on them in a dictatorship or who are catered to by the government in a republic. But there is no government for the happy few. Such a government would be a republican system directed by an elite of witty people who are superior in intelligence but who never adopt bureaucratic or pompous manners; people who are not concerned about keeping their position or being reelected, and who would rather sacrifice their political career than suppress a witticism. Considering the generally sad situation created by "serious" politicians, such a state would probably be no worse and would at least have the advantage of being amusing.

But "til that happy day," when such a state will come about, what politics are the happy few to pursue? It is not so much the politics of survival, as Irving Howe suggests,[11] as the politics of happiness, because their survival is not threatened by politics. Julien and Fabrice are imprisoned not because of political actions but because they shot or killed someone for personal reasons; and they are definitely not political prisoners.

It is thus not the politics of survival they pursue but the politics of self-preservation, in the strictest sense of the word, that is, the preservation of the self, of their intimate being. Their aim is to find an oasis, a sort of Eldorado without walls, where they can preserve and protect their intimate private life from the madness that surrounds them. That is the meaning of Fabrice's retirement to the Charterhouse of Parma, of La Sanseverina's retreat to Vignano, of Lucien Leuwen's projected retreat to Fontainebleau, and of Julien Sorel's final retreat in prison.

It is reported that one day, during rush hour on a Los Angeles freeway, a driver stopped his car, got out, and shouted, "Sanity!"

Stendhal found himself in a similar situation. In the confusion of blind, reactionary, narrow-minded, selfish, and savage political life, he was shouting, "Civilization!" And it must be understood that the civilized person is one who refuses to return to the cave, regardless of who inhabits it.

Chapter Eight
Napoléon le Petit
The Second Republic and Second Empire, 1848–70

After the collapse of the July Monarchy, the revolutionary crowd invaded the Chamber of Deputies, an act that put an end to any possibility of a continuation of the Orleanist dynasty. The crowd demanded a republican government, which was hastily formed as the provisional government. Its leading members included the poet Lamartine, the radical Ledru-Rollin, and the Socialist Louis Blanc.

The new government established universal suffrage, thereby increasing the number of eligible voters from two hundred and fifty thousand to nine million; and it abolished slavery, leading to chaotic conditions in the French colonies. To combat unemployment, the government set up national workshops, but these were not very effective. The taxes necessary to pay for them and for the national debt hit the peasants the hardest, and since the peasants had the largest share of the new voting privileges, the Constituent Assembly turned out to be heavily conservative.

Disappointed with their lack of success at the polls, the revolutionary leaders Barbès and Blanqui attempted a revolt in May, which was easily stopped, and the leaders fled the country or were imprisoned. The June 1848 uprising was far more serious, since it was staged almost without leaders by the unemployed and starving workers. This one was ruthlessly crushed by Cavaignac.

The most important article in the new constitution provided that the president of the Republic was to be directly elected by the voters and would have executive powers. Grévy warned his colleagues that this might lead to a new Napoleon, a warning all the more appropriate, since Napoleon's heir apparent was waiting in the wings. And, sure enough, Louis-Napoleon won the election for president by a large majority, defeating his nearest rival, Cavaignac, by four million votes.

The new president of the Second Republic took an oath to uphold its constitution, appointed a conservative administration, and set out to tour the country. The May 1849 elections returned a comfortable conservative majority, but the left-wing forces garnered far more votes than had been expected. The left once again attempted an abortive uprising in Paris, which led to some repressive measures. The right to vote was reduced by eliminating all those who had been found guilty by the courts, and a law on education by Falloux was approved. It granted religious orders the right to open schools without certification by the state and it put control of the university in the hands of religiously dominated councils. This measure led to a struggle between religious and secular education, a conflict that plays such an important role in Zola's novel *Vérité,* to be discussed in volume II of this study.

The constitution also prohibited the reelection of the president, and although the Assembly voted in favor of revising this article, the necessary two-thirds majority could not be obtained. Since his term was to end in 1852, Louis-Napoleon decided to take matters into his own hands.

A coup d'état was organized for 2 December 1851, which also happened to be the anniversary of Napoleon I's victory at Austerlitz. The Assembly, accused of conspiracy, was dissolved, and opponents of the government were arrested in their homes. About three hundred deputies met to protest and were likewise arrested. Victor Hugo and several republicans formed a committee to organize resistance, and barricades rose up in Paris. At one of these, Dr. Baudin, a deputy, was killed. Several hundred republicans joined in the fighting, but a contingent of thirty thousand troops quickly quelled the uprising. In Paris, 380 rebels were killed and in the entire country 26,884 were arrested. Soon 3,500 of these were freed, and an amnesty in 1859 reduced the number of political prisoners to 1,800. Some atrocities were committed, the most serious of which took place on the boulevard Poissonnière, where soldiers shot into a crowd of people who were simply watching. Victor Hugo first fled to Brussels, from there to Jersey, and later to Guernsey. He did not return to France until 1870, when the Second Empire had fallen.

Compared to more recent revolutions and atrocities, one may be inclined to consider the 1851 coup d'état a moderate one, but the Second Empire was never able to shake off a guilt complex kept alive by Victor Hugo's vituperations from abroad. This, however, did not prevent 7,800,000 voters from approving, by plebiscite, the establishment of the Second Empire, against 250,000 "no" votes.

Historians tend to be less severe than Victor Hugo in judging the new emperor. He was forty-five years old when he took over the reins of

France under the name of Napoleon III. Since he had spent most of his previous life outside of France, he spoke "German like a Swiss, English like a Frenchman, and French like a German."[1] Although heavy and short, he did not lack dignity; in fact, he exerted a surprising charm on people, especially on women. Joined at first by his English mistress, in 1853 he married a young Spanish lady, Eugénie de Montijo, who bore him a son. Their court was far more elegant and witty than that of Louis Philippe. While he seemed to follow a hypnotic course concerning what he considered his preordained political goals, in most other respects Napoleon III was a humanitarian influenced by the peculiar socialism of the Saint-Simonians with whom he had associated in his earlier days.

The beginnings of the Second Empire were very promising. The expansion of the railroad network and modernized banking methods improved France's economic conditions considerably. Haussmann directed the works that turned Paris from a medieval city with narrow, winding streets into a modern metropolis with wide boulevards. Napoleon III had promised a peaceful empire and, although he did not engage in major campaigns, he pursued a policy of encouraging national groups to gain independence. He entered the Russo-Turkish war against Russia ostensibly to protect holy places, but his real purpose was to acquire some glory and improve relations with England. The conquest of Sebastopol in 1855 was greeted with joy, even though France gained nothing by that victory.

The emperor was equally fortunate in his Italian war. He had had close associations with the Italian Carbonari, so it was only natural that he would aid them in their struggle against the Austrians. Resounding victories were scored at Magenta and Solferino, and the peace treaty eventually resulted in the annexation by France of Savoy and Nice. Although Napoleon III was not particularly interested in colonies, Algeria remained under French control and Senegal was later added. An expedition to Syria led to the construction of the Suez Canal, beginning in 1859.

During these events, not only was peace kept with England, the traditional enemy, but a free-trade treaty was signed with Great Britain. While Napoleon III carried out a successful program in trade, his military luck began to abandon him. By supporting a Polish revolt against Russian rule in 1863, a possible alliance with Russia was rendered impossible, and by agreeing to remain neutral in the Austro-Prussian war of 1866 in return for a vague promise of territory, Napoleon III played into the hands of Bismarck. An expedition to Mexico in support of the Hapsburg prince Maximilian against the anticlerical government of Juarez drew applause from Catholic groups but ended in disaster when French troops had to be withdrawn in 1867 and Maximilian was killed by the Mexicans.

From 1860 on, the Empire was becoming more liberal. Debate on the speech from the throne was permitted, the budget was voted on by sections instead of in its totality, and the opposition was able to contest for votes in elections. Constitutional reforms were announced in 1867 and the press given greater freedom in 1868.

Just then economic conditions worsened. The cotton industry slumped, the silk industry was hit by silk worms, and in the vineyards phylloxera wreaked havoc. By then Morny, the emperor's half brother, had died, and the most powerful minister was now Rouher, a conservative thinker. The greatest challenge his administration faced was to find a way to stand up to an increasingly powerful Prussia. The economic crisis, however, and the cost of past wars and of rebuilding Paris left little money for rearmament, which was violently opposed by monarchists and republicans alike.

The 1869 elections resulted in an alarmingly large vote for the opposition. Napoleon III now dropped Rouher and replaced him with the liberal Ollivier. This move helped provide a victory for the government in the plebiscite of 1870, which approved the proposed constitutional reforms by 7.358 million votes against 1.572 million.

In the end it was neither political opposition nor Victor Hugo's poetic shafts from Guernsey that brought down the Second Empire, but war. In June 1870, the Spanish throne was offered to a Hohenzollern prince, which France considered an insult. Peace seemed to be assured when the acceptance of the Spanish offer was withdrawn by the father of the prince. But, under pressure from the empress and her circle, the French ambassador at Berlin demanded that the announced withdrawal be guaranteed by the Prussian king. The latter refused in firm but polite terms, but Bismarck, his prime minister, seized on this opportunity to make a statement to the press implying that Wilhelm I had rejected the French demand in an insulting manner.

On 19 July 1870 France confidently declared war on Prussia. But the patriotic flag-waving soon gave way to disillusionment. In a quick series of defeats France lost Alsace and saw Lorraine invaded. Bazaine, who had not distinguished himself in the Mexican campaign, was appointed commander-in-chief and suffered defeat at Gravelotte. General MacMahon and the emperor now marched their troops to relieve Bazaine at Metz, but Bazaine did not move and, as a consequence, MacMahon and Napoleon III were defeated at Sedan. On 1 September 1870 the emperor surrendered with 84,000 soldiers, 2,700 officers, and 39 generals. The Second Empire had lasted no longer than the July Monarchy. The nephew left France in shambles just as his glorious uncle did in 1814. Apparently nineteenth-century regimes were destined to come to an end either by revolution or by war. Eighty-one years had gone by since the Bastille was taken. After two short-lived republics, the Terror, the Consulate, two Napoleonic emperors, two Bourbon kings, one Orleanist king, and a total of three revolutions, would even those born in 1789 live long enough finally to see what had been the raison d'être of the French Revolution: a lasting republic?

Chronology

1848:   Provisional government set up; government of Cavaignac.
        (4 November): constitution of Second Republic; (10 December): Louis-Napoleon elected president.

1849:   Expeditionary force sent to Rome.

1850:   Left-wing victories in by-elections.

1851:   Legislative Assembly fails to vote constitutional reforms; (2 December): coup d'état of Louis-Napoleon.

1852:   Plebiscite on Empire; Louis-Napoleon proclaimed emperor as Napoleon III.

1853:   Marriage of Napoleon III and Eugénie Montijo; Victor Hugo: *Les Châtiments*

1854–1856:   Crimean War. Peace Congress in Paris.

1859:   Construction of Suez Canal begun; War of Italian Unification; victories at Magenta and Solferino; Armistice at Villafranca.

1860:   Annexation of Savoy and Nice.

1861:   Expedition to Mexico.

1864:   Maximilian proclaimed emperor in Mexico.

1867–1868:   French troops withdrawn from Mexico; execution of Maximilian.

1869:   Opening of Suez Canal.

1870:   Plebiscite approves constitutional reforms; France declares war on Prussia; French defeats at Gravelotte and Sedan; (1 September):Napoleon III surrenders; Provisional Government of National Defense set up; resistance organized by Gambetta and Freycinet.

1871:   Prussian shelling of Paris; (28 January): armistice.

Victor Hugo

His Opposition to Napoleon III

Béranger did not like the Restoration government and he made that abundantly clear in his songs. But he remained in France. And he was jailed, not once but twice.

Victor Hugo did not like the Second Empire government and he made it abundantly clear in his poems. But he did not want to get jailed. So he left France.

Like all historical or literary parallels, this one is flawed. Béranger was jailed for seditious and irreligious songs (or at least considered so by the Restoration government); Victor Hugo was expelled for open resistance to the coup d'état of 2 December 1851. Béranger was popular but held no political office; Hugo was France's leading literary figure and had had a long career in politics: in the upper house during the July Monarchy, and as a member of the Assembly during the Second Republic.

What the two poets had in common was that they had, with all their might, developed and perpetuated a legend of Napoleon I— heavily weighted with comparisons unfavorable to the Restoration—it amounted, in fact, to hero worship, even to idolatry.[2] And these dithyrambic homages to Napoleon the Conqueror, the Great Man, the Lawgiver, the Hero, the Emperor, the General Close to His Soldiers and Beloved by Them, the Savior of the Revolution, the Recognizer of Merit, were bound to produce in the reader's mind an image of what France had been and should still be. No one, not even the most fervent Bonapartist, had done more than Victor Hugo to endow the name of Napoleon with the sort of magic that paved the way to power for his far less glorious nephew.

From all evidence it appears that Hugo was favorable to the election of Louis-Napoleon as president of the Second Republic and that he maintained close relations with him and voted for measures proposed by him against the Republic and in preparation for the establishment of the Second Empire. On the question of why Hugo broke with Louis-Napoleon and became an ardent champion of the Republic, the poet, usually so anxious to reveal his soul, remains rather vague. Pierre de Lacretelle, an unsympathetic critic of Hugo, is not the only one who attributes Hugo's change of attitude to a personal resentment after a rebuff from the future Napoleon III.[3]

Be that as it may, what interests us today is not principally Hugo the statesman and legislator but Hugo the artist, who could successively wax enthusiastic over the Restoration, the July Monarchy, and the Second Republic. And when he turned against Napoleon III, he did so with all the fiery intensity of which he was capable. Regardless of any possible personal motives, Hugo did not have to force his poetic imagination to find reasons for condemning the man who had destroyed the young Republic (and thereby the goals of the French Revolution), violated his oath of office, shed innocent blood, and imprisoned or exiled opposition leaders.

So intense was Hugo's hatred of the perpetrator of these acts that he devoted three works, often repetitive, to testify against the man and his regime: *Napoléon le Petit* (1852), *Les Châtiments* (1853), and *Histoire d'un crime* (published in 1877 but written in 1851–52). Despite their documentary appearance, the two prose works cannot be considered more than the personal account of an eyewitness, too obviously prejudiced and far too personally involved to serve as an authentic document of the December 1851 coup d'état. *Les Châtiments,* if anything, is even more personal and prejudiced, but it has achieved immortality as a work that, in its best poems, transcends history to become the passionate outcry of a patriotic exile.

Napoléon le Petit: Les Châtiments

What, indeed, could a man, even a Victor Hugo, living unhappily exiled in Brussels or Jersey or Guernsey, do against an emperor who bore the magic name of Napoleon, and controlled the government, the army, and the country of France? He could write, tell what he considered the truth, urge resistance to and overthrow of the government, or call on foreign powers to intervene. But there was no notable resistance in France, and neither Belgium nor England showed any enthusiasm for invading France, just to please Victor Hugo.

Still, the poet did not give up hope. He believed profoundly in the power of ideas, of the word, of truth. These abstract and moral values, he felt, would eventually triumph over the most powerful but evil enemy. Hugo expresses this concept in one of his best poems in *Les Châtiments*.

The Trumpets of the Mind

When Joshua 'gainst the high-walled city fought,
He marched around it with his banner high,
His troops in serried order followed nigh,
But not a sword was drawn, no shaft outsprang;
Only the trumpets the shrill onset rang.
At the first blast, smiled scornfully the king,
And at the second sneered, half-wondering:
"Hop'st thou with noise my stronghold to break down?"
At the third round the ark of old renown
Swept forward, still the trumpets sounding loud,
And then the troops with ensigns waving proud.
Stepped out upon the old walls children dark,
With horns to mock the notes and hoot the ark.
At the fourth turn braving the Israelites,
Women appeared upon the crenelated heights—
Those battlements embrowned with age and rust—
And hurled upon the Hebrews stones and dust,
And spun and sang when weary of the game.
At the fifth circuit came the blind and lame,
And with wild uproar clamorous and high,
Railed at the clarion ringing to the sky.
At the sixth time, upon a tower's tall crest,
So high that there the eagle built his nest,
So hard that on it lightning lit in vain
Appeared in merriment the king again:
"These Hebrew Jews musicians are, me-seems!"
He scoffed, loud laughing, "but they live on dreams."
The princes laughed submissive to the king,
Laughed all the courtiers in their glittering ring,
And thence the laughter spread through all the town.

At the seventh blast the city walls fell down.[4]

[Sonnez, sonnez toujours, clairons de la pensée.

Quand Josué rêveur, la tête aux cieux dressée,
Suivi des siens, marchait, et, prophète irrité,
Sonnait de la trompette autour de la cité,
Au premier tour qu'il fit, le roi se mit à rire;
Au second tour, riant toujours, il lui fit dire:
"Crois-tu donc renverser ma ville avec du vent?"
A la troisième fois l'arche allait en avant,
Puis les trompettes, puis toute l'armée en marche,
Et les petits enfants venaient cracher sur l'arche,
Et, soufflant dans leur trompe, imitaient le clairon;
Au quatrième tour, bravant les fils d'Aaron,
Entre les vieux créneaux tout brunis par la rouille,
Les femmes s'asseyaient en filant leur quenouille,
Et se moquaient, jetant des pierres aux Hébreux;
A la cinquième fois, sur ces murs ténébreux,
Aveugles et boiteux vinrent, et leurs huées
Raillaient le noir clairon sous les nuées;
A la sixième fois, sur sa tour de granit
Si haute qu'au sommet l'aigle faisait son nid,
Si dure que l'éclair l'eût en vain foudroyée,
Le roi revint, riant à gorge déployée,
Et cria: "ces Hébreux sont bons musiciens!"
Autour du roi joyeux, riaient tous les anciens
Qui le soir sont assis au temple, et délibèrent.

A la septième fois, les murailles tombèrent.][5]

Hugo is truly a pen warrior. What Napoleon I did with the sword, he will do with the pen. And he will besiege France the way Joshua besieged Jericho. The little emperor may be able to keep out armies but he cannot keep out ideas and the truth expressed by the word.[6] More than that, the poet assigns himself a role similar to that of General de Gaulle after the fall of France in 1940. He considers himself a one-man government in exile and his pen will overcome the tyrant and liberate France, which he views, rightly or wrongly, as occupied by a small group of evil men with Napoleon III in the role of a cruel, pleasure-craving, and bloodthirsty pasha.

The usual method of exposing such a situation had been satire and irony: an apparent agreement with the unjust ruler undermined by subversive side remarks, inappropriately placed adverbs, tongue-in-cheek modifications; or by a character ostensibly disavowed by the author. This is how Montesquieu, Crébillon fils, Voltaire, and, to some extent, Stendhal had expressed their opposition.

But such a manner requires an attitude of detachment, a light tone, a sense of humor; in short, the ability to consider hated tyranny as just another example of human aberration and folly. Hugo possessed none of these characteristics. He was serious-minded, a heavyweight in tone, and so intently involved in the situation he was attacking that irony, on the rare occasions he attempted it, fell with the force of a sledge hammer.

A casual glance at the table of contents of Les Châtiments might give the impression that Hugo is employing satire to chastise Napoleon III. The first six books are entitled, in sequence: "Society Is Saved"; "Order Is Reestablished"; "The Family Is Restored"; "Religion Is Glorified"; "Authority Is Sacred"; "Stability Is Assured." These slogans sum up the accomplishments claimed by the Second Empire. In each section we find poems that show the contrary to be true or the achievement to be unworthy. The last book, entitled "The Saviors Will Take Flight,"[7] comforts the victims of the regime by predicting certain punishment of the guilty. These seven books are preceded by "Nox," a long poem containing the major themes of Les Châtiments. The last book is followed by "Lux," which closes the work antithetically.[8]

In "Nox," a powerful poem, we can conveniently follow Hugo's accusations and predictions. Part 1 describes the coup d'état carried out at night by soldiers turned into brutes by wine and under the orders of a bloodthirsty bandit.

> Fire! fire! later, royal people, you'll go to the polls!
> Slash all rights, slash the law, the head of honor rolls!
> On all boulevards let blood in rivers spread!
> Fill your canisters with wine, and coffins with the dead!
> Who wants some brandy? When the weather turns so cold,
> One has to drink. Soldiers, kill that man, he's old.
> Kill that child. Who there is that weeping dame?
> The mother? Kill her. Let those people, full of shame,
> Tremble, and let their heels be soaked in blood.
>
> [Feu! Feu! Tu voteras ensuite, ô peuple-roi!
> Sabrez le droit, sabrez l'honneur, sabrez la loi!
> Que sur les boulevards le sang coule en rivières!
> Du vin plein les bidons! des morts pleins les civières!

Qui veut de l'eau-de-vie? En ce temps pluvieux
Il faut boire. Soldats, fusillez-moi ce vieux.
Tuez-moi cet enfant. Qu'est-ce que cette femme?
C'est la mère? tuez. Que tout ce peuple infâme
Tremble, et que les pavés rougissent ses talons!
(*Châtiments,* p. 14)]

Part 2 of "Nox" describes the days following the coup d'état. More bloodshed is revealed, and the judges who prostitute their function, accepting money and honors in return for sentencing innocent people, are condemned.

Part 3 deals with one of the major themes of *Les Châtiments:* a comparison between the Great and the Little Napoleon, and the accusation that the little one cynically uses the name of his great predecessor to advance his own evil cause. Hugo makes Napoleon III express his sinister scheme.

"Napoleon reigned for fifteen years, braving frowns
        Of storms from all direction.
All the kings adored him, he walked on their crowns,
        They asked him for protection.

"He took, off'ring every one a brand new chance,
        Madrid, Moscow, and Berlin.
I'll do better: I shall use the neck of France
        To dig my fingers in.
.   .   .   .
"We shall, my uncle and myself, divide up history.
        The one of us who's brighter
Is I, for sure. He'll have the part of glory,
        I'll make the treasury lighter.

I'll use his name, at birth it was my wage;
        Of splendor there's no lack.
The dwarf pulls to the giant up. He can have his page,
        But I'll take the back.
.   .   .   .
"I'm the owl, this eagle with my claws I'll seize,
        I so low, he so much higher,
I have him! I choose the greatest of his anniversaries;[9]
        That's the date which I require.

"That day I shall be like a stealthy man who came,
A coat to keep eyes away;
No one will guess that I'll heap only shame
On such a glorious day.

"More easily my enemies I shall be besting,
With blows destroy their citadels,
Since on that day all of France'll be resting
On its bed of laurels."

And so he came, with eyes such as debauchees earn,
Whom furtive gait befits,
And this evil night thief lit his dirty lantern
On the sun of Austerlitz!

[Napoléon quinze ans régna, dans les tempêtes,
Du Sud à l'Aquilon.
Tous les rois l'adoraient, lui, marchant sur leurs têtes,
Eux, baisant son talon;

"Il prit, embrassant tout dans sa vaste espérance,
Madrid, Berlin, Moscou;
Je ferai mieux: je vais enfoncer à la France
Mes ongles dans le cou!
. . . .
"Nous nous partagerons, mon oncle et moi, l'histoire.
Le plus intelligent,
C'est moi, certe! il aura la fanfare de gloire,
J'aurai le sac d'argent.

"Je me sers de son nom, splendide et vain tapage,
Tombé dans mon berceau.
Le nain grimpe au géant. Je lui laisse sa page,
Mais j'en prends le verso.
. . . .
"Moi, chat-huant, je prends cet aigle dans ma serre.
Moi si bas, lui si haut,
Je le tiens! je choisis son grand anniversaire;
C'est le jour qu'il me faut.

"Ce jour-là, je serai comme un homme qui monte
Le manteau sur ses yeux;
Nul ne se doutera que j'apporte la honte
A ce jour glorieux;

"J'irai plus aisément saisir mon ennemie
     Dans mes poings meurtriers;
La France ce jour-là sera mieux endormie
     Sur son lit de lauriers. "

Alors il vint, cassé de débauches, l'oeil terne,
     Furtif, les traits pâlis,
Et ce voleur de nuit alluma sa lanterne
     Au soleil d'Austerlitz!
                    (*Châtiments*, pp. 16–17)]

Part 4 describes the joy of the victorious criminals: soldiers, politicians, priests, who celebrate, each in his own way, with drink, low women, or hypocritical sermons. But part 5 presents a contrast by describing the victims, innocent people of all ages and conditions, in mass graves, or others not yet buried. Part 6 abruptly transports us to Notre-Dame, where a Te Deum is celebrated for Napoleon III. It is so disgusting that

On a cross, set up in the back of the sanctuary,
So that he would not flee, Jesus had been nailed.
This scoundrel with his murd'rous crime had God regaled.

[Sur une croix dressée au fond du sanctuaire
Jésus avait été cloué pour qu'il restât.
Cet infâme apportait à Dieu son attentat.
                    (*Châtiments*, p. 20)]

Part 7 represents an interlude during which the sea tries to calm the poet. Finally, parts 8 and 9 predict the triumph of the French Revolution, [10] and the punishment of the assassins, not by the guillotine but by satire.

These topics reccur in many variations throughout *Les Châtiments:* descriptions of the "crime"; descriptions of the dead, victims of the vulgar corruption, debauchery, enjoyments and enrichments of the victors; comparisons between the Great and the Little Napoleon; calls to resistance; and prediction of punishment of the guilty.

The question is how Victor Hugo manages to turn these repeated subjects into lasting poetry. He uses his powerful imagination to transform dry, abstract, or political concepts into living beings or dynamic objects. Liberty is a dog chained by police commissioner Carlier ("Nox," pt. 1); Humanity is the mother of the Revolution ("Nox," pt. 8); in

"L'Empereur s'amuse" (bk 3, no. 10; p. 137) France is a woman married to an assassin. Law has been turned into a specter, Justice into a prostitute ("Le Bord de la mer," bk 3, no. 15, p. 149). The three parties that Hugo evokes most frequently (the Second Empire, the First Empire, and the people) are represented by three horses: a racehorse, a war horse, and a jade. The racehorse is a snob and praises religion; by contrast, the jade is hungry, thirsty, cold, and unhappy; and the war horse indignantly exclaimes, "Vive l'Empereur!" meaning Napoleon I ("Les Trois Chevaux," bk 6, no. 16; pp. 285–86). These are only typical examples and many more can, of course, be found in *Les Châtiments*.

Monotony is avoided by lyric poems, such as "Stella" (bk 6, no. 15), or personal professions of faith in his cause, the most striking being "Ultima Verba" (bk 7, no. 17), which rings with a conviction and a defiance the like of which has rarely been cast against a tyrant. Whatever the temporary success of the hated Napoleon III, Hugo will never give up his struggle.

> My noble comrades, I shall keep your cult;
> Though banished, the Republic still unites our gaze,
> I'll transform into glory every insult,
> I'll paint in infamy whate'er they praise.
>
> . . . .
>
> Yes, so long as he'll be there, wherever he may stand,
> Oh France! Beloved France o'er which I weep,
> I shall not see again your sweet and saddened land,
> Home of my loves and where my parents sleep.
>
> . . . .
>
> I welcome bitter exile, whatever be its term,
> And do not care to know in any form or way
> If someone yielded who seemed to be quite firm,
> Or if others left who were supposed to stay.
>
> If but one thousand shall remain, count on my hands.
> If there are but one hundred our revenge to fan,
> Yes, if only ten remain, I'll be the tenth;
> And if there remains but one, I'll be that man!
>
> [Mes nobles compagnons, je garde votre culte;
> Bannis, la République est là qui nous unit.
> J'attacherai la gloire à tout ce qu'on insulte;
> Je jetterai l'opprobre à tout ce qu'on bénit!
>
> . . . .

Oui, tant qu'il sera là, qu'on cède ou qu'on persiste,
O France! France aimée et qu'on pleure toujours,
Je ne reverrai pas ta terre douce et triste,
Tombeau de mes aïeux et nid de mes amours!
. . . .
J'accepte l'âpre exil, n'eût-il ni fin ni terme;
Sans chercher à savoir et sans considérer
Si quelqu'un a plié qu'on aurait cru plus ferme,
Et si plusieurs s'en vont qui devraient demeurer.

Si l'on n'est plus que mille, eh bien, j'en suis! Si même
Ils ne sont plus que cent, je brave encor Sylla;
S'il en demeure dix, je serai le dixième;
Et s'il n'en reste qu'un, je serai celui-là!
(*Châtiments,* "Ultima verba," bk. 7,
no. 16; pp. 348–49)]

These lofty passages should not make us forget that Hugo's pre-dominant tone is one of invective,[11] angry shouts, or anathema. One could compile an impressive dictionary of insults by drawing on the terms the poet uses to assail his enemy: bandit ("Nox," pts. 1 and 8; bk 1, no. 6), night thief ("Nox," pt. 3), traitor (bk 1, no. 5), brigand, pirate, (bk 1, no. 8, pt. 3), flagrant criminal, vile adventurer, Napoleon the Little (bk 2, no. 7, pt. 7), scoundrel (bk 3, no. 7), and so on.

Another drawback is the crushing number of detailed references to contemporaries, especially cabinet members, judges, bankers, senators, and priests, the vast majority of whom are completely forgotten today, so that the reader constantly has to consult notes.

Somewhat surprisingly, Hugo does not make great use of the form that lends itself ideally to poetry of flagellation: the iambic meter, employed by André Chénier and, in Hugo's time, by Auguste Barbier. Iambic verses occur in only six or seven poems, and even then the shorter line does not lash out the way Chénier's do. His preferred meter remains the alexandrine verse, which he uses to convey his sweeping images, symbols, and antithesis.

The famous poem "L'Expiation" (bk. 5, no. 13) contains so much poetic splendor that, by itself, it can silence all the criticism leveled against Hugo—who André Gide said is France's greatest poet—alas! The hallucinatory retreat at the end of the Russian campaign—with the obsessive "il neigeait" evoking the horror and the misery of the Russian winter for those soldiers whose once lively and conquering pace has slowed down to a step-by-step retreat and whose once admired discipline has given way to disorderly rout—is magnificently described by an artist who was a verbal painter and composer.

It snowed. A white blanket covered the dead.
For the first time the eagle hung its head.
Sad days! The emperor slowly turned his back
On smoking Moscow, burnt down and all black.
It snowed. Bitter winter now announced its reign:
White plain was followed by 'nother white plain.
Nor chiefs nor banners order could keep;
Yesterday the Grande Armée, and now only sheep. . . .
It snowed, kept snowing on. . . .

The scene shifts to Napoleon, who sees

A whole army fading away in the night.
The emperor stood and watched the sight.
He was like a tree gigantic in size
Whose grandeur 'til then spared from demise.
Misfortune, the somber woodsman, with ax raised,
Stood ready. And he, live oak, forlorn gazed,
Quiv'ring at the specter of revenge so tall,
As around him he saw all his branches fall.
Chiefs, soldiers, all dying, each one in turn.

[Il neigeait. On était vaincu par sa conquête.
Pour la première fois l'aigle baissait la tête.
Sombres jours! l'empereur revenait lentement,
Laissant derrière lui brûler Moscou fumant.
Il neigeait. L'âpre hiver fondait en avalanche.
Après la plaine blanche une autre plaine blanche.
On ne connaissait plus les chefs ni le drapeau.
Hier la grande armée, et maintenant troupeau. . . .
Il neigeait, il neigeait toujours! . . .
Toute une armée ainsi dans la nuit se perdait.
L'empereur était là, debout, qui regardait.
Il était comme un arbre en proie à la cognée.
Sur ce géant, grandeur jusqu'alors épargnée,
Le malheur, bûcheron sinistre, était montée;
Et lui, chêne vivant, par la hache insulté,

> Tressaillant sous le spectre aux lugubres revanches,
> Il regardait tomber autour de lui ses branches.
> Chefs, soldats, tous mouraient. Chacun avait son tour.
> (*Châtiments,* "L'Expiation,"
> part 1; pp. 223–24)]

Next Hugo turns to Waterloo. To the French, that little Belgian town will forever mean: "Waterloo! Waterloo! Waterloo! morne plaine!" ("L'Expiation," part 2) He pays a glowing tribute to Napoleon's soldiers, and especially to the Imperial Guard, which marched into battle,

> Calmly, smiling at the English hail of bullets. . . .
> In the twinkling of an eye,
> Like wind carries burning straw away,
> Vanished the sound that was the Grand Armée.
> And that plain, alas, where now we bow our head,
> Saw flee those before whom the universe had fled!
>
> [Tranquille, souriant à la mitraille anglaise. . . .
> En un clin d'oeil,
> Comme s'envole au vent une paille enflammée,
> S'évanouit ce bruit qui fut la grande armée,
> Et cette plaine, hélas! où l'on rêve aujourd'hui,
> Vit fuir ceux devant qui l'univers avait fui!
> ("L'Expiation," part 2, pp. 226–27)]

Hugo goes on to describe the emperor's exile and suffering during his imprisonment. At each of these trials Napoleon cries out that God has punished him, but a voice answers, "Not yet."

He dies and finally his remains are brought back to France for burial. One night he wakes up in his grave and witnesses strange happenings. The voice is heard again and tells him that the moment of punishment has arrived. Unsavory people have taken hold of him and have turned him into a spectacle.

> They took you. You died the way a star expires,
> Napoleon the Great, emperor; now born again
> As Bonaparte, circus rider of the Beauharnais clan.[12]
> Now you're one of them, they've got you in their harness.
> In public they call you a great man, in private, ass.
> All over Paris they drag, down there below,
> Their swords, which, if occasion demands, they'll swallow.

As passers-by assemble their show tent to admire,
They say: "Come in and see the spectacle Empire!
The pope's a member of the troupe, how's that?
Far better still, the czar's here too, not bad?
Oh, the czar is but a sergeant, the pope only a bonze;
Look here: we have that stately man in bronze!
We are the nephews of the Great Napoleon!"

[Ils t'ont pris. Tu mourus, comme un astre se couche,
Napoléon-le-Grand, empereur; tu renais
Bonaparte, écuyer du cirque Beauharnais.
Te voilà dans leurs rangs, on t'a, l'on te harnache.
Ils t'appellent tout haut grand homme, entr'eux, ganache.
Ils traînent sur Paris, qui les voit s'étaler,
Des sabres qu'au besoin ils sauraient avaler.
Aux passants attroupés devant leur habitacle,
Ils disent, entends-les:—Empire à grand spectacle!
Le pape est engagé dans la troupe; c'est bien.
Nous avons mieux; le czar en est; mais ce n'est rien.
Le czar n'est qu'un sergeant, le pape n'est qu'un bonze.
Nous avons avec nous le bonhomme de bronze!
Nous sommes les neveux du Grand Napoléon!—
                    ("L'Expiation," part 7, pp. 232–33)]

Horrified, Napoleon exclaims:

"Who are you?" "I am your crime," the voice replied.
At that the tomb was kindled by a strange light,
Like when God's vengeance brightens up the night;
And like the words that lit up before Belshezzar,
Two words on the dark flashed in the eyes of Cesar.
Bonaparte, trembling like an orphan in despair,
Lifted his pale face and read: EIGHTEENTH BRUMAIRE. [13]

[—Qui donc es-tu? —Je suis ton crime, dit la voix.
La tombe alors s'emplit d'une lumière étrange
Semblable à la clarté de Dieu quand il se venge;
Pareils aux mots que vit resplendir Balthazar,
Deux mots dans l'ombre écrits flamboyaient sur César;
Bonaparte, tremblant comme un enfant sans mère,
Leva sa face pâle et lut: DIX-HUIT BRUMAIRE!
                    ("L'Expiation," part 7, p. 234)]

The ending of this magnificent poem illustrates one of Hugo's several dilemmas. The concept of divine punishment for Napoleon the

Great makes for tempting poetic images but at the same time weakens the position Hugo has taken. All along he has held up Napoléon le Grand as the standard against which to measure Napoléon le Petit; at the same time he has set himself up as a defender of the Republic. Now it turns out that "le Grand" has perpetrated the very act for which Hugo condemns "le Petit." It makes for a nice parallel, with Hugo punishing "le Petit" while God punishes "le Grand," but it does not strengthen Hugo's case.

Another disturbing question is this: If Napoleon III was such a gray mouse, why did it take a mountain of aggressive and vituperative poetry to crush him? One does not have to drop an atomic bomb to eliminate an ant hill. Yet Hugo compares his Little Napoleon to such historical monsters as Philip II (of Spain), Henry VIII, and Cesar Borgia. The poet cannot have it both ways—one is either a big monster or a little monster.

While these may be literary flaws, a far greater dilemma confronted Hugo in his attitude toward the French. A sincere patriot, he believed in his people. How else could he have appealed to them to resist the tyrant? But there were at least two sets of statistics that could not be ignored. In 1848 Louis-Napoleon had been elected president of the Second Republic, crushing his closest opponent (Cavaignac) by 5,434, 226 votes to 1,448,107. And the plebiscite of 1852 approved the Second Empire by 7,800,000 votes to only 250,000 against. Obviously, the plebiscite was not as reliable as the presidential vote, and Hugo was entirely justified in his skepticism of the official result; but the first figure made the second look more respectable.

So what had happened to the French, a majority of whom were obviously supporting Napoleon III? Hugo treats this behavior as a sign of decadence and aberration, but he implies that it is only of a temporary nature. Soon the people will wake up, see this sham empire for what it is, and throw off their shackles. At times, however, he experiences moments of discouragement.

> Since all souls have grown weak,
> Since they grovel and memories no longer seek
> What is true, pure, beautiful, and brave,
> The indignant eyes of history,
> Honor, law, rectitude, and glory,
> And those who are in the grave;
>
> I love you exile! Sorrow, I love you.

[Puisque toute âme est affaiblie,
Puisqu'on rampe; puisqu'on oublie
Le vrai, le pur, le grand, le beau,
Les yeux indignés de l'histoire,
L'honneur, la loi, le droit, la gloire
Et ceux qui sont dans le tombeau;

Je t'aime, exil! douleur, je t'aime.
(*Châtiments,* "Puisque le juste est dans
l'abîme," bk. 2, no. 5; p. 85)]

But he never loses his faith in the people, whom he compares to a
sleeping lion who will eventually wake up.

They do not seem to know, those poor, dwarfish conquerors,
Who jumped on ramparts from the depths of their cavern,
That, when an illustrious people one wants to govern,
A people never deaf to honor's beck and call,
One is all the more heavy as one is small! . . .
Oh! these cursed men, these miserable men.
They'll finally succeed to make the people mad
By always pushing down the lion's head.
The beast is lying down, stretched out and tired;
It dozes in the shade to which it has retired;
Its red and savage snout, I grant, is still;
True, its huge and monstrous paw bodes no ill;
But they excite it so to make its claws display,
I think they're wrong to play around that way.

[Ils ne savent donc pas, ces pauvres nains vainqueurs,
Sautés sur le pavois du fond d'une caverne,
Que lorsque c'est un peuple illustre qu'on gouverne,
Un peuple en qui l'honneur résonne et retentit,
On est d'autant plus lourd qu'l'on est petit! . . .
Ah! ces hommes maudits, ces hommes misérables
Eveilleront enfin quelque rébellion
A force de courber la tête du lion!
La bête est étendue à terre, et fatiguée;
Elle sommeille, au fond de l'ombre reléguée;
Le mufle fauve et roux ne bouge pas, d'accord;
C'est vrai, la patte énorme et monstrueuse dort;
Mais on l'excite assez pour que la griffe sorte,
J'estime qu'ils ont tort de jouer de la sorte.
(*Châtiments,* "O drapeau de Wagram! ô pays de Voltaire!,"
bk. 5, no. 5; pp. 199–200)]

We know from history that it was neither Victor Hugo nor the French people who put an end to the Second Empire, but Prussian troops in 1870. At the height of the disaster Hugo returned to France and was given a hero's welcome. He was now more than France's national poet—he had prophesied the downfall of the Second Empire and he had turned out to be right, even if it had taken a French military defeat to achieve it. He was elected deputy of Paris with the second highest vote on 8 February 1871 and took his seat in the Assembly, which was meeting in Bordeaux. But only a month after his election he resigned over a dispute concerning the invalidation of Garibaldi's election. In 1872 he was defeated in a partial election, but he finally gained a seat in the Senate in 1876. On his death, in 1885, he was given a national funeral.

We began this chapter by contrasting Béranger and Victor Hugo. Rather than oppose them, it may be more appropriate to compare their similarities, for monarchies and empires reeled under their unrelenting attacks: Béranger with his light and satiric songs, Hugo with his weighty and tragic poems. Béranger was directly involved in both the overthrow of the Restoration government and the establishment of the July Monarchy, whereas it was not Hugo who brought about the fall of the Second Empire, but Prussian troops. But both undermined the prestige of their opponents by their constant attacks. If Hugo's unceasing poetic trumpet sounds had not brought down the walls of the Second Empire, he had certainly helped shake loose the ground on which the walls rested. One can legitimately speculate that Hugo may have weakened the loyalty of the French Army to Napoleon III and, hence, the willingness of the soldiers to risk their lives in defense of the Second Empire.

Literary attacks of such proportions have an effect that goes far beyond the historical moment at which they appear. Hugo's *Les Châtiments* exerted a great influence on General Boulanger[14] and this may have changed the course of French history. And what Paul Stapfer claims for Victor Hugo's work can be said in general of all great opposition works. "It has rendered impossible, not perhaps a surprise move by a dictatorship which, one night, may strangle a republic, but any lasting restoration of monarchy; one can start again but not consolidate the folly and the crime stigmatized for all centuries to come in the immortal book of *Les Châtiments*."[15]

Notes and References

Introduction

1. Albert Camus, *Discours de Suède* (Paris: Gallimard, 1958), 38.
2. See Charles F. Lenient, *La Satire en France au Moyen Age* (Paris: Hachette, 1859) and *La Satire en France; ou, La Littérature militante au XVIe siècle* (Paris: Hachette, 1866).
3. Léon Levrault, *La Satire: Evolution du genre* (Paris: Delaplane, 1904), 45.
4. William F. J. Bottiglia, *Voltaire's "Candide": Analysis of a Classic*, Studies on Voltaire and the Eighteenth Century, vol. 7a (Geneva: l'Institut et Musée Voltaire, 1959), 16–17.
5. Especially in the case of Aragon, whose novels were often written or published long after the events described in them. The reason for choosing Aragon was that he presents a theory that requires a considerable span of history to explain the causes that led to World Wars I and II. Similarly, Stendhal's *Lucien Leuwen*, written during the July Monarchy but published much later, was preferred to novels by Balzac, because Stendhal was more intimately and more militantly involved in the politics of the period; furthermore, the inclusion of *Lucien Leuwen* permitted a more complete evaluation of Stendhal as a protest writer, since his other great novels are also discussed.
6. J. E. Flower, *Writers and Politics in Modern Britain, France, and Germany* (New York and London: Holmes and Meier, 1977), 4.
7. The most notable work dealing with "committed" writing is no doubt Jean-Paul Sartre's "Qu'est-ce que la littérature?" in *Situations II* (Paris: Gallimard, 1948). In addition to numerous articles on the subject, summaries and definitions can be found in: Maxwell Adereth, *Commitment in Modern French Literature: A Brief Study of "littérature engagée" in the Works of Péguy, Aragon, and Sartre* (London: Gollancz, 1972); David L. Schalk, *The Spectrum of Political Engagement: Mounier, Benda, Nizan, Brasillach, Sartre* (Princeton: Princeton University Press, 1979), especially 23–25; Susan Rubin Suleiman, *Authoritarian Fiction* (New York: Columbia University Press, 1983), 6–17; and Predag Matvejevitch, *Pour une poétique de l'événement*, Editions 10/18 (Paris: Union général d'Edition, 1979).
8. Stendhal, *Le Rouge et le noir*, in *Romans et Nouvelles*, Bibliothèque de la Pléiade (Paris: Gallimard, 1952), 1:576.
9. Théophile Gautier, preface to *Mlle de Maupin* (Paris: Droz, 1946), 31.
10. Charles Baudelaire, *Oeuvres complètes*, Bibliothèque de la Pléiade

(Paris: Gallimard, 1954), 1095–96. Baudelaire was not attacking circumstantial literature per se, but he felt that it needs to be combined with a more permanent element, as evidenced in this passage from *Le Peintre de la vie moderne*.

The beautiful is made up of an eternal, invariable element . . . and a relative, circumstantial element, which, if you will, can be, in turn or altogether, the period, the fashion, morality, passion. Without this second element, which is like the amusing, titillating, stimulating wrapping of the divine cake, the first element would be indigestible, hard to appreciate, unadaptable, and inappropriate to human nature.

[Le beau est fait d'un élément éternel, invariable . . . et d'un élément relatif, circonstanciel, qui sera, si l'on veut, tour à tour ou tout ensemble, l'époque, la mode, la morale, la passion. Sans ce second élément, qui est comme l'enveloppe amusante, titillante, apéritive du divin gâteau, le premier élément serait indigestible, inappréciable, non adapté et non approprié à la nature humaine. (*Oeuvres complètes*, 883)]

11. Stéphane Mallarmé, "Crise de vers," in *Oeuvres complètes*, Bibliothèque de la Pléiade (Paris: Gallimard, 1945), 361. Mallarmé's circumstantial poems were of a personal and playful nature and not tied to events. Not all poets shared these views. Goethe considered, toward the end of his life, that true poetry is the poetry of circumstance (*Gelegenheitsgedicht*), as reported by I. V. Kiréievsky, "Observations sur l'état actuel de la littérature" (1845), in *Oeuvres complètes d'I. V. Kiréievsky* (Moscow, 1911), 1: 122–23.

12. Honoré de Balzac, "Comédiens sans le savoir," in *Oeuvres complètes*, Bibliothèque de la Pléiade (Paris: Gallimard, 1955), 7: 47.

13. John Lucas, ed., *Literature and Politics in the Nineteenth Century* (London: Methuen, 1971), 2.

14. Letter to Madame Roger Des Genettes, dated, Croisset, octobre? 1864, in Gustave Flaubert, *Correspondance*, new ed., enl., 5th ser. (1862–68) (Paris: Conard, 1929), 5: 160.

Chapter One

1. Jean de La Bruyère, "De l'Homme," §128, in *Oeuvres complètes*, Bibliothèque de la Pléide (Paris: Gallimard, 1951), 353.

2. Jean-Baptiste Tavernier, *Les Six Voyages en Turquie, en Perse, et aux Indes*, 2 vols. (Amsterdam: Von Someren, 1676); François Bernier, *Voyages de F. Bernier . . .* , 2 vols. (Amsterdam: Marrett, 1699); Jean Chardin, *Voyages en Perse et autres lieux de l'Orient*, 10 vols. (Amsterdam, 1711); Charles Dufresny, *Les Amusements sérieux et comiques* (Paris: Barbin, 1699); Giovanni

Paolo Marana, *L'Espion du Grand Seigneur et ses relations secrètes envoyées au Divan de Constantinople . . . ,* 6 vols. (Paris: Barbin, 1684).

3. Paul Valéry, *History and Politics,* Bollingen series 45.10, trans. Denise Folliot and Jackson Mathews (New York: Bollingen Foundation, 1962), 223.

4. All references are to Montesquieu, *Lettres persanes* (Paris: Garnier-Flammarion, 1964). Since many editions of this work exist, identifications contain both the letter numbers and the 1964 edition's page numbers.

5. Montesquieu, "Some Reflections on *The Persian Letters*" (1754), in Montesquieu, *The Persian Letters,* ed. and trans. J. Robert Loy (New York: Meridian Books, 1961), 40.

6. "He made people talk during his life; everybody kept silent at his death." [Il a bien fait parler des gens pendant sa vie; tout le monde s'est tu à sa mort (*Lettres persanes,* letter 92, p. 151).]

Chapter Two

1. Montesquieu obviously refers to the Jansenists in this remark about Louis XIV: "He loves his religion, but he cannot stand those who say that he must observe it rigorously." [Il aime sa religion, et il ne peut souffrir ceux qui disent qu'il la faut observer à la rigueur. (*Lettres persanes,* letter 37, p. 73)]

2. For over two hundred years Crébillon fils received scant attention from literary critics, although his short novel *Le Sopha* (1736) was probably read under the covers by more French lycée students than any other book. My former colleague Robert-Peter Aby has not received proper credit for his efforts to bring Crébillon out from under the bed covers in his unpublished Ph.D. dissertation, "The Problem of Crébillon fils" (Stanford University, 1955). Fortunately, critics have finally woken up from their long sleep and realized that Crébillon's novels, chiefly *Les Egarements du coeur et de l'esprit* (1736), *La Nuit et le moment* (1755), and *Le Hasard du coin du feu* (1763), must be considered important works, not only in eighteenth-century French literature but in the evolution of the French novel as well. At the same time, the critics have made the startling discovery that, far from being a licentious novelist, Crébillon deserves to be called a moralist. For that point of view, see Hans-Günter Funke, *Crébillon fils als Moralist und Gesellschaftskritiker* (Heidelberg: Carl Winter Universitätsverlag, 1972).

3. Robert Peter Aby argues convincingly that the person responsible for Crébillon's arrest was probably the duchesse de Maine, great-aunt-in-law (legitimized) of the king, a *femme savante* who presided over a courtly salon at Sceaux. Crébillon depicts her under the guise of the ugly fairy Concombre, to whom poor Tanzaï has to make love in order to regain his lost manhood. Concombre rules over the Island of the Wasps. From wasps it is no far cry to the honeybee, the emblem of the duchesse de Maine (Aby, "Problem," 27, 121). As for Crébillon's release from prison, it has been suggested that the

queen was instrumental in it, somewhat surprisingly so, since she was such a
fervent defender of the bull *Unigenitus* that she was called Unigenita by its
opponents. But she was no doubt pleased by the flattering portrayal of herself
in Crébillon's heroine Néadarné. See the introduction by Palissot de Monte-
noy, in *Oeuvres complètes de Monsieur de Crébillon, Fils,* new ed., rev. and corr.,
12 vols. (Maestricht: Jean-Edmé Dufour et Phil. Roux, 1779).

    4. The French text used is that in Claude-Prosper Jolyot de Crébillon
fils, *L'Ecumoire* (Paris: Le Divan, 1930). The above translation is mine. Subsequent translations, sometimes slightly altered or modernized by me, are taken
from Crébillon fils, *The Skimmer; or, The History of Tanzaï and Néadarné* (London: Printed for F. Galicke near Temple-Bar, 1742).

    5. See Aby, "Problem," 126; and Crébillon fils, *L'Ecumoire; ou, Tanzaï et
Néadarné: Histoire japonaise,* ed. Ernest Sturm (Paris: Nizet, 1976), 313 n.
115.

    6. The French proverbial expression *avaler le calice* (to accept a sacrifice;
avaler = to swallow) may have been in Crébillon's mind.

    7. On a more literal level, the skimmer may be an allusion to the
preamble in the bull *Unigenitus,* where the pope declares that he will expose
the condemned propositions of Father Quesnel's book in order "to separate the
wheat from the chaff." It is also not excluded that Crébillon may have chosen
the skimmer in part for scatalogical allusions. *Ecumoire* can be read as *é-cu-moi,*
which evokes the vulgar term *cul* (ass), a word in which the final consonant is
not pronounced. Hence the licking of the skimmer would take on a vulgar
meaning and ultimately suggest to the trained and not entirely puritan mind
homosexual overtones. To those accustomed to playing with words (and
Crébillon certainly was), the word *écumoire* also contains the syllable *écu,* which
was a money value at the time; hence the author may also be playing with the
inference that what was at stake for the defenders of the bull was not so much
religious dogma as money, which equals power.

    8. Crébillon leaves little doubt about the phallic nature of the skimmer.
The bead of jewels suggests the slang term for testicles (*les bijoux*). It is
interesting to note that Diderot wrote his novel *Les Bijoux indiscrets* (1748) to
prove that it is easy to write licentious novels, and in it he makes several
references to Crébillon fils and to *L'Ecumoire.*

    9. In Moustache's narration of her adventures, Crébillon produced a
parody of Marivaux's style, which critics call *le marivaudage.* Marivaux was
flattered at first, but on further examination he became annoyed and counter-
attacked Crébillon in passages of his novel *Le Paysan parvenu* (1735–36).
There are in reality two parts to the views expressed in these passages: one
concerns style, and there the parody seems to have been written in fun rather
than animosity; the other concerns reflections that interrupt the telling of the
plot, i.e., author interventions. On this subject the couple in *L'Ecumoire*
resembles very closely that in *Le Sopha.* In both novels the male heroes

(Tanzaï, the sultan) demand the facts first and a minimum of interruptions, whereas the women (Néadarné, the sultana) display far more literary sensitivity in their appreciation of the author's reflections. Crébillon occupies an important position in the history of author interventions, a subject that was to become of great interest to novelists from Diderot (*Jacques le fataliste*) to Stendhal.

10. Since Crébillon's *L'Ecumoire* may not be easy to find, the passages in question are quoted below. The first contains the advice Moustache offers to women who want to hold on to their man.

Love is only what we make it to be. If we leave it the way nature gave it to us, it would be too even, without refinement, it would have no voluptuousness. We owe this gift only to ourselves; we must make it difficult to make it pleasant. Our power over men depends on us, and if we happen to lose it, we have only our lack of skill to blame for it. If they withdraw it from us, it is not of their doing. Alas! Poor people that they are, they would never be able to figure this out by themselves. Made for slavery, they cast off one chain only for another; they feel that they are made to be dominated. But suppose we want them to remain attached to us. Let us never offer them perfect happiness; let us fulfill their desires without destroying them. In the midst of the greatest sensuous pleasures, make sure that something is missing, were it only a sigh. Desire dies only when it is completely satisfied, and that is a fate it suffers only when we choose not to avoid it.

[L'amour n'est que ce que nous le faisons. Si nous le laissions comme la nature nous le donne, il serait trop uni, sans délicatesse, il serait sans volupté. Nous ne devons ce bien qu'à nous-mêmes: il fallait le rendre difficile, pour le rendre agréable. Notre empire sur les hommes dépend de nous, et quand il nous arrive de le perdre, ce n'est jamais qu'à notre peu d'adresse que nous devons nous en prendre: s'ils nous en privent, ce n'est pas leur faute. Hélas! Les pauvres gens qu'ils sont, ils n'y penseraient pas d'eux-mêmes. Déterminés pour l'esclavage, ils ne quittent une chaîne que pour rentrer dans une autre, ils sentent qu'ils sont faits pour être toujours dominés. Mais voulons-nous les fixer? Ne leur offrons jamais un bonheur parfait; comblons leurs désirs, mais ne les anéantissons pas. Au milieu des plus grandes voluptés, qu'il leur manque quelque chose, ne fût-ce qu'un soupir. Le désir ne meurt que d'être comblé, et c'est une maladie qui ne lui arrive que quand nous ne voulons pas la lui épargner. (*L'Ecumoire,* pp. 174–75)]

The second passage is a reflection by the author at the moment when Néadarné is about to be "cured" by Jonquille. Whereas the first passage presents a female's point of view, this one expresses a male's attitude:

It is rare that a woman of the world finds herself in a dangerous situation against her wishes; her virtue is never exposed to violence because of circumstances, and though more than one has claimed that, when granting her suitor a certain rendezvous at which she succumbed, she would not have granted it if she had not believed she would preserve her honor, one must always believe that she had no doubts about what would happen. The proof of this? If a man who has been granted one of those innocent rendezvous fails to take advantage of it, the beautiful and virtuous lady who was locked up in a room with him will walk out on him and leave him almost no hope. Women have many resources to save their virtue: their habit of hiding their feelings, and the principles of propriety and pride, which muffles them. Our timidity, our respect for them, and almost always our ignorance of what idea they have of us, and our fear of displeasing them—that makes up the power of that fearsome virtue that impresses us so much. . . . By herself, a woman may not linger on mental pictures that might offend her sense of propriety, but let a suitor appear and please, and then see what she thinks of virtue! If she still struggles, it is not for the sake of defending it; she would lose too much by that. But she must cede with honor and put some grandeur into her weakness—falling with decency, in short—and be able to excuse herself in her own mind when thinking about her licentiousness. Few women will agree with this truth, but that does not change the fact that it is a permanent one.

[Il est rare qu'une femme du monde se trouve dans un cas dangereux pour elle, sans qu'elle le veuille; sa vertu n'est jamais violentée par les circonstances et quoique l'on ait entendu dire à plus d'une, qu'en donnant à son amant tel rendez-vous où elle succomba, elle ne l'aurait pas fait, si elle n'avait pas cru s'en tirer à son honneur, on devra toujours croire qu'elle ne doutait pas de ce qui arriverait et la preuve de cela, c'est qu'un homme à qui l'on aura donné un de ces innocents rendez-vous, n'a qu'à n'en point faire usage, pour être brouillé presque sans ressource avec la vertueuse beauté qui se sera renfermée avec lui. Les femmes ont pour sauver leur vertu bien des ressources. L'habitude où elles sont de voiler leurs mouvements, et ce principe de bienséance et d'orgueil qui les étouffe. Notre timidité, notre respect pour elles, et presque toujours l'ignorance où nous sommes des idées qu'elles ont avec nous, et la crainte de leur déplaire, voilà ce qui fait ordinairement les forces de cette formidable vertu qui nous en impose. . . . D'elle-même, une femme peut ne se pas arrêter aux images qui pourraient blesser sa pudeur, mais qu'un amant se présente et qu'il plaise, qu'est-ce alors pour elle que la vertu? Si elle combat encore, ce n'est plus pour la sauver, elle y perdrait trop. Mais il faut céder avec honneur, et mettre du grand dans sa faiblesse: tomber décemment, en un mot, et pouvoir s'excuser soi-même quand on réfléchit à son désordre. Peu de femmes tombent d'accord de cette vérité, mais cela n'empêche pas qu'elle soit constante. (*L'Ecumoire*, pp. 225–27)]

   11. Translation mine.

Chapter Three

1. Crébillon pére had attacked the doubtful origins of royalty in *Sémiramis* (1718), 2: 3, in these verses:

> A generous warrior, crowned by his courage,
> Is as good as a king named by law's choice;
> The first so honored owed it only to his voice.

> [Un guerrier généreux, que sa vertu couronne,
> Vaut bien un roi, formé par le secours des lois;
> Le premier qui le fut n'eut pour lui que sa voix.]

2. Ronald S. Ridgway, *La Propagande philosophique dans les tragédies de Voltaire,* Studies on Voltaire and the Eighteenth Century, no. 15 (Geneva: l'Institut et Musée Voltaire, 1961), 133.

3. Ibid., 235.

4. Quoted in Léon Fontaine, *Le Théâtre et la philosophie au XVIIIᵉ siècle* (Paris: Baudry, 1879), 245.

5. An example of this view can be found in Christian Wolff, *Reasonable Meditations about God, the World, and the Soul of Man* (1720). "But since nothing can happen without a sufficient cause, then such a cause must exist to explain why God preferred one world to another. Since the various worlds, being things of one kind, cannot be otherwise distinguished save by the degree of their perfection, hence this cause cannot be other than a greater degree of perfection encountered by God in this world which he preferred to others. And from this it follows that the supreme perfection of the world is the motive cause underlying his will."

Alexander Pope, in his *Essay on Man* (1734), expressed a similar view.

> All nature is but art, unknown to thee;
> All Chance, Direction which thou canst not see;
> All Discord, Harmony not understood;
> All partial Evil, universal Good;
> And, spite of Pride, in erring Reason's spite;
> One truth is clear; Whatever is, is right.

From a strictly rational point of view, the idea that ours is the best of all possible worlds is nearly irrefutable. The argument goes something like this: Since God is omnipotent and omniscient, he necessarily has the attribute of supreme reason; hence, when creating our world, he chose among the options and obviously chose the best.

6. The text used is that in Voltaire, *Romans et contes,* Editions Folio (Paris: Gallimard, 1972). Chapters as well as the 1972 edition's pages will be indicated, since many editions of *Candide* exist.

7. Jean Sareil, *Essai sur "Candide"* (Geneva: Droz, 1967), 44.

8. Voltaire, *Romans et contes,* 386.

9. According to most commentators, the Bulgarians represent the Prussians, and the Avars the French. This seems to be confirmed by the recruiters' interest in Candide's height, which corresponds to the desire of Frederick the Great to have tall soldiers. But it is not quite logical that the Prussians should destroy a Westphalian castle and that the French should avenge the victims.

10. David Worcester, *The Art of Satire* (Cambridge: Harvard University Press, 1940), 14, 31, 111.

11. H.-A. Taine, *Histore de la littérature anglaise* (Paris: Hachette, 1882), 4: 40–41.

12. Erich Auerbach, in *Mimesis: The Representation of Reality in Western Literature,* trans. Willard R. Trask (Princeton, New Jersey: Princeton University Press, 1953), 410, criticizes Voltaire improperly when he writes: "He is always inclined to simplify, and his simplification is always handled in such a way that the role of sole standard of judgment is assigned to sound, practical sense. . . . From among the conditions which determine the course of human lives none but the material and natural are given serious consideration. Everything historical and spiritual he despises and neglects."

These remarks miss the point of satire, and to accuse the historian who wrote such works as *Le Siècle de Louis XIV* and *Essai sur les moeurs* of despising everything historical strikes us as preposterous. As for spiritual matters, it all depends on what is meant by that term. If it refers to religion in the traditional sense, then Voltaire may be guilty, but if spiritual values include aesthetics and philosophy, then Voltaire can stand comparison with most writers (and critics, for that matter).

13. See Rousseau, *Discours sur l'origine de l'inégalité parmi les hommes* (1755). The same concept is contained in Montesquieu's account of the history of the Troglodytes, in *Les Lettres persanes.* Ferocious, savage, unjust in their early stages, they become decimated due to selfishness, which prevents an exchange of essential goods and so leads to disease, to which a doctor abandons them after having been refused payment. The tribe is regenerated thanks to two men who are humane and virtuous. Through their teachings and efforts a small, idyllic family-based society flourishes, where virtue, work, piety, and unselfishness provide a state of happiness and justice. But when the population increases to such an extent that the Troglodytes, tired of assuming their responsibilities, choose to be ruled by a king, this utopian situation is destined to end (*Lettres persanes,* letters 11–14).

14. A secondary aspect of the garden group in *Candide* is the retreat from the turbulence of an adventuresome and ambitious life in favor of a calm existence in the company of congenial individuals. The theme of withdrawal runs through French literature and can be found in *La Princesse de Clèves* (1678) by Mme de Lafayette, in the idyllic little group at Clarens in Rousseau's *La*

Nouvelle Héloïse, and later in the kind of life desired or chosen by Stendhal's young heroes after tumultuous adventures.

15. Emile Faguet, *La Politique comparée de Montesquieu, Rousseau et Voltaire* (Paris: Société française d'Imprimerie et de Librairie, 1902), 133.

16. Roland Barthes, preface to Voltaire, *Romans et contes,* 12.

17.   Sleep you content, Voltaire, and does your hideous smile
        Flit o'er your fleshless skull in mockery the while?
        [Dors-tu content, Voltaire, et ton hideux sourire
        Voltige-t-il encor sur tes os décharnés?]
                                            (Alfred de Musset, *Rolla,* part 4)

Translation by Marie Agathe Clarke, in *The Complete Writings of Alfred de Musset* (New York: Hill, 1905), 2: 21.

Chapter Four

1. It should be noted that Figaro is not just an ordinary valet. In his adventurous career he has been a barber, a veterinarian, a playwright, a journalist, and a croupier.

2. Quoted in Félix Gaiffe, *Le Mariage de Figaro* (Amiens: Malfère, 1928), 52–53.

3. Quoted in Beaumarchais, *Le Mariage de Figaro,* Nouveau Classiques Larousse (Paris: Larousse, 1971), 1: 16–17.

4. Molière's *Dom Juan* (1665) was prohibited after a short run, but the great comic playwright put ridiculous and conceited noblemen on stage in *Le Misanthrope* (1666) and a dishonest one in *Le Bourgeois Gentilhomme* (1670).

5. See, for example, Lesage's play *Crispin rival de son maître* (1707).

6. Beaumarchais uses the legal argument about the contract to launch a direct attack on the government, but he is careful to couch it in a play on words. Figaro, who acts as his own lawyer, and Bartholo, who represents Marceline, argue over the following sentence in the promissory note: ". . . which sum I shall repay upon her demand in this castle, or else I shall marry her." [. . . laquelle somme je lui rendrai à sa réquisition, dans ce château, ou je l'épouserai. (*Le Mariage de Figaro,* 3.15)]. The question is whether the word *ou* has an accent (*où* = where) or not (*ou* = or else). Figaro, who maintains that it has no accent, gives an example that plays on the identity of grammatical and political terms. " '*Either* you write nothing that pleases, *or else* the fools will disparage you'; or else the fools, the sense is clear; for in the case just cited, *fools* or *wicked people* are the substantive that governs." ["*ou* vous n'écrirez rien qui plaise, *ou* les sots vous dénigreront"; ou bien les sots, le sens est clair; car, audit cas, *sots* ou *méchants* sont le substantif qui gouverne (*Le Mariage de Figaro,* 3.15).] Beaumarchais purposely works the argument up to the last sentence, which implies that those who govern are fools or wicked people.

180 SUBVERSIVE TRADITION, VOLUME I

7. Quoted in Gaiffe, *Le Mariage de Figaro*, 88.
8. Quoted in René Jasinski, *Le Mariage de Figaro* (Paris: Les Cours de Lettres, 1948), 345–46.
9. Ibid., 346–47.
10. The Château d'Aguas Frescas, for example, had originally been called the Château de Fraîche Fontaine.
11. Victor Hallays-Dabot, *Histoire de la censure théâtrale*, 133.
12. Charles-Augustin Sainte-Beuve, *Les Grands Ecrivains français* (Paris: Garnier, 1930), 39. Originally in *Lundi* (29 June 1852).
13. Jules Michelet, *Histoire de France* (Paris: Marpon et Flammarion, 1879), 19: 231–32. Michelet illustrates in this judgment the misconceptions and attitudes so frequently found in writers of the far left and the far right. (1) He completely misses the point of *Le Mariage de Figaro* because he has a closed mind and tunnel vision that sees only revolution at the end. The goal pursued by Figaro is not revolution but reward based on merit: Figaro does not aspire to lead his nation, nor does he set himself up as a model. (2) Michelet displays both a frightful absence of a sense of humor and a distrust for witty people. Figaro's complaint that "unable to degrade wit, they take vengeance by mistreating it" applies equally to ultraconservatives and ultraliberals. For both, everything must be serious, and whoever laughs or makes fun of things is considered dangerous. Instead of welcoming an author who, whatever his own objectives, would aid their cause, these extremist thinkers reject him, either because he did not do enough, or because he did not do it their way, or because his intentions were not pure enough.

Chapter Five

1. See Hippolyte-Adolphe Taine, *Les Origines de la France contemporaine*, 36th ed. (Paris: Hachette, 1947).
2. See Jules Michelet, *Histoire de la Révolution française*, 8 vols. (Paris: Marpon et Flammarion, 1879).
3. The middle classes' usurpation of the Revolution from the lower classes is reported by most liberal historians of the Revolution with more or less undisguised regret. Yet this usurpation was inevitable, since those who took the Bastille and acted as the early shock troops of the Revolution were obviously incapable of running a government of any sort. While there was no lack of atrocities committed by the leaders of the Revolution, one shudders to imagine what it would have been like if the people who carried heads atop pikes had been put in charge.
4. Quoted in Pierre Dominique, *Les Polémistes français depuis 1789* (Paris: La Colombe, 1962), p. 73.
5. Ibid., p. 73.
6. For example: Antoine-Marie Le Mierre, *Barnevelt* (1790); Jean-François La Harpe, *Mélanie* (1791); Pierre Laujon, *Le Couvent* (1790); Harny de

Guerville and Charles-Nicolas Favart, *La Liberté conquise; ou, Le Despotisme renversé* (1791); Jacques Boutet de Monvel, *Les Victimes cloîtrées* (1791). See Théodore Muret, *L'Histoire par le théâtre*, 1st ser., 3 vols. (Paris: Amyot, 1865).

7. Quoted in J. Christopher Herold, *Mistress to an Age* (Indianapolis and New York: Bobbs-Merrill, 1958), 219.

8. The text used is André Chénier, *Oeuvres complètes*, Bibliothèque de la Pléiade (Paris: Gallimard, 1950). Page numbers refer to this edition.

9. Herold calls *Delphine*, quite aptly, a "great bad novel," ibid., 236.

10. Quoted in ibid., 93.

11. David G. Larg, *Madame de Staël; La Seconde Vie (1800–1807)* (Paris: Champion, 1928), 276.

12. The manuscript of this primitive version of *Les Martyrs* was discovered and later published by the Société Chateaubriand in *Les Martyrs de Dioclétien*, Cahiers Chateaubriand, no. 3 (Paris: Librairie classique Belin, 1951). For relevant passages and comments, consult Béatrix d'Andlau, *Chateaubriand et "Les Martyrs": Naissance d'une épopée* (Paris: Corti, 1952), especially chap. 9.

13. Chateaubriand, "Les Martyrs de Dioclétien," 189.

14. From Craven L. Betts, trans., *Songs from Béranger* (New York: Frederick A. Stokes, 1888).

15. Pierre Jean de Béranger, *Oeuvres complètes* (Paris: Fournier Aîné, 1840), 9–10.

Chapter Six

1. Stendhal refers to this project in a veiled manner as the "Secret Note" in *Le Rouge et le noir*, part 2, chaps. 21–24. See Pierre-Georges Castex, *Stendhal: Le Rouge et le noir*, Les Cours de Sorbonne (Paris: Centre de Documentation universitaire, 1973), 36ff.

2. Béranger castigates the treatment of Napoleon's veterans by the Restoration in songs such as *Nouvel Ordre du jour* and *Le Vieux Drapeau*.

3. Another political poet, Auguste Barbier, well known at the time for his *Iambes*, protested against this romanticized portrayal of Napoleon in *L'Idole*, stanza II, dated May 1831, in *Iambes et poèmes*, ed. Ch.-M. Garnier (Oxford: Clarendon Press, 1907), 14:

> What? Napoleon again, with his huge image?
> Oh! How much blood and tears and outrage
> That rude and harsh warrior has cost
> For a few branches of laurel now lost! . . .
> Now you are reborn from your dark fall: . . .
> Napoleon is no longer the thief of a crown,
> That usurper without shame and decency
> Who, under the cushions of his throne,
> Throttled the throat of liberty.

[Encore Napoléon! encore sa grande image!
Ah! que ce rude et dur guerrier
Nous a coûté de sang et de pleurs et d'outrage
Pour quelques rameaux de laurier! . . .
Maintenant tu renais de ta chute profonde: . . .
Napoléon n'est plus ce voleur de couronne,
Cet usurpateur effronté
Qui serra sans pitié, sous les coussins du trône,
La gorge de la liberté.]

Some 125 years after Barbier, Jean Anouilh launched an even stronger attack against the lasting legend of Napoleon, in his play *La Foire d'empoigne*. (See vol. 2, Chap. 8 of this study [1871–1971].)

4. From William Young, trans., *Songs of Béranger* (Edinburgh and London: William Blackwood and Sons, 1878). Unless otherwise stated, translations of Béranger are taken from this source.

5. The French is more comic than translation can express. The English expression "It's all Greek to me" is paralleled in French by a statement about ignorance of Hebrew, so that in the French original God admits he does not know Hebrew. I slightly changed two verses of the otherwise fine translation, which reads: "All this in sermons sublime without doubt, / Though what they mean I could never make out," in order to convey some sense of the humor in them.

In the third verse from the end, the word *spy* does not exactly render the meaning of *mouchard,* which designates an informer. The reference here is obviously to those who inform the Congrégation about improper behavior. The humor is that even God fears these informers and that his liberal behavior may get him excommunicated.

Finally, the title of the song is untranslatable. "Jupiter" is too awe-inspiring a term for "Le Bon Dieu," which is a familiar and affectionate way of referring to a gentle and well-disposed God.

6. Translation mine.

7. Stendhal dedicates *La Chartreuse de Parme* to "the Happy Few." We shall see later that he includes in that group not only the small number of readers who will appreciate his novel but the intimate group of his characters who search for happiness.

8. For an understanding of Julien's surprising behavior, it is necessary to realize that he is acting in an alternate state of consciousness. For a brief description of that state and its use by other authors, see Leo Weinstein, "Alternate States of Consciousness in Flaubert's *Madame Bovary* and Kafka's *A Country Doctor,*" in *Voices of Consciousness,* ed. Raymond Cormier (Philadelphia: Temple University Press, 1977), 215–29.

9. Stendhal, *Le Rouge et le noir,* in *Romans et nouvelles,* Bibliothèque de la Pléiade (Paris: Gallimard, 1952), vol. 1. Page numbers refer to this edition.

10. Franz Kafka is usually not associated with Stendhal but rather with Flaubert; yet there are some striking resemblances in their novels: (1) they tend to be unfinished (*The Castle, Lucien Leuwen*); (2) the characters stumble on opportunities that they could not discover by design; (3) their situation seems hopeless and all doors closed, but in reality they are not completely so; (4) they fail to understand what they are really seeking, and are pursuing a false road. I attempted to point out this aspect of Kafka's work in "Kafka's Ape: Heel or Hero?" *Modern Fiction Studies* 8 (Spring 1962): 75–79.

11. Like certain modern liberals, Stendhal could not stand the "people," even though he realized that they were the only class left that still possessed energy. "I abhor the rabble (to have dealings with it)," he admits, "while at the same time, under the name of *people*, I passionately wish for their happiness. . . . I detest whatever is dirty, and the people are always dirty in my eyes" (Stendhal, *Vie de Henri Brulard*, Editions 10/18 [Paris: Union générale d'Editions, 1964], 175).

12. " 'Oh,' he exclaimed, 'Napoleon was indeed the man sent by God for young Frenchmen! Who will replace him?' " ["Ah! s'écria-t-il, que Napoléon était bien l'homme envoyé de Dieu pour les jeunes Français! Qui le remplacera?" (p. 304).]

13. Even Taine, one of the earliest critics to recognize the excellence of Stendhal, failed to emphasize this contradiction in Julien Sorel. In his epoch-making article of 1865, Taine characterized Julien as a "superior mind," but later, in 1886, judged him to be odious. It is surprising that Taine, who speculated about the true calling of the philosophers he attacked (Victor Cousin should have been an oratorical disciple of Bossuet, etc.) and who saw Napoleon as an artist locked up in politics, did not apply this sort of analysis to Julien Sorel.

14. The allusion is probably to Rothschild. Stendhal may have chosen the name Thaler to designate a count who bought his title with money. The *Thaler* (or *Taler*) was an old German silver coin. See also Stendhal's reference to German *Thaler* in *Lucien Leuwen*, in *Romans et nouvelles* 1:1042.

Chapter Seven

1. Stendhall called the work variously "Leuwen," "L'Orange de Malte," "Le Télégraphe," "Lucien Leuwen," "L'Amarante et le noir," "Les Bois de Premol," "Le Chasseur vert" and "Le Rouge et le blanc."

2. Stendhal, *Lucien Leuwen*, in *Roman et nouvelles*, Bibliothèque de la Pléiade (Paris: Gallimard, 1952), vol. 1. Page numbers refer to this edition.

3. If *Lucien Leuwen* were required reading in American schools, a great number of governmental investigations could be avoided and much time that is now wasted could be saved.

4. Ranuce-Ernest's fear of enemies under his bed recalls Montesquieu's

remark about the "invisible enemies" (the Jansenists) that haunt Louis XIV (*Les Lettres persanes*, Lettre 24). And the prince of Parma takes advantage of his subjects' vanity as did Louis XIV.

5. In their desire for retreat in intimate company, Stendhal's young heroes continue a theme already treated in Voltaire's *Candide* and Rousseau's *La Nouvelle Héloïse*. But Julien, Lucien, and Fabrice envisage neither the productive circle of individuals in Candide's garden nor the didactic and rhetorical seminars on education or domesticity that seem to delight Rousseau's intimate group at M. de Wolmar's estate at Clarens. Stendhal, in his *Vie de Henry Brulard*, 297, provides a revealing look into his idea of intimate life.

A salon with eight or ten people, where the women have all had lovers, where the conversation is gay, full of anecdotes, and where a light punch is served at half past midnight is the place where I feel most at home. There, in my circle of friends, I much prefer listening to somebody else talk than talk myself. With pleasure I fall into the silence of *happiness* and, if I speak, it is only in order to *pay my admission ticket,* an expression used in the sense that I introduced in Parisian society.

[Un salon de huit ou dix personnes dont toutes les femmes ont eu des amants, où la conversation est gaie, anecdotique, et où l'on prend du punch léger à minuit et demi, est l'endroit du monde où je me trouve le mieux, là dans mon centre j'aime infiniment mieux entendre parler un autre que de parler moi-même. Volontiers je tombe dans le silence du *bonheur* et, si je parle, ce n'est que pour *payer mon billet d'entrée,* mot employé dans ce sens que j'ai introduit dans la société de Paris.]

6. Like Julien Sorel, Lucien Leuwen is an artist—not an administrator or a politician, as his father realizes (*Lucien Leuwen,* p. 1110). It is interesting to note the contrast between Stendhal's young men, who do not know their real calling, and those of Balzac (Rastignac, Rubempré, Bianchon), who are very sure of theirs and never vary from it.

7. See Leo Weinstein, "Stendhal's Count Mosca as a Statesman," *PMLA* 80 (June 1965), 210–16. Balzac's famous article on Stendhal first appeared in *La Revue parisienne* (25 September 1840).

8. Stendhal, *La Chartreuse de Parme,* in *Romans et nouvelles,* vol. 2. Page numbers refer to this edition.

9. Just to amuse ourselves, we might engage in the game of speculating whether any real statesmen have come close to Stendhal's ideal. There was the example of Chateaubriand, who was minister of foreign affairs during the Restoration, but Stendhal did not care much for the works of Chateaubriand (whom he called "le grand Lama") and even less for his politics. Lamartine, more liberal and a leading figure in the provisional government after the revolution of 1848, might have come closer, but Stendhal would not have

been impressed by his political skill and would probably have found him too serious. If it had not been for his opportunistic politics, Talleyrand would have come close to representing the kind of statesman Stendhal preferred. Among modern statesmen, perhaps Léon Blum, prime minister (1936–37) of the liberal Popular Front, would have been a candidate. Although very cultured and, interestingly, author of an excellent study on Stendhal, Blum was hardly a model of elegance and wit. Great modern diplomats such as Sir Anthony Eden or Dean Acheson, the architect of the Marshall Plan, both of whom were liberal and elegant, would probably have appealed to Stendhal. Unfortunately, no American presidents are among the candidates. Lucien Leuwen muses, "Washington would have bored me to death, and I would much rather be in the same salon as M. de Talleyrand." [Washington m'eût ennuyé à la mort, et j'aime mieux me trouver dans le même salon que M. de Talleyrand (*Lucien Leuwen*, 823).]

Stendhal's view of American presidents still has some validity, not so much because these men are necessarily boring as because Americans want their president to be a sort of benignly smiling buddha. Any obviously jocular remark by an American president is at once transformed into a major crisis by a totally humorless press and television, and this seems to upset the people. This dehumanization of their presidents explains the shocked reaction of the American people when the man in the White House reveals any human failings.

10. Similar opinions about America occur repeatedly in Stendhal's novels. In *La Chartreuse de Parme* (431), Mosca muses, "On the other hand, in America, in the republic, you have to do the boring job of seriously courting shopkeepers all day long; and you get to be as stupid as they; and then, there is no Opera." [D'un autre côté, en Amérique, dans la république, il faut s'ennuyer toute la journée à faire la cour sérieuse aux boutiquiers de la rue, et devenir aussi bête qu'eux; et là, pas d'Opéra.]

11. That is how Irving Howe entitles his chapter on Stendhal in his now classic study, *Politics and the Novel* (New York: Horizon Press, 1957; New York: Avon Books, 1970).

Chapter Eight

1. Quoted in André Maurois, *Histoire de la France* (Paris: Wapler, 1947), 454

2. See Jules Garsou, *Victor Hugo poète napoléonien (1830–1848)* (Paris: Le Carnet, 1902). Balzac, too, engaged in Napoleon worship, for example in the recital of a former veteran in *Le Médicin de campagne* (1833).

3. Pierre de Lacretelle, *Vie politique de Victor Hugo* (Paris: Hachette, 1928), especially chapters 3 and 4.

4. Translation by Toru Dutt, in Victor Hugo, *Works* (Boston: D. Estes, n.d.), 23: 168–69. The title was added by the translator.

5. Victor Hugo, *Les Châtiments* (Paris: J. Hetzel, n.d.), bk. 7, no. 1, 294–95. Page numbers in text refer to this edition.

6. Hugo believes in the power of the word. It is no coincidence that the first poem of book 1 of *Les Châtiments* contains that very theme.

> France! when humiliated you lie,
> A tyrant's foot on your forehead,
> The voice will come forth and cry:
> And, trembling, your chains you'll shed.
>
> The exiled, who on the shore appears,
> When at the stars and sea has gazed,
> Like those whom in dreams one hears
> Will speak in darkness, his voice high raised.
>
> And his voice, which like thunder lands,
> His words shining like the light,
> Will be like mysterious hands
> Holding swords glimmering in the night.
>
> They will make the marble freeze,
> The mountains they will cause to shiver,
> And the tallest of the trees
> In the black of night will quiver.
>
> They will be the tocsin's sound,
> The shout that not a raven braves,
> The unknown breath that turns around
> The blades of grass on silent graves.
>
> They will shout: "On scoundrels, shame,
> Shame on murderers, on oppressors."
> To call out souls they'll aim
> Like one appeals to warriors.
>
> On races that transforming keep,
> Somber storm, their claims they'll stake.
> And if the living fall asleep,
> Those who are dead will then awake.

(This and all remaining translations in this chapter are mine.)

> [France! à l'heure où tu te prosternes,
> Le pied d'un tyran sur ton front,
> La voix sortira des cavernes;
> Les enchaînés tressailleront.

Le banni, debout sur la grève,
Contemplant l'étoile et le flot,
Comme ceux qu'on entend en rêve,
Parlera dans l'ombre tout haut;

Et ses paroles qui menacent,
Ses paroles, dont l'éclair luit,
Seront comme des mains qui passent
Tenant des glaives dans la nuit.

Elles feront frémir les marbres
Et les monts que brunit le soir;
Et les chevelures des arbres
Frissonneront sous le ciel noir.

Elles seront l'airain qui sonne,
Le cri qui chasse les corbeaux,
Le souffle inconnu dont frissonne
Le brin d'herbe sur les tombeaux.

Elles crieront: Honte aux infâmes
Aux oppresseurs, aux meurtriers!
Elles appelleront les âmes
Comme on appelle des guerriers!

Sur les races qui se transforment,
Sombre orage, elles planeront;
Et si ceux qui vivent s'endorment,
Ceux qui sont morts s'éveilleront.

(Jersey, août 1853, *Châtiments,* bk. 1, no. 1; pp. 29–30)]

7. "Les Sauveurs se sauveront." Hugo makes a play on words that can suggest not merely that the Saviors will have to flee, in their turn, but also that they will save only themselves, not France.

8. In the 1870 edition of *Les Châtiments,* a poem written on the occasion of Hugo's return to France was placed at the beginning of the volume.

9. The coup d'état of 2 December 1851 took place on the anniversary of Napoleon I's victory at Austerlitz.

10. In his hatred, Hugo even finds excuses for the Terror. He goes to extremes to convince us that Napoleon III's "crime" is inexcusable. "There are massacres in history, abominable ones, no doubt, but they had their raison d'être; the Saint Bartholomew and Dragonnade massacres can be explained by religion, the Sicilian Vespers and the September killings can be explained by patriotism, suppressing the enemy, extinguishing the foreigner; crimes for a good motive. But the bloodshed of the boulevard Montmartre is a crime committed for no reason" (*Histoire d'un crime,* vol. 2, 3ᵉ Journée, chap. xvi).

11. Paul Stapfer, in *Victor Hugo et la grande poésie satirique en France,* Société d'Editions littéraires et artistiques (Paris: Librairie Paul Ollendorff, 1901), 285, suggests a definition of invective that may not correspond to what one finds in a dictionary but that very aptly fits the case of Hugo: "the exclamation that relieves and consoles impotent reason, the violent summary of everything it would vainly try to prove."

12. Napoleon III was the son of Louis Bonaparte and Hortense de Beauharnais.

13. Date of Napoleon I's coup d'état (9–10 November 1799).

14. See vol. 2, chap. 1 of this study (1871–1971).

15. Stapfer, *Victor Hugo,* 348.

Selected Bibliography

PRIMARY SOURCES

Beaumarchais, Pierre Augustin Caron de. *Le Mariage de Figaro*. In *Théâtre*. *Lettres relatives à son théâtre*. Bibliothèque de la Pléiade. Paris: Gallimard, 1949.

Béranger, Pierre-Jean de. *Oeuvres complètes*. Paris: Fournier Aîné, 1840.

————. *Songs of Béranger*. Translated by William Young. Edinburgh and London: William Blackwood and Sons, 1878.

————. *Songs from Béranger*. Translated by Craven L. Betts. New York: Frederick A. Stokes, 1888.

Chateaubriand, François-René, vicomte de. *"Les Martyrs" et "Dernier des Abencérages."* Paris: Hachette, 1900.

————. *Les Martyrs de Dioclétien*. Cahiers Chateaubriand, no. 3. Paris: Librairie classique Belin, 1951.

Chénier, André. *Oeuvres complètes*. Bibliothèque de la Pléiade. Paris: Gallimard, 1950.

Crébillon (fils), Claude-Prosper Jolyot de. *L'Ecumoire*. Paris: Le Divan, 1930.

————. *L'Ecumoire; ou, Tanzaï et Néadarné:* Histoire japonaise. Critical edition. Edited by Ernest Sturm and Marie-Clotilde Hubert. Paris: Nizet, 1976.

————. *The Skimmer; or, The History of Tanzaï and Néadarné*. London: Printed for F. Galicke near Temple-Bar, 1742.

Hugo, Victor. *Les Châtiments*. Paris: J. Hetzel, n.d.

————. *Works*, vol. 23. Translated by Toru Dutt. Boston: D. Estes, n.d.

Montesquieu, Charles-Louis de Secondat, baron de La Brède et de. *Lettres persanes*. Paris: Garnier-Flammarion, 1964.

Staël-Holstein, Anne-Louise-Germaine Necker, baronne de. *Corinne; ou, l'Italie*. Paris: Garnier Frères, n.d.

————. *Delphine*. Paris: Charpentier, n.d.

Stendhal. *La Chartreuse de Parme*. In *Romans et nouvelles*, vol. 2. Bibliothèque de la Pléiade. Paris: Gallimard, 1952.

————. *Lucien Leuwen*. In *Romans et nouvelles*, vol. 1. Bibliothèque de la Pléiade. Paris: Gallimard, 1952.

————. *Le Rouge et le noir*. in *Romans et nouvelles*, vol. 1. Bibliothèque de la Pléiade. Paris: Gallimard, 1952.

Voltaire, *Candide*. In *Romans et contes*. Editions Folio. Paris: Gallimard, 1972.

SECONDARY SOURCES

Aby, Robert-Peter. "The Problem of Crébillon fils." Diss., Stanford University, 1955.

Andlau, Béatrix d'. *Chateaubriand et "Les Martyrs": Naissance d'une épopée.* Paris: Corti, 1952.

Aubarède, Gabriel d'. *André Chénier.* Paris: Hachette, 1970.

Bachman, Albert. *Censorship in France from 1750 to 1780: Voltaire's Opposition.* New York: Institute of French Studies, 1934.

Barr, Mary Margaret. *Quarante Années d'études voltairiennes: Bibliographie analytique des livres sur Voltaire (1926–1965).* Paris: Colin, 1968.

Bergerhoff, E. B. O. *Evolution and Liberal Thought and Practice in the French Theater, 1680–1757.* Princeton: Princeton University Press, 1957.

Bottiglia, William F. *Voltaire's "Candide": Analysis of a Classic.* Studies on Voltaire and the Eighteenth Century, vol. 7a. Geneva: l'Institut et Musée Voltaire, 1959.

Brown, Gordon. *Les Idées politiques et religieuses de Stendhal.* Paris: Jean Bernard, 1939.

Brussely, Manuel. *The Political Ideas of Stendhal.* New York: Columbia University Press, 1933.

Castex, Pierre-Georges. *Stendhal: Le Rouge et le noir.* Les Cours de Sorbonne. Paris: Centre de Documentation universitaire, 1973.

Cazamian, Louis. *Le Roman social en Angleterre (1830–1850).* Paris: Société nouvelle de Librairie et d'Edition, 1903.

Charles-Brun, Jean. *Le Roman social.* Paris: V. Giard et E. Brière, 1910.

Cobban, Alfred. *A History of Modern France.* 3 vols. Baltimore: Penguin Books, 1957–1965.

Crocker, Lester G. *An Age of Crisis: Man and World in Eighteenth Century French Thought.* Baltimore: Johns Hopkins University Press, 1959.

Curtius, E. R. *Die literarischen Wegbereiter des neuen Frankreich.* Potsdam: Kiepenhauer, 1923.

Descotes, Maurice. *La Légende de Napoléon et les écrivains français du XIXᵉ siècle.* Paris: Lettres modernes, Minard, 1967.

Des Granges, Charles-Marc. *La Comédie et les moeurs sous la Restauration et la Monarchie de Juillet.* Paris: Fontemoing, 1904.

Desnoiresterres, Gustave. *La Comédie satirique au XVIIIᵉ siècle: Histoire de la société française par l'allusion, la personnalité et la satire au théâtre: Louis XV, Louis XVI, La révolution.* Paris: Perrin, 1885.

Dimier, L. *Les Maîtres de la contre-révolution au XIXᵉ siècle.* Paris: Librairie des St-Pères, 1907.

Dominique, Pierre. *Les Polémistes français depuis 1789.* Paris: La Colombe, 1962.

Selected Bibliography191

Dufrenoy, Marie-Louise. *L'Orient romanesque en France: 1704–1789*. 2 vols.Montreal: Beauchemin, 1946.
Faguet, Emile. *La Politique comparée de Montesquieu, Rousseau et Voltaire*. Paris:
Société Française d'Imprimerie et de Librairie, 1902.
Fontaine, Léon. *Le Théâtre et la philosophie au XVIIIᵉ siècle*. Paris: Baudry, 1879.
Funck-Brentano, Frantz, and Paul d'Estrée. *Figaro et ses devanciers*. Paris:
Hachette, 1909.
Funke, Hans-Günter. *Crébillon fils als Moralist und Gesellschaftskritiker*. Heidel-
berg: Carl Winter Universitätsverlag, 1972.
Gaiffe, Félix. *Le Mariage de Figaro*. Amiens: Malfère, 1928.
Gale, John E. "The Literary Image of Napoleon III in the Works of Victor
Hugo." Thesis, University of Colorado, 1967.
Garsou, Jules. *Béranger et la légende napoléonienne*. Brussels: Weissenbruon,
1897.
————. *Victor Hugo poète napoléonien (1830–1848)*. Paris; Le Carnet, 1902.
Gausseron, Jacques. *André Chénier et le drame de la pensée moderne*. Paris: Edition
du Scorpion, 1963.
Gay, Peter. *Voltaire's Politics: The Poet as a Realist*. Princeton: Princeton Univer-
sity Press, 1959.
Guex, Jules. *Le Théâtre et la société française de 1815 à 1848*. Diss, Université de
Lausanne, 1900.
Hallays-Dabot, Victor. *La Censure dramatique et le théâtre: Histoire des vingt
dernières années (1850–1870)*. Paris: Dentu, 1871.
————. *Histoire de la censure théâtrale en France*. Paris: Dentu, 1862.
Hazard, Paul. *Crise de la conscience européenne*. 3 vols. Paris: Boivin, 1935.
Heimbecher, Hans-Joachim. "Victor Hugo und die Ideen der grossen franzö-
sischen Revolution." *Romanische Studien* 15, no. 27 (1932): 1–323.
Heisler, Marcel. *Stendhal et Napoléon*. Paris: Nizet, 1969.
Herold, J. Christopher. *Mistress to an Age*. Indianapolis and New York: Bobbs-
Merrill, 1958.
Howe, Irving. *Politics and the Novel*. New York: Horizon Press, 1957; New
York: Avon Books, 1970.
Imbert, H.-F. *Les Métamorphoses de la liberté; ou, Stendhal devant la Restauration
et le Risorgimento*. Paris: Corti, 1967.
Jasinski, René. *Le Mariage de Figaro*. Paris: Les Cours de Lettres, 1948.
Lacretelle, Pierre de. *Vie politique de Victor Hugo*. Paris: Hachette, 1928.
Larg, David G. *Madame de Staël: La Seconde Vie (1800–1807)*. Paris: Cham-
pion, 1928.
Lenient, Charles F. *La Satire en France au Moyen Age*. Paris: Hachette, 1859.
————. *La Satire en France; ou, La Littérature militante au XVIᵉ siècle*. Paris:
Hachette, 1866.
Leroy, Maxime. *Stendhal politique*. Paris: Le Divan, 1929.
Levrault, Léon. *La Satire: Evolution du genre*. Paris: Delaplane, 1904.

Liprandi, Claude. *Au coeur du "Rouge": L'Affaire Lafargue et "Le Rouge et le noir".* Lausanne: Edition du grand Chêne, 1961.

Loggins, Vernon. *André Chénier: His Life, Death, and Glory.* Athens, Ohio: Ohio University Press, 1965.

Lucas-Dubreton, Julius. *La Chanson, la politique, la société.* Paris: Hachette, 1934.

————. *La Restauration et la Monarchie de Juillet.* Paris: Hachette, 1926.

Lumbroso, Alberrto. *Béranger e Napoleone.* Rome: Mades e Mendel, 1895.

McGhee, Dorothy M. *Voltaire's Narrative Devices Considered in the Author's "Contes philosophiques."* Menasha, Wisconsin: Bontee, 1933.

Marcus, Willy. *Die Darstellung der französischen Zustände in Montesquieus "Lettres persanes" verglichen mit der Wirklichkeit.* Breslau: Nischkowsky, 1902.

Martino, Pierre. *L'Orient dans la littérature française au XVIIe et XVIIIe siècles.* Paris: Hachette, 1906.

Matvejevitch, Predag. *Pour une poétique de l'événement.* Ed. 10/18. Paris: Union Générale d'Editions, 1979.

Menche de Loisne, C. *L'Influence de la littérature française de 1830 à 1850 sur l'esprit public et les moeurs.* Paris: Garnier Frères, 1852.

Meyer, Maurice. *Commentaire des "Lettres persanes" de Montesquieu.* Paris: Fournier, 1841.

Michelet, Jules. *Histoire de France.* Vol. 19. Paris: Marpon et Flammarion, 1879.

————. *Histoire de la Révolution française.* 8 vols. Paris: Marpon et Flammarion, 1879.

Mornet, Daniel. *Les Origines intellectuelles de la Révolution française (1715–1787).* Paris: Colin, 1933.

————. *La Pensée française au XVIIIe siècle.* Paris: Colin, 1926.

Muret, Théodore. *L'Histoire par le théâtre.* 1st ser., 3 vols. Paris: Amyot, 1865.

Nixon, Edna. *Voltaire and the Calas Case.* London: Gollancz, 1961.

Nöckler, Alfred. *Crébillon der Jüngere, 1707–1777: Leben und Werke.* Leipzig: Dr. Seele, 1911.

Parquez, Jacques. *La Bulle "Unigenitus" et le jansénisme politique.* Paris: Les Presses modernes, 1936.

Pelletan, Camille. *Victor Hugo, homme politique.* Paris: Ollendorff, 1907.

Poitou, Eugène. *Du Roman et du théâtre contemporains et de leur influence sur les moeurs.* Paris: Durand, 1857.

Pomeau, René. *Politique de Voltaire.* Paris: Colin, 1963.

Ridgway, Ronald S. *La Propagande philosophique dans les tragédies de Voltaire.* Studies on Voltaire and the Eighteenth Century, no. 15. Geneva: l'Institut et Musée Voltaire, 1961.

Roustan, Marius. *Les Philosophes et la société française au XVIIIe siècle.* Lyon: Rey, 1906.

Saint-Auban, Emile de. *L'Idée sociale au théâtre.* Paris: Stock, 1901.

Sainte-Beuve, Charles-Augustin. *Les Grands Ecrivains français.* Paris: Garnier, 1930.

Sareil, Jean. *Essai sur "Candide."* Geneva: Droz, 1967.

Scarfe, Francis. *André Chénier: His Life and Work (1762–1794).* Oxford: Clarendon Press, 1965.

Schick, Ursula. *Zur Erzählungstechnik in Voltaires "Contes."* Munich: Fink, 1968.

Stapfer, Paul. *Victor Hugo et la grande poésie satirique en France.* Société d'Editions littéraires et artistiques. Paris: Librairie Paul Ollendorff, 1901.

Steiner, George. *The Death of Tragedy.* New York: Knopf, 1961.

Suran, Théodore. *Les Esprits directeurs de la pensée française du Moyen-Age à la Révolution.* Paris: Schleicher, 1903.

Taine, Hippolyte-Adolphe. *Les Origines de la France contemporaine.* 11 vols. 36th ed. Paris: Hachette, 1947.

Tison-Braun, Micheline. *La Crise de l'humanisme: Le Conflit de l'individu et de la société dans la littérature française moderne.* 2 vols. Paris: Nizet, 1958.

Vaarlot, Jean. "La Philosophie et la politique dans les 'contes' de Voltaire." *Pensée* n.s. 88 (November–December 1959): 41–50.

Valéry, Paul. "Préface aux *Lettres persanes.*" In *Variété.* In *Oeuvres,* Vol. 1. Editions Pléiade. Paris: Gallimard, 1957.

———. "Stendhal." In *Variété II,* 75–139. Paris: Gallimard, 1940.

———. *The Collected Works in English.* Bollingen Series 45, vol. 10: *History and Politics,* Translated by Denise Folliot and Jackson Mathews. New York: Bollingen Foundation, 1962.

Wade, Ira O. *Clandestine Organization and Diffusion of Philosophic Ideas in France from 1700 to 1750.* Princeton: Princeton University Press, 1938.

Walter, Gérard. *André Chénier: Son milieu et son temps.* Paris: Laffont, 1947.

Weinstein, Leo. "Altered States of Consciousness in Flaubert's *Madame Bovary* and Kafka's *A Country Doctor.*" In *Voices of Consciousness: Essays on Medieval and Modern French Literature in Memory of James D. Powell and Rosemary Hodgin.* Edited by Raymond J. Cormier, 215–29. Philadelphia: Temple University Press, 1977.

———. *Hippolyte Taine.* New York: Twayne, 1972.

———. "Kafka's Ape: Heel or Hero?" *Modern Fiction Studies* 8 (Spring 1962): 75–79.

———. "Stendhal's Count Mosca as a Statesman." *PMLA* 80 (1965): 210-16.

Weiss, J. J. *Le Théâtre et les moeurs.* Paris: Calman-Lévy, 1889.

Worcester, David. *The Art of Satire.* Cambridge: Harvard University Press, 1940.

Wright, Gordon. *France in Modern Times: From the Enlightenment to the Present.* 3rd ed. New York and London: W.W. Norton, 1981.

Zeraffa, Michel. *Roman et société.* Paris: Presses universitaires de France, 1971.

Index

Aby, Robert-Peter, 173nn2, 3; 174n5
Acheson, Dean Gooderham, 185n9
Adereth, Maxwell, 171n7
Alembert, Jean Le Rond d', 23, 38, 43
Andlau, Béatrix d', 181n12
Anouilh, Jean, 182n3
Anthony, 40
Aragon, Louis, xii, 139, 171n5
Archilochus, 88
Aristotle, 38
Artois, comte d' (brother of Louis XVI), 66, 67
Artois, comte d' (brother of Louis XVIII). *See* Charles X
Aubigné, Agrippa d', x, 88
Auerbach, Erich, 178n12
Augier, Emile, xii

Balzac, Honoré de, xi, xii, xiv, 141, 145, 171n5, 172n12, 184nn6, 7; 185n2
Barbès, Armand, 149
Barbier, Auguste, xiv, 163, 181–82n3
Barbusse, Henri, 139
Barre, chevalier de la. *See* La Barre
Barry, Jeanne Bécu, comtesse du, 36, 82
Barthes, Roland, 60, 179n16
Baudelaire, Charles, xiv, 171–72n10
Baudin, Alphonse, 150
Bayle, Pierre, 38
Bazaine, Achille, 152, 153
Beauharnais, Hortense de, 188n12
Beaumarchais, Pierre Augustin Caron de, 17, 39, 61, 64–75, 179nn3, 6
Benda, Julien, xiv
Benedict XIII, pope, 22
Béranger, Pierre-Jean de, xii, 86, 98–101, 104, 105–18, 124, 154, 169, 181nn14, 15; 181n2, 182n4
Bernier, François, 8, 172n2

Berry, Caroline de Bourbon-Sicile, duchesse de, 130
Berry, Charles, 103, 104
Billaud-Varenne, Jean Nicolas, 82
Bismarck, Otto von, 152
Blanc, Louis, 149
Blanqui, Louis Auguste, 149
Bloy, Léon, xii
Blum, Léon, 185n9
Boileau, Nicolas, x, 3
Bonaparte. *See* Napoleon I
Bonaparte, Louis (father of Napoleon III), 188n12
Bordeaux. *See* Chambord
Borgia, Cesar, 167
Bossuet, Jacques Bénigne, 183n13
Bottiglia, William F., 171n4
Boucher, François, 61
Boulanger, General Georges, 169
Bourbon, Louis Henri, duc de, 6, 7
Bourgogne, Marie-Adelaïde de Savoie, duchesse de, 8
Boutet de Monvel, Jacques, 181n6
Brissot, Jacques Pierre, 81, 82
Broglie, Achille Léon Victor, duc de, 129
Broglie, Victor François, duc de, 42, 50
Bruneau, Mathurin, 106
Byng, Admiral George, 50

Cabanis, Georges, 120
Calas, Jean, 59, 60
Calonne, Charles Alexandre de, 63, 64
Campan, Jeanne Louise Genet, 66
Camus, Albert, ix, 171n1
Carlier, P. Ch. J., 161
Carrier, Jean-Baptiste, 90
Casimir-Périer, Auguste, 129
Castex, Pierre-Georges, 181n1
Catinat, Nicolas, 14
Cavaignac, Jean-Baptiste, 149, 153, 167